THE IMPACT OF RACISM ON
AFRICAN AMERICAN FAMILIES

The Impact of Racism on African American Families
Literature as Social Science

PAUL C. ROSENBLATT
University of Minnesota, USA

Routledge
Taylor & Francis Group

LONDON AND NEW YORK

First published 2014 by Ashgate Publishing

2 Park Square, Milton Park, Abingdon, Oxfordshire OX14 4RN
52 Vanderbilt Avenue, New York, NY 10017

Routledge is an imprint of the Taylor & Francis Group, an informa business

First issued in paperback 2020

British Library Cataloguing in Publication Data
A catalogue record for this book is available from the British Library

The Library of Congress has cataloged the printed edition as follows:
Rosenblatt, Paul C.
   The impact of racism on African American families : literature as social science / by Paul C. Rosenblatt.
      pages cm
   Includes bibliographical references and index.
   ISBN 978-1-4724-1558-5 (hardback)
   1 American fiction--African American authors--History and criticism.
   2. African American families in literature. 3. Racism in literature. 4. Domestic fiction, American--History and criticism. 5. African Americans families--Social conditions. 6. Literature and society--United States. I. Title.
   PS374.N4R59 2014
   813.009'896073--dc23

                                                                    2013032356

ISBN 978-1-4724-1558-5 (hbk)
ISBN 978-0-367-60094-5 (pbk)

Contents

Acknowledgments

It is impossible to write a book like this, without having had support, input, advice, perspectives, stimulation, and criticism from many people. Ideally I would thank here the dozens of people who have stimulated me, educated me, helped me, etc., but I have not done a good job of keeping track of them all. In fact, I think much of the input registered with me unconsciously and not in a way that allows attribution to specific people. However, there are a few people who have been most influential who I want to single out for thanks. I thank Emily Wright-Rosenblatt for her great knowledge of this literature, her leading me to new books, her knowledgeable comments about the books I have read, her educating me about big picture and disciplinary views of the literature in general and of specific works in the literature, her infectious enthusiasm for the literature, her wisdom about and knowledge of the racial system, and her tolerance for my being a beginner and going in the directions I have chosen to go. I probably would not have done this project without her stimulation and help. But then what I have done is not necessarily anything like what she would consider appropriate. I also want to thank my friend and colleague Oliver J. Williams for welcoming and supporting my work on this project and for educating me about the importance of family stories in African American families. I want to thank John Barner and Michael Ames for wonderfully helpful advice about earlier versions of this book. I want to thank Terri Karis for her wisdom and support and for her ongoing education of me about whiteness, the racial system, and African American families. And I want to thank Ashgate Commissioning Editor Neil Jordan and two anonymous reviewers he commissioned for support and for stimulating me to think about things in new and, I think, very constructive ways. My thanks to you all in helping get as far as I have, and of course the errors and limitations are entirely mine.

Chapter 1

Novels as Resources for Understanding the Impact of Racism on African American Families

How does racism come home to and influence everyday relationships in African American families? For centuries African American families have lived in a racial system that made life difficult for them. Even today, 150 years after the end of slavery, and with economic, educational, occupational and other advances for many African Americans, racism remains a reality. It may be more often than in the past disguised and covert (Bonilla-Silva, 2010), but it is still a reality. There is substantial evidence that African Americans are disadvantaged compared to European Americans on such indices of well-being as life expectancy, infant survival rate, quality of health care, housing quality, earnings, and accumulated assets. On indicators that things are not good, African Americans have, for example, higher levels of unemployment, incarceration, experiences of discrimination in hiring, experiences of police profiling, and attendance in poorer quality schools.

But in all the richness of documentation about the influence of the racial system on African Americans there is surprisingly little social science research on how racism affects everyday family interaction. The most substantial literature in the area is about African Americans raising children to face a racist world (see Chapter 8 for an overview of that literature). Other than that, we only have a scattering of research on how racism might intrude into everyday interaction in African American families—for example, Banks-Wallace and Parks (2001), Hughes and Chen (1997), Rosenblatt and Wallace (2005a, 2005b), St. Jean and Feagin (1998). While thousands of social science writings are about the influence of racism on African American individuals or reflect what racism has done to African Americans collectively (e.g. Dodson, 2007; Nobles, 2007), arguably there is need for additional research that traces the impact of racist events on what goes on in everyday African American family relationships.

If an African American father/husband is denied employment on the basis of his race or if a mother/wife is demeaned and disrespected on the job by racist slurs, how is their everyday family life affected by these experiences of racism? How does it come home? How does it show up in their family conversations? Does it show up in neediness that puts claims on other family members, preoccupation that distances them from others in the family, irritability that leads to family tensions, or words of support from others in the family? What might a person say to other family members about an experience of racism, and if a person says anything about an experience of racism how might that affect other family members? These are questions that social science can and should address, and we certainly have relevant literature, particularly in regard to parenting. But we need to explore a wider range of ramifications of the effects of racism on interactions in African American families. One trove of potentially useful observations about African American family life is the corpus of novels written by African American authors about African American families. Many African American-authored novels contain rich depictions of African American family life, and many of those novels depict the influence of racism on African American family life (cf. Wall, 2005, p. 8). Thus, African American-authored novels potentially can help to fill the gap in the social science literature concerning how racism may come home to everyday African American family life. This book turns to such novels for ideas about the impact of racism on African American families. How do African American novelists telling stories about African American families write about racism coming home to and affecting everyday life in African American families?

Novels as a Source of Knowledge for the Social Sciences

Can social science questions be addressed with validity by analyzing novels? One way to think of novels as legitimate for social science analysis is to think of novelists as like social scientists in being astute observers of the social world. Novelists, like social scientists, may often work at getting good access to the kinds of lives they write about and at developing excellent observational skills. Also, some novelists rely on methods for learning about the world that are like methods social scientists use (Phillips, 1995). The resonance of many novels with their readers is often that they have to offer accounts that parallel common human experiences (Cosbey; 1997) and that they pay close attention to everyday life (Rogers, 1991, pp. 49–50). Related to that, not infrequently novelists who write about families draw on details of experiences in their own families (Goldin, 2008). Because so many novels have good grounding in everyday life, the sociologist Jon Frauley wrote about the usefulness to sociologists of respecting the analytical power of fiction: "Looking at fiction can help us understand more about our own social reality, as works of fiction are anchored, moored, or rooted in reality and deal with real issues such as racism, violence, or marginalization" (2010, p. 52). So a case can be made that a novel can be rich in insightful and persuasive elements that link to and stimulate social science analysis and theoretical constructions (Cosbey; 1997). And in fact novels have not infrequently been used as illustrative material in sociology courses (e.g. Carlin, 2010; Cosbey; 1997; Hegtvedt, 1991).

Of course, we must be cautious about how we use the models, understandings, characterizations, and conceptualizations that novels offer. With many novels having autobiographical elements (Rogers, 1991, pp. 48–9) that provide grounding in social realities, we need to be alert to the subjectivities and unique aspects of novels that could make them a questionable basis for building confident and broadly applicable views of human social life. It is also important, in using fiction as a source of social science insights, ideas and data, to be aware of the conventions and stance used by each novelist (Watson, 1995). Related to this, Hathaway (2004) warned about what she called a "touristic reading," assuming that a fictional text is an authentic and accurate account of the culture it describes. So novels must not be used uncritically in social research. They deserve the same skepticism, disciplined scrutiny, and questioning as conventional social research.

From another angle, a case can be made that fiction deserves to be taken seriously in social science analysis because the boundary between fiction and nonfiction or between imaginative story-telling and apparently objective research is, from a post-modern view, blurry (Borenstein, 1978; Hegtvedt, 1991; Rogers, 1991; Watson, 1995; Wilson, 1979). As part of the blurriness, both fiction and apparently objective social research rest on subjectivities about what to pay attention to and what to report, subjectivities in the language used in describing matters, and subjectivities in the interpretations given to the observations that become incorporated into the writing (Borenstein, 1978; Rosenblatt, 2002). As another part of the blurriness, fiction and social science share cultural roots, not only about everyday life but about what to focus on and be concerned about (Rogers, 1991, p. 176). Also, social science research arguably draws on some of the same imaginative well springs and often even speaks to the same events as fiction (Borenstein, 1978). Then, too, many writers of fiction have been influenced by psychology and the social sciences (Rogers, 1991, pp. 177–8), and many social scientists have been influenced by novels they have read (see, for example, Carlin, 2010). Further, fiction and social science draw on information sources that are at base subjectivities (for example, what witnesses to events believe they saw and heard, what people say that they think and feel; autobiographical and other memories) and they are embedded in the same culture(s) with the same language resources, areas of obliviousness, and biases. Social science research may be inspired and grounded in the researcher's life experiences, observations, and stories heard just as much as would be true for the work of a novelist. Some would argue that in disciplined social science research there is greater clarity than can be found in fiction about what is attended to, in what situations it occurs, how it is expressed, and what its consequences are. However, one might also argue that the language and rhetoric of disciplined observation and objectivity in reports of social research obscure the ways that social research has the same cultural and experiential roots and subjectivities as fiction.

One could argue that perhaps the most important difference between social research and fiction is that we social researchers write as though we offer something like objective truth much more often than do writers of fiction. But it is conceivable that fictional accounts of events represent as accurately or perhaps in certain domains of human life even more accurately (Watson, 1995) the experiences, feelings, perceptions, memories, and words of people and the complexities of a culture and social life, because social research can be trapped in conventions and limitations that can obscure nuance, complexity, subjectivity, and difference. For example, the standard model for a social research journal article typically emphasizes the objective version of the researcher's voice and devotes a great deal of the report to social science language. One consequence is that one rarely sees many extended quotes from participants, and the quotes that are offered typically have been edited to suppress the complexity of actual speech and interactions that is undergirded by the complexity of people's struggle to understand things and to relate to one another. By contrast, the fictional representations of African American experience on which this book is based are often rich in individual speech, dialogue, the interior life of individuals, complex and multiply interpretable interactions among family members, and the struggle to make sense of things individually and in interaction with others. This allows novelists to bear witness to and construct accounts of events that may too often have been ignored or glossed over in social science reports about African Americans that do not represent African American experience and understandings well (Mitchell, 2002, pp. 9–11). The sociologist Richard Biernacki (2012) has offered a related perspective, arguing that the "coding" and other data reduction of the social sciences can distort or lose so much that by contrast humanistic research, with its careful documentation and footnoting may be better at exploring.

To the extent that novels are based on life experiences and informal observations of novelists, one can also make the case that novels are in a sense based on nonreactive measures (Webb, Campbell, Schwartz, et al., 1981) of what happens in African American families when one, some, or all family members encounter racist experiences. People who are being studied may be reactive to a formal research process in which a researcher intrudes into a family's life. Thus, the researcher's presence may change things. For example, the researcher's questions may get lines of thinking going, may upset people, or otherwise influence them in ways that might change what they say or do. By contrast, the unobtrusiveness of a novelist whose work mines her or his memories may avoid reactive effects. And that is another potential advantage of turning to novels for data.

Carlin (2010) has argued that a key to using fiction in sociological analysis is the close reading and the work of the analyst. And he frames the issue in terms of what Garfinkel (2002) called the "corpus status," whether an item counts as a member of a particular category. What Carlin offers is not a blanket statement about the pros and cons of using fiction in social science research but instead what I think is a sense of two things: (1) when all the analytic work is done, whether there is anything there that is valuable depends on what the analyst has produced and (2) whether something like a novel counts as research data depends on the politics of the social sciences as they relate to how the case is made regarding the corpus status of novels as legitimate research material. Carlin focused on the use of novels in teaching sociology, but I would contend that we can extend his analysis to a work like the present one, which attempts to make the case for fiction as a source of ideas in social science research and offers a set of ideas as meaningful and important.

Social Science Precedents for Turning to Novels for Ideas

The idea of using literature as a source of insights into people's lives is not new. Social science, psychological, and cultural studies scholars have often turned to fiction for insights. Among important examples are Ragan and Hopper's analysis of ways to leave a lover (1984), Whitson's analysis of cross-social-class romances (2002), Czarniawska's analysis of gender discrimination in organizations (2006), Riley's (1968) use of English novelists' accounts of childbirth as social history, Harris's (1982) analysis of domestics in black American literature, Meyer's (1965) analysis of Midwestern farm novels, Griffin's (1995) analysis of African American migration narratives, Goldsmith and Satterlee's (2004) exploration of the psychology of traumatic experiences, Hornbostel's (1988) analysis of the lives of women in farming, and Alberts' (1986) analysis of couple conversations in Harlequin romance novels. Also, Lipsitz (2011) used a single novel, Paule Marshall's *Brown Girl, Brownstones*, as an element in his analysis of how racism takes place.

Fiction has been used as evidence for research focused on a particular culture, for example, on the contemporary culture of Korea (Rosenblatt and Yang, 2004; Ryang, 2012). It has also been used to explore social and psychological matters that have a broader generality than the particulars of any specific work of fiction, for example, the complexities of human self-reflection (Hook and Horvath, 2005), the central issues in economic development (Lewis, Rodgers, and Woolcock, 2008), human emotional complexity (Goldsmith and Satterlee, 2004), family processes in dealing with the death of a loved one (Rober and Rosenblatt, 2013), and the fate of close relationships in consumer societies (Brinkmann, 2009). So it is not surprising that some social scientists advocate the use of fiction as data (Phillips, 1995; Watson, 2011) and use it. Moreover, in some sociological approaches fiction has been very important in providing illustrations and insights—for example, certain approaches in French sociology (Ellena, 1998), some of the work of Alfred Schutz (Srubar, 1998), Goffman's work (Bynum and Pranter, 1984), and conversational analysis (McHoul, 1987).

Ruggiero (2003) used novels as data in a wide ranging exploration of the sociology of crime, and in one chapter he used works by the African American authors James Baldwin and Richard Wright to explore the sociology of hate crimes directed at ethnic minorities, the sociology of differential treatment of ethnic minorities in the criminal justice system, and the sociology of crime in the context of large differences between ethnic groups and neighborhoods in opportunities for jobs of any sort, decent-paying jobs, and illicit jobs. Although Ruggiero's focus was not on families but on how society functions, his focus on what drives, permits, and excuses white hate crimes directed at African Americans touched on issues that come up in this book. This is so in part because some African American families in the novels analyzed in this book have conversations about white hate crimes and because to tell his story of hate crimes Ruggiero told how intimidation, humiliation, and impoverishment experienced at the hands of whites play out in certain fictional African American families. Further, Ruggiero's sociological analysis emphasizes how much white aggression against African Americans is to African Americans as a category of person, not as individuals. And that fits what this book is about in that many African American-authored novels depict a society in which the problems African Americans face are not about the particulars of individual relationships with whites but about being treated as members of a despised, feared, and denigrated category. So Ruggiero's analysis of the sociology of hate crimes based on fiction by Baldwin and Wright provides a strong precedent for this book, even though Ruggiero's focus was not on family relationships.

Works that use novels to explore real life social issues are based on assumptions about the relationship between fictional representations of social life and what can be said to actually go on in social life, and those assumptions have had their critics. Ulrich (1986), for example, questioned the relationship between communication as depicted in fiction and communication in real life. But even if characters in the novels analyzed for this book and the novelistic depiction of their interactions deviate in some ways from what actually could be witnessed in everyday life, there still may be considerable validity to what is described in novels and also to the underlying conceptualizations in novels. These descriptions and conceptualizations could come out of what the authors experienced themselves and observed in others. They could come out of how the authors make sense for themselves about the world. They may be part of common sense in the larger culture and in African American communities. They could even represent something like ethnographic research, astute and careful observations by writers who have had long-term access to African American families, communities, churches, revivals, stores, gossip sessions, kitchens, front porches, workplaces, bars, juke joints, living rooms, clubs, hairdressers, funerals, playgrounds and so on.

What Novels Teach Us and What We Know When We Think We Know Something

I think with social science research we never can claim truth and certainty. I believe that the best we can hope to offer are ideas, awareness, perspectives, and engaging forms of documentation. The world is too complicated, people are too diverse, our social research methods are too fallible and limited, things change too fast, there are too many different valid but mutually inconsistent ways of investigating things, and there are too many plausible alternative interpretations of the findings of much of social research for us to claim certainty. But that does not mean the explorations of this book should be dismissed as unpromising. There is so little in the social sciences on how racism affects the inner workings of African American family life that I think we need all we can find, and the novels are collectively an interesting, even moving and inspiring source of ideas, awareness, perspectives, and insights. The novels probe the inner workings of African American families in ways that social science rarely does.

Turning to Novels for Insights on the Impact of Racism on African American Families

Earlier in this chapter it was asserted that we are so short of information on how racism affects the daily lives of African Americans that we might as well turn to novels for insights. But that assertion is too tepid an endorsement of using novels to explore African American family life. In fact, in researching the impact of racism on African American families, novels may be especially valuable resources. Stanfield (2011) went so far as to argue that during the rise of modern social science many of the most important analyses of racism were written by novelists such as Toni Morrison and James Baldwin. Similarly, Dilworth-Anderson, Burton, and Johnson (1993), three eminent scholars of the African-American family, argued for turning to African-American novels for valuable new ways of thinking about African American families, and cited three novelists whose works are used in this book, Zora Neale Hurston, Alice Walker, and Gloria Naylor, as writers who offer great insight into African American families.

There are many reasons for us to believe that novels provide analyses of racism that we should take seriously. Not many social science researchers have been interested in this area of research, and white researchers (historically the vast majority of social researchers) have not necessarily had good or long-term access to African American families. The questions addressed in social research have often been macro questions, not questions about family dynamics and processes. The social sciences have historically not been free of the racial biases of the larger society, and that raises questions about the validity and insight of considerable social science research, particularly from the past, dealing with African Americans. One can assume that family novels written by African Americans are free from the biases of the dominant white society. In fact, not only are African American novels a resource to cover an area that has been neglected, the weakness of the social sciences in this area may have motivated some African American authors to write novels. John Edgar Wideman, one of whose novels is a source of data in this book, said that a key reason he wrote his novels about African American families was to counter the invalidity of social science claims about African American families (Guzzio, 2011, p. 98).

In some novels about African American families, racism may be irrelevant or a tangential influence. But many novels about African American families deal directly and sometimes extensively with how racism affects African American families. In fact, a few of the novelists whose works are analyzed in these pages made clear that they intended for their writing to expose racism and other forms of injustice (e.g. Petry, 1950). They did this even though there would be some risk in terms of being able to publish their books (in a country where most editors and publishers were white), see their published work favorably reviewed (in a country where most reviewers were white), and see the published work sell well (in a country where most book buyers were white). But, as Ralph Ellison said, writing in order to please white audiences would be very bad writing (Ellison, 1955).

In the novels analyzed in this book, the authors seem to me to have striven for a fundamental authenticity in characterizing African American individuals and families. And there is evidence of that from writings about what some of the novelists were trying to do. Ensslen (1984, p. 151), for example, wrote about Ernest J. Gaines trying "to capture the spirit of authentic oral reports of former slaves" as a kind of "folk autobiography" in *The Autobiography of Miss Jane Pittman*. Bröck (1984) wrote that Paule Marshall tried to capture in *Brown Girl, Brownstones* the kitchen talk she heard from her mother and her mother's friends. Ludwig (2007) wrote about Toni Morrison's novels as a vehicle for Morrison's criticism concerning the social conditions of African Americans. Guzzio (2011, p. 98) wrote about John Edgar Wideman seeming to say that all of his novels were about his family. In fact, many of the novels analyzed in this book have been said to have autobiographical (and hence, experiential) elements. Porter (1996), for example, wrote about the autobiographical elements of James Baldwin's *Go Tell It on the Mountain*. Monteith (2006) and Fox (2009) wrote about the autobiographical elements of Sarah E. Wright's *This Child's Gonna Live*. Russell (1990) wrote about the autobiographical aspects of Gwendolyn Brooks' *Maud Martha* (p. 65) and Alice Walker's *Meridian* (p. 128). Dorothy West talked about autobiographical elements of her novel, *The Living Is Easy* (McDowell, 1997; Mitchell and Davis, 2012; Sherrard-Johnson, 2012).

Even when, as with some of the novels of Toni Morrison, there are allegorical or magical realist qualities to stories (as when impossible things like a person flying are described), or as with Langston Hughes writings in which snow, cold, and tornadoes may be symbols of racism (Schultz, 2007), the descriptions of many events and characters in these novels are arguably close to what authors remember or otherwise believe to be true about their personal life and the lives of people around them.

Family Systems Theory

This book is in part a work of family systems theory (Rosenblatt, 1994). It builds on family systems thinking and provides family systems framing for understanding what the novels suggest about African American family relationships in the context of racism. The most fundamental idea in family systems theory is that family members are interconnected, so what affects one family member will affect others and one family member's action or reaction will affect others. Families exist in and are linked to larger systems (Bronfenbrenner, 1979), social, political, and other institutions, groups of people beyond the family, the physical environment, and everything else outside of the family. And the external systems are not only responsible for dreadful things like discrimination in hiring, police brutality, and racist insults but also for good things like the support of a caring and affirming community.

Systems interact, so the family has an impact on what is going on around it as well as being impacted by what goes on around it. And there are examples in the novels of families having an impact on the larger systems with which they are in contact. But when it comes to racism, there is so much more power on the side of racism (fire power, economic power, police power, judicial power, the power to ignore, the power to misunderstand, control of the mass media, etc., even the power built into how in the larger culture African Americans are defined) that most of the observable impact in the relationship between the racist larger society and African American families is the impact of racism on the families and not the reverse.

In family systems thinking, family interactions, family patterns, ways of sharing life with other family members, and ways of getting along and not getting along with each other in the family are governed by family rules (Rosenblatt, 1994). The rules are often unspoken, and quite possibly they are not even in the awareness of family members. But family members ordinarily act in accordance with the rules, and if they do not, other family members may object and try to move them back into conformity with the rules. Family rules can be understood to be layered in the sense that there are very specific and surface rules, for example, the family eats dinner together. And then there are more abstract, less obvious, and often more powerful meta-rules; for example, one meta-rule that governs many more specific and limited rules may be that a family member must not become too different from other family members. The rules of a family come from the families of origin of the adults in the family, come from the community and culture, and come from family member cumulative struggles and interactions with each other. And in the case of African American families in the world of the novels, some family rules develop because of what it takes to live in the racial system. Among examples of such rules in this book are that in quite a few African American families in the novels parents work at socializing their children to be relatively safe and out of trouble in relationship to whites. For example, parents might teach their children the racial system etiquette that whites expect or even demand from them.

Family systems theory also alerts us to the importance of processes of determining who is in and who is out of a family (Rosenblatt, 1994). With any family, the lines that define who is in the family and who is not may be blurry. And people may have their own definitions of family that are different from a dictionary or social science definition (Gubrium and Holstein, 1990). African American families, perhaps especially in difficult circumstances, may have family or family-like relationships with neighbors, coworkers, members of their church congregation, and others who are not family by a conventional dictionary definition (Duck, 2012; Hines and Boyd-Franklin, 1996; Stack, 1974; Stewart, 2007). And in fact in the novels there are a number of instances in which people have family like relationships though they are not family for each other by conventional definitions—for example, the parenting of the three orphaned children (the three Deweys) by Eva Peace in Toni Morrison's novel *Sula*, or the joining together of Mattie Michael and her young son Basil with Eva Turner and her grandchild Lucielia in Gloria Naylor's novel *The Women of Brewster Place*.

Related to the issue of defining who is and is not family, a related and important concept of family systems theory is that of family boundary (Rosenblatt, 1994). Families differ quite a bit in how much they let information and family members into the outside world and how much they let outsiders, outsider information, and anything else from the outside into the home. For low-income, urban African Americans the boundaries between family and community may be blurry (Collins Sims, 2013), so, for example, crucial connections for a person may be outside the family, and difficulties in the family are often quickly known in the community. And for African Americans in a world where racism disrupts family life, many people, adults as well as children, may find themselves moving from one family to another (see Chapter 10).

Bateson (1967) wrote about systems analysis as being in part about the limitations on one part of a system that comes from links to other parts. Extending his perspective, one can say that African American families might not only be directly impacted by the racial system but might also be affected in the sense that what they can do and how they can adapt are limited by the racial system in which they are embedded. For example, there may be few economic alternatives available to them, few jobs, and limited places in which to live. And the limitations at one level maintain the larger racial system and the place of African American families in it and at another level limit what African American individuals and families can do and who they can be in that system.

Chapter 2

Reading Novels as a
Social Science Researcher

This book relies on the insights in 27 African American-authored novels that include accounts of African American family life. In these novels, racism intrudes on, shapes, limits, harms, or otherwise affects family life. Many of the 27 novels focus on characters who have to be good students of how racism operates in order to get along and perhaps even to survive. The novels analyzed were published from the Harlem Renaissance (which flourished in the 1920s) to 2006.

Choosing the Novels

I wanted to work with widely read, influential African American novels, but there is no agreed upon list of such novels. My search began with a review of syllabi on the internet for college and university courses dealing with African American literature. Turning to syllabi has its limits, but Young (2006, p. 12) argued that the canon for African American literature much more than literature by white authors, has been established by college and university syllabi. I looked also for novels that were mentioned often in internet lists of recommended or important novels by African American authors, library holdings of African American novels, and Wikipedia and other articles that provide lists of what are considered the major novels by African Americans. I wanted to research novels that are widely read and widely recognized, partly because widespread reading and recognition are indirect measures of the insights novels offer. I wanted novels read in courses that focus on African American life and culture, because for me that is a measure of the resonance and validity of the books.

The novels mentioned frequently in syllabi and on internet lists were usually more than 20 years old. Older novels were quite acceptable to me, because the racism of the past was part of the lives of many older people and because racism persists—for example, employment discrimination (Royster, 2007), discrimination in housing and real estate (Satter, 2009; Squires, 2007), and internalized racism in the form of valuing white physical features remains common in African American families (Parmer, Arnold, Natt and Janson, 2004). But I wanted to include more recent novels touching on how racism might impact African American family life. To identify those novels, I looked at what online book sellers were selling, and data (if online sellers provided it) on how well the various novels by African

American authors were selling. In total, from my initial list and from the search for more recent novels, I had 103 novels as candidates for use in this project.

As I searched for novels, I discovered that many novels had little or no family content, so I weeded them out, a total of 36 books. I also chose not to use eight genre novels (science fiction, western, or detective novels, plus a novel written for children), because I thought that their narrative might be too responsive to canons about what is a good story in their genre. Eight other novels were not enough about African Americans or were set too much outside the United States. Ten novels were set too much before the twentieth century, and one was surrealist. So in total I chose not to use 63 books that had been candidates for analysis in this work. That left 40 novels. I started going through them one by one, taking notes and organizing ideas. After I had read 27 novels I decided to stop, because they cumulatively seemed to me to provide substantial amounts of material for what I wanted to write. Stopping at 27 is analogous to stopping at that number of cases in a qualitative interview study, knowing from one's preliminary familiarity with the data what one's major themes would be and knowing that the cases one has will provide strong data with regard to the themes. For qualitative interview studies, 27 cases is quite a lot. For example, Kvale and Brinkmann (2009, p. 113) suggested that 15 +/- 10 cases is typical in interview research.

I did not choose novels because they featured the effects of racism, but I wanted novels that dealt at least to some extent with families. As it happened, many of the novels I chose had a great deal to say about racism as it relates to families. I agree with Davis (2002) that recent novels by African American authors are less likely to deal much if at all with African American struggles against racist oppression, but I do not think that means racism is no longer a powerful factor in Africa American life. I am inclined to think that means that more often than in the past African American novelists who write about families have chosen to focus on family life and not so much on white people and white dominated institutional contexts of family life. And in focusing on family life they could be understood to be saying that what family members do and do not do in relationship to one another is what people have relatively great control of and responsibility for, that the phenomenology of everyday life is much more about what goes on between intimates than it is about the external environment, and it is in the context of family that people's lives play out. Thus, the focus of one of the more recent novels analyzed in this book, Bernice L. McFadden's *The Warmest December* (2001), is on an adult daughter's pain, alcoholism, and struggle to heal in the context of her father's alcoholism, violence, and cruelty. McFadden could conceivably have stepped back and framed the father's alcoholism, violence, and cruelty in terms of life in a racist society, but she focused tightly on the psychological struggles of the daughter and the dynamics of the family. Nonetheless, the more recent novels analyzed in this book have at least something to say about how racism and interactions with white people affect family life. The 27 novels are listed at the end of this book, so readers who want to check the quotes or their context in this book can find the proper pages in the editions of the novels that I used.

Because I used three novels by Toni Morrison, and two each by James Baldwin, Ernest J. Gaines, Bernice L. McFadden, Gloria Naylor, and Alice Walker, the 27 novels represent the work of 20 authors. Although for the most part the books by the same author seem to me to tell different stories about how racism may affect African American families, I try to be careful throughout this book not to treat the two or three books by the same author as independent cases, because of course they are not.

Novelists with Stories to Tell about Life in a Racist Society

Some of the novelists said (perhaps only years after they published a novel) that they wrote what they wrote because they had things to say about life in a racist society. For example, James Baldwin wanted the world to know what was going on in racist America. Toni Morrison talked about her emphasis on black culture (including black language) in the United States (Ferguson, 2007, pp. 286–7), but then black culture as she conceptualized it seems to be partly in response to, in defense against, and constrained by the racial system. Novelists who focused on struggles with racism could hope that their writings might help to change things. They might well have lived with strong emotions and vivid images that they wanted to put to paper. Besides, to the extent that stories that novelists tell often come from their experience and the experiences of others in their lives, it is not at all strange that African American novelists would write stories that included experiences with racism.

Is there some kind of threat to truth or validity from novelists inspired by their strong feelings about racism? One might argue that they were writing to make change and so were exaggerating or otherwise writing biased accounts. But there is nothing in these novels that seems discrepant from the historical record, sociological research findings, news accounts, and other records of African American life. The structure in the stories (accounts of struggles to live in a Jim Crow world, struggles with racism, struggles with racism-imposed poverty, struggles with police brutality and an unfair criminal justice system, and so on) fit what is in the historical, journalistic, and social science record. In a sense, the novels that have much to say about how racism affects African American families are not trying to persuade readers but are bearing witness to harsh realities (cf. Durrant, 2004). Furthermore, the novels are not only about racism. Every novel depicts people who are complex, autonomous individuals whose lives involve much more than whatever it takes to deal with white people, racism, and the limitations imposed on them by white people and institutions. So I doubt that any of the novels offers an invalid view of the racial system and of African American families.

By contrast, some of the novelists wanted to tell a story that did not focus primarily on struggles with racism. For example, Terry McMillan, writing seemingly for an audience of young, urban, upwardly mobile or middle-class Black women seems to intentionally emphasize other things than racial conflict (Smiles, 2010). Paule Marshall, author of *Brown Girl, Brownstones*, said that she wanted to tell the story of a young urban woman in the context of her community, not to tell a story in which racism defined the central characters (Bröck, 1984). One novel that says almost nothing about racism is Zora Neale Hurston's *Their Eyes Were Watching God*. Meisenhelder described it as a book that examines "models of black male and female identity and the larger social world they both reflect and shape" (1999, p. 62). In the dialogue of the characters, racism is a minor irritant and concern. Although a reader can bring to bear on the novel personal knowledge of how white racism sets the constraints on the characters in the novel, white people are almost absent from the novel, and racism is scarcely mentioned. When *Their Eyes Were Watching God* was published, some African American reviewers criticized it for "ignoring the harmful effects of racism" (Spencer, 2006). But Gates (2006) argued that Hurston made a deliberate choice to resist a way of writing and thinking that she thought made African American life seem so responsive to racial oppression that African Americans seemed to be depicted as people whose lives, thoughts, actions, and feelings were simply reactions to white people and to racial oppression.

Similarly, Gloria Naylor in writing *Mama Day* paid little attention to racism. And perhaps speaking indirectly for writers who chose not to say much about racism, Toni Morrison wrote in *The Song of Solomon* the following about Guitar, the most didactic, analytic character in that book and the one who most talks about the US racial system:

> He was bored. Everybody bored him. The city was boring. The racial problems that consumed Guitar were the most boring of all. He wondered what they would do if they didn't have black and white problems to talk about. Who would they be if they couldn't describe the insults, violence, and oppression that their lives (and the television news) were made up of? If they didn't have Kennedy or Elijah to quarrel about? ... Every job of work undone, every bill unpaid, every illness, every death was The Man's fault. (p. 108)

One could take Guitar's thoughts about racism as connected to why African American authors might not write much about racism. Writing about racism would take away from the other areas of life and limit the scope of what characters talk about. Racism could become an excuse central to meaning systems in ways that could disempower characters and limit the ways they could take charge of their lives and make sense of things. Focusing on the impact of racism could make it seem that African American life is one of reaction to what whites do, and that would make whites the center of the story and make African Americans seem to lack agency in creating their own lives, families, and communities (Schryer, 2011, pp. 55–81).

Is there some kind of threat to truth or validity from novelists choosing to say little or nothing about racism? I would argue that theirs is as legitimate a perspective and way of looking at African American life as an approach that focuses a great deal on racism.

Analyzing Novels Spanning Decades, Regions of the Country, and Social Classes

The novels analyzed in this book tell stories about people in diverse eras, regions of the country, and economic situations—at one extreme, stories of impoverished southern African Americans trapped and abused as sharecroppers and servants during the Jim Crow era, at the other extreme, an African American middle class living in recent times in material comfort. And yet there are common issues and themes across eras, regions, and economic situations. Across all the changes in economics, laws, discourses about race, educational opportunities, public roles for African Americans, and media depictions of African Americans, the racial system of the United States has not disappeared. It is reflected in persisting racial differences in life expectancy, wealth, income, incarceration, unemployment, access to quality healthcare, and thousands of other indicators of well-being. Here is something from a novel published in 1989, an account of a young African American physician and his wife that speaks to the persistence of the racial system:

> They gave dinner parties and spent time with other young couples like themselves, first- or second-generation Black success stories, who knew they were symbols to whites of how far Blacks had come and proof to other Blacks of how much still remained to be done. (Golden, *Long Distance Life*, p. 219)

There have been historical changes of great importance for African Americans (and hence for everyone else in the United States), and included in that there have been remarkable changes in how much African American-authored fiction is published. Nonetheless, I believe that across the writing eras spanned by the novels analyzed for this book, the fundamental influence of racism on African American families has not changed in such significant ways that it would be necessary to separate novels from, say, the Harlem Renaissance (the 1920s) or the Black Arts Movement (the 1960s) from more recent novels. Family context and forms of racism may change, laws may change, the hiring patterns of many employers may change, educational barriers may be eliminated for some African Americans, and the resources available to some African American families may now be very substantial, but racism still occurs and can still come home to African American families. Despite the powerful and diverse forms of denial by many in the country (Bonilla-Silva, 2010), racism is still a powerful and pervasive force.

Literary Criticism Focused on the Novels

Hundreds of articles, book chapters, book reviews, and books have been written about the novels analyzed in this book. This literature is filled with solid and careful analyses of what the novels might mean, who the characters are, and how the authors came to write what they wrote. Reviewing much of this literature has confirmed my initial readings of the novels but also, at times, given me new and valuable insights. Still, my focus is so specific and so different from the foci that are common in critical writings about the novels that most of the works of criticism I have looked at do not address what this book focuses on, the influence of racism on African American family life. And so I cite only a small fraction of that work. This book puts together two perspectives that have not often been taken in literary analysis, a focus on racism and a focus on family dynamics. Although racism is at the heart of some of the novels and provides context for all of them, most analyses of these texts focus on other matters than racism. Related to this, Bouson (2000) has written about how unsettling and even discomforting scholarly study of racism is (p. x). That might be one of the reasons why there are not more published analyses of the novels that address racism. Bouson (2000, p. 3) has, in particular, commented on how critical analysis of the novels of Toni Morrison has largely stayed away from the elements of racism in her works. Similarly, in my reading of literary criticism dealing with the novels, family dynamics are virtually never at the focus, though a few specific family events (for example, Cholly's incestuous rape of Pecola in Morrison's *The Bluest Eye*) are ingredients for critical discussion. To the extent that literary analysis of the novels touches on issues of social science and psychology it is typically about individual psychology (gender identity, for example, or individual psychological development), not about family dynamics. I cite relevant literary criticism in this book, but given the focus of this book, not so much is relevant.

Are the Novels Independent of One Another?

If there are underlying similarities among the novels in how racism is depicted as affecting family life, it could be because the novelists have had similar experiences and have heard similar stories. But then it also could be that some of the novelists knew and were even good friends with others of the novelists, and that allowed for mutual influence. For example, among the authors whose novels are used in this book, Zora Neale Hurston and Dorothy West were, for a while, good friends (Mitchell and Davis, 2012; Newkirk, 2009, p. 284) and Hurston and Langston Hughes worked together on a literary journal and knew each other well (Newkirk, 2009, pp. 279–80). Still another force for similarity among the novels is that many of the novelists almost certainly read the works of others of the novelists and may have been influenced by what others wrote. For example, Gloria Naylor, two of whose novels provide data for this book, talked about how much she was influenced by reading another book used as data in this project, Toni Morrison's

The Bluest Eye (Goldstein, 1983), and Naylor has written that she knew all of Toni Morrison's novels almost by heart (Naylor, 1985). Then too, Paule Marshall talked about how much she was influenced by Gwendolyn Brooks' *Maud Martha* (Bröck, 1984), and Alice Walker, who resurrected interest in the work of Zora Neale Hurston, has been said to have taken up themes in her own writing that were central to Hurston's work (Howard, 1993).

Although there were many possibilities for authors of some of the novels to have been influenced by authors of other of the novels, my belief is that most or all what the novelists bring to their novels about how racism comes home to families arises from personal experiences and their sense of the experiences of other African Americans. That is, they are not somehow imitating one another's work or drawn into a common authorial subculture but are each drawing on personal experiences and the experiences of many other people who they know or know about. Then if there is similarity between novels about some matter, I believe the similarity is about racism expressing itself in more or less the same way across the differences of experience and awareness of multiple authors. The similarity is also, I think, about the similarity across places and times in how African American families deal with the various insults, limitations, and forms of damage racism causes.

Analyzing and Writing about the Novels

In analyzing the novels I have carried out what I would call a thematic analysis, the kind of analytic process I have done with in-depth interview material (e.g. Rosenblatt, Karis, and Powell, 1995; Rosenblatt and Wallace, 2005a, 2005b; Rosenblatt and Wieling, 2013). I read and reread the novels with a great deal of openness to what the novelists had to say about racism affecting African American families. As my reading progressed, I developed thematic conceptual categories for the material, and some of these grew, as the material accumulated, to become chapter titles and headings within chapters.

I read the novels as a literalist, although some of them at places or throughout have an allegorical, magical, or satirical character. I think it is legitimate to do a literalist reading of such works because the allegories, magical tales, and satires are invariably wrapped around stories about people living everyday lives. So in my analyses I still have the everydayness to analyze for family life and experiences of racism. That is not to deny the validity, power, and insight of readings that would focus on the allegorical, magical, and satirical but only to say that for the purposes of this book I look at everyday lives as represented in the novels.

Since this book focuses on the intersection of racism with African American family life, there are far fewer quotes in what follows from novels that offer little content at that intersection, and those novels do not provide as many of the examples and insights. That means some of the novels contribute far more to the discussions in this book than others do. Such a difference in how much a given case contributes to a research report is, I think, quite common in qualitative interview research, with some interviewees contributing much more material than others that illustrates concepts and processes and that inspires and informs analysis and discussion.

Deciding what is Racism

Deciding what is racist in the novels was both very easy and very challenging. What was easy was that there were instances in which the author or one or more characters says explicitly that something was racist. I treat those statements as accurate. Also, there are actions of white people in the novels directed at black people that seem clearly to be attacking, discriminatory, unjust, demeaning, insulting, dismissive, hurtful, harmful, frightening, or oppressive. I counted those also as racist. There are also institutional forms of racism that impact the characters. With institutional racism there are situations where there is no particular white person who is depicted in a novel passage as acting racist, but an African American individual or family in contact with the institution seems to me to have been victimized by discriminatory, unfair, cruel, oppressive, or hurtful action or inaction. For example, if the canned patriotic speech given to an African American child to read at a school ceremony says nothing about racism and the difficulties African Americans face but instead says that all Americans are treated equally by government institutions and have the same economic opportunities, I counted that as institutional racism. Or if railroads have a policy of requiring African Americans to sit in segregated cars, I counted that as institutional racism.

To complicate things, racism has shifted over the years. For example, some of the most blatant racist acts that were commonplace, particularly in the US south, have for the most part disappeared. However, there is arguably a "new racism" (e.g. Bonilla-Silva, 2001, pp. 89–136; 2010) that is often covert or masked in comparison to the racism of the past. Whites and institutions that express racism nowadays are more likely to avoid using what whites might consider to be racist language, and the mechanisms for reproducing racial inequality are defined and justified in nonracist terms. In some sense, what has changed with the new racism are the justifications used to frame what can be seen as mistreatment of African Americans, the language used to talk about African Americans who are injured by institutionalized racism, and what white people who benefit from the new racism and/or who have some role in making it happen say about themselves (Bonilla-Silva, 2010). To some extent my analysis of the experience of racism in the novels means looking at different kinds of incidents for novels set in recent times versus novels set years ago. But then many forms of the "new racism" are not in the more recent novels. I think that is in large part because many forms of the new racism are about white denial and that is not central to what happens in a story about African Americans living their lives.

Because quite a few passages from the novels that are quoted in this book include material on what I counted as racist, the reader is in a position to evaluate what I counted as racist, to decide whether or not there was validity to my classifying something as racist.

In the novels there are passages that the novelists may have understood to be about racism but that are not clearly to me to be about racism. I have chosen to treat passages like that as not being about racism. To illustrate, in *The Street*, Ann Petry wrote this about a bar, the Junto, in Harlem:

> The inside of the Junto was always crowded ... because the white bartenders in their immaculate coats greeted the customers graciously. Their courteous friendliness was a heart-warming thing that helped rebuild egos battered and bruised during the course of the day's work. (p. 143)

I chose to interpret the reference to "egos battered and bruised during the course of the day's work" as meaning that life can be bruising for anyone, even though Petry might have meant that dealing with white people batters and bruises the African Americans who frequent the Junto. As another example, in the first chapter of *The Street*, Lutie, the main character, thinks about her extremely meager savings and earnings and about the near illiteracy of the African American building "super" who rents her an apartment. Lutie does not say that her savings and earnings are so slim because she is an African American in a racist society, or that the super is so poorly educated because he is an African American in a racist society. But Petry might have believed that an African American reader, or any reader, would understand that Lutie was thinking about racism. It may be a limitation of this book that I read passages like these cautiously, as not being about racism, but I would rather not make inferential leaps that take me beyond what an author explicitly wrote.

On Not Focusing on the Core of Some of the Novels

As was said earlier in this chapter, some of the novels focus on matters very different from racism as it affects families. However, every novel seems to me to be about lives in which there are at least undercurrents of racial relationships and difficulties with whites. In every novel, the social scenery and situations have been set in part by white racism—a family's economic situation, its history, the work available to the African American characters, where they live, the kind of formal education they have, and so on. Even Paule Marshall, who said that she wanted to base *Brown Girl, Brownstones* on the kitchen talk of her mother and women relatives and friends that she heard growing up and to depict characters who were not defined by racism, said that the women whose kitchen talk she heard "Spent most of their day working as domestics in the homes of white people, being exploited, being disregarded, being considered the pariah of a society" (Bröck, 1984, p. 196). So it is not surprising that the kitchen talk she heard to some extent was about the diminishments, pain, constraints, and frustrations of menial and difficult work in a white racist world. That does not mean the women's lives were determined by racism, but their kitchen talk could be understood as in part about taking charge of their lives in dealing with and getting perspective on the racism that made life difficult for them. Arguably, even Hurston made racial oppression (along with sexual oppression) an important, though masked, part of *Their Eyes Were Watching God* (Meisenhelder, 1999). Also, as is discussed in Chapter 7, every novel describes at least some African American characters in terms of skin color and other physical features that have meaning in racialized US society, so the characters are depicted in a cultural world that makes skin color, hair texture, etc. important (to the characters, the author, and the author's imagined readers). And every novel, whether racism is central to the story line or, at the other extreme, is hardly mentioned at all, recognizes ways in which racism and oppression by whites have altered or limited the lives of African Americans.

What Is Family?

I had to decide what in the novels to count as "family." Many family scholars argue against using a narrow or closed definition of "family" (e.g. Gubrium and Holstein, 1990). And research on African Americans has documented very well (ever since pioneering work by Stack, 1974) how much African Americans may create synthetic families, families in which kin terms might be used for people who are not kin and in which the people acting like family to each other are not literally family as defined by birth, marriage, or adoption. In an open perspective on family, a family can be any relationships a person defines as family. In this book, I am open to what seems to be "family" to each novelist and the characters in each novel. Hence, "family" includes people who are lovers, sexual partners, housemates, nonrelatives caring for children and the children they care for, or people who have other kinds of connections that they call "family" or that seem to me to be enduring and family-like in terms of emotional connection and interdependence.

Punctuating a Complex World in Order to Understand It

In analyzing family systems and families as part of a larger societal system there is the issue of system punctuation (Rosenblatt, 1994). A system is made up of many elements. To understand and write about a system, we typically cannot immediately grasp the whole system but must take a step by step approach to examine its elements and their links. This means that we must begin by looking at some piece of the system. The choice of where to begin is the punctuation of the system. The choice of where to punctuate the system can affect what we pay attention to and what we ignore, and also what seems most important in the system. So our choice of where to punctuate the system can leave us far short of seeing and understanding the system fully and can lead us to feature or to subordinate what might, from other perspectives, be seen quite differently. For example, if we look at the effects on a family of Dad being denied a job because he is African American, we punctuate the racial system by focusing on the job denial, and that could lead us to pay less attention to or even ignore, among many things, Dad's history of encounters with racism, what he has heard from family and friends about their experiences trying to find or hold jobs, the economic precariousness of the family, health problems Dad might have as a result of where he is forced to live and the health care available to him, or how racism might have left Dad poorly educated to do many jobs. We must punctuate somewhere in order to begin to understand family systems and larger systems, but that punctuation can make us not so aware of the many different ways in which the racial system limits and shapes lives and causes harm.

Novelists must also punctuate in order to tell their stories. And the analyses in this book are inevitably shaped by the punctuation the novelists gave to family systems and the larger systems affecting them. I cannot abandon novelist accounts to see a family system or larger systems in ways not given in the novel. For example, in Ann Petry's *The Street*, one of the crucial family system story lines is that Jim is unable to find a job, and so his wife Lutie must go to work as a maid for a well-off family in Connecticut, leaving Jim and their son Bub behind in New York City, and that leads to Jim having an affair with another woman. As Petry tells the story (and as I develop more fully in Chapter 3), the racial system that denies Jim work is a driving force for the couple to live apart, which is a driving force for Jim to enter into an affair. But conceivably there could be much else about the system in which Lutie and Jim are a couple that could account for Jim's affair. Petry does not touch on such potentially relevant matters as whether Jim felt he needed a woman to do household chores, how sexual abstinence was understood in the family system he created with Lutie or in his family of origin, and whether Jim and Lutie had the inclination and social skill to talk through their issues about him being unemployed, her going far away to work, or his potential to have an affair. In interacting with a real family it often is possible to elicit information from the members about these and related matters, but with a novel we are limited to what is given in the text.

Also, a crucial part of understanding a family system with which one is in direct contact is learning that each member has her or his own perspectives and punctuation of things and her or his understanding of other members' perspectives and punctuation. With a novel, typically we are given some of the perspectives of the main character, and sometimes some of the perspectives of other characters and of the novelist as narrator. But having partial perspectives and not necessarily perspectives from all characters limits what we can know about a system. Further the novels are for the most part about African American characters and members of African American families. So we do not have much about how whites in the worlds of the novels understand the racial system. All this means that this book works not only with an incomplete and patchwork view of the racial system but also with an incomplete and patchwork view of African American families as they deal with the racial system.

In summary, this book is about family systems and larger systems punctuated by the novelists and then punctuated by me and based on stories that give incomplete information about how the characters punctuate things. I think the novels are more than rich enough to help us to move forward in understanding how racism may come home to families, but everything could be understood in other ways that are missed by the novelists and by me.

What Kind of Knowledge Does This Book Offer?

This book offers a knowledge of possibility, what is possible in African American families affected by racism. It does not offer anything like the truths that some might claim from systematic research on a representative sample of live families. It does not offer the capacities to dig deeper and to probe for certain aspects of veracity or evasion that can come when one can interview people in depth. The novels, as was laid out in Chapter 1, are potential treasures in illuminating aspects of African American life that have not been well studied. But in my opinion, what we have from the novels are things to think and theorize about, things to look for, issues to be concerned about in African American families and issues for further research, but not more.

African American Writers in a White Dominated Publishing World

Toni Morrison, James Baldwin, Ann Petry, Alice Walker, and the other authors whose work provide the data for this book offered their insights into US society and African American life. Reviewers praised their books. Their books succeed in part because of the insights the books offer. But have African American writers been free to tell their truths in a white-dominated publishing world? This is an issue of validity for the analyses in this book. If African American authors are blocked from saying their truths, the novels may not be valid representations of African American family life in a racist society.

There is considerable evidence that in the past African American writers were under pressure from white gatekeepers in publishing to write some things and not others (*Journal of Blacks in Higher Education*, 1995; Washington, 2001). James Baldwin, for example, told about a white publisher who refused to publish a Baldwin book manuscript because it was not what the publisher thought white readers wanted to read, an "official version of the black experience" (Baldwin quoted in Troupe, 1988). Young (2006) offered many examples of white editors and publishers manipulating, controlling, and altering what might be called the wrappings of novels by African American authors, for example, title and advertising. Young also gave examples of African American writers, including some of the most widely read, such as Toni Morrison, being forced to rewrite substantial parts of books.

It is common in writer relationships with editors, literary agents, and publishers for authors to have to revise manuscripts substantially, but to the extent that white editors or publishers have tried to make African American novels more palatable to themselves and to white readers about racial matters that goes beyond what white writers have to deal with. It is of a piece with the racial system in which white people, across many domains, control, manipulate, silence, and demean African Americans (Young, 2006, p. 4). Burrows (2004, p. 136), citing Morrison (1987), saw the similarities in the muting of African American experience in books by African American authors to the muting of slave narratives written in slave times to enlist white support for ending slavery. In the slave narratives, the most horrible, debasing, brutal aspects of slavery would often be veiled as a result of pressures from white publishers and sponsors.

From another perspective, some, perhaps many, African American novelists whose work provide the data for this book may have written with double consciousness, the dual realities that DuBois (1989, p. 3) said were part of the life of black people in white America (Young, 2006). A double consciousness may provide an African American author with an internalized white editorial presence to shape what the author wrote. For example, Toni Morrison wrote about having learned what it takes to publish through her work as an editor with Random House publishing company, and some of "what it takes" was to deal successfully with white gatekeepers by meeting their white standards (Duffey, 2002). Apparently Langston Hughes was under pressure from the white woman who provided financial support for him to revise earlier versions of his novel *Not Without Laughter* to be less threatening to white people (Shields, 1994). Zora Neale Hurston received support from that same woman (Story, 1989), so Hurston, like Hughes, might have been at times influenced to write in ways that were less threatening to white people. Furthermore, Hurston wrote about what white publishers would not publish (1950). She said that white readers, and hence white publishers, lacked curiosity about blacks, did not want to know about black emotions and internal life, and did not want to know about the lives of upper class blacks. Or if white publishers were willing to publish a story about, say, the romantic life of upper class blacks it would have to be complicated by the race struggle (which allows whites to be in the story). And, according to Hurston, if one wrote a story with upper class black protagonists, white publishers insisted that the protagonists would go down to defeat (which puts the black protagonists in a place below white publishers and many white readers). One would hope publishing has come a long way since 1950, when Hurston published her essay, but at least as recently as the early 1990s, it was widely believed in the publishing industry that black people do not read or buy books, and white people will not read black authors or buy books by them (Grimes, 1996). Such beliefs may have led to continuing pressure on black authors to mute what they might have to say about racism.

On the other hand, Young (2006) emphasized that despite the influence and power of white publishers and editors, some African American-authored book manuscripts have come through the publishing process with as little change as might occur to an excellent manuscript by a white author. And some white publishers were champions of African American authors, taking the economic risks not only because they thought there was a market but also because they thought works of those authors should be published (Young, 2006). Also, independent presses owned by African Americans, most notably Third World Press, have published important African American novels.

Even after an African American-authored novel is published, white people may act in ways that keep it from succeeding and being read. For example, there were white people who demanded that books by African American authors, such as Toni Morrison's *Beloved* and *Song of Solomon* and Ernest Gaines' *A Lesson before Dying*, be kept out of high school libraries and off high school reading lists (Reynolds, 2003). Sometimes the effort to ban such books was ostensibly about profanity or explicit sexual content, but sometimes it was that the books seemed anti-white. Morrison talked about white critics who applied white standards to her work and hence were unfairly negative about it (Morrison and McKay, 1983).

I believe the novels relied on in this book ring true and have psychological, sociological, and artistic validity. But I also believe that given the possibilities of white gatekeepers limiting which fiction authored by African Americans about African American life is published and becomes well known, we need to understand that there may have been truths and insights so thoroughly censored that they are difficult or impossible to find in this project. Some very insightful novels may never have been published. Even for novels that have been published, what did white gatekeepers insist on changing or deleting? I do not want to disparage in any way the novels that I rely on in this book and other novels by African American authors that have made it into print. What made it into print offers so much condemnation of white racism, so much insight into the unfairness of the racial system, so much rage at white people, so much pain about what racism has done, and so much insight into the ways that racism has affected African American families that it is obvious that white censorship based on white defensiveness has not been total. There is a lot in African American novels for us to understand and consider concerning the effects of the racial system on African American families. But still, I wonder what might be missing.

White People Writing about African Americans

There are compelling reasons to be wary of white people writing about African Americans (hooks, 1989a). White social scientists are diverse, but there is a long history of white social science pathologizing and blaming African Americans for their differences from whites, their poverty, and anything else that could be defined as a problem (see, for example, Dodson, 2007; Nobles, 2007). White scholars may take standpoints when studying African Americans that offer white realities, miss or misunderstand African American realities, and ignore, minimize, or distort the effect of past and present racism on African Americans. Even many white scholars who ostensibly seem interested in racial justice and contributing to an understanding of the racial system actually seem to support the status quo (a point made by, for example, hooks, 1989a; the essays in Long, 2005, Welcome, 2004; and the essays in Zuberi and Bonilla-Silva, 2008). So it is possible that this book could be construed to blame African Americans, to support a racist status quo, to be clueless about important African American experiences and perspectives, to minimize or distort the influence of past and present racism, or to be trapped in my own positionality as a white male academic. I have no intention of doing any of those things, but it is possible for someone to see me as clueless, to see a deficit model in this book, to see ignorance, or even to see support of the racial system as it exists built into the basic question of this book: How do African American novelists telling stories about African American families write about racism coming home to and affecting life in African American families? Asking how bad things come home to African American families could be about identifying pathology and deficit or keeping the system as it is. But I see this book as about African American families in a societal system, and so if the system bruises, undermines, shapes, limits, or otherwise harms an African American family, the account of the situation is about the system as well as the family. Then the pathology, if that is an appropriate term to use, is in the white dominated system, not the African American family. And illuminating the racial system is a key step in doing away with the pathology of the system.

In a society where white people can be oblivious to much that goes on racially and where many white people are well defended against their own guilt and the ways in which they are complicit in and benefit from a system that oppresses African Americans (Rosenblatt, 2009), I must be concerned, as should be the reader, about my limits and biases. One limit is that as a white person I do not necessarily understand the racism and oppression that is written about in the novels. I may miss important elements of a scene in a novel that the author and many African American readers would see and understand. But the novels are so clear at so many places about racism and its impact on African Americans that I can still provide a substantial account of insights and understandings in the novels about how racism affects African American family life.

Another concern about whiteness that leads to questions about my work in this book is a concern that Zora Neale Hurston raised about the "'arrogance' of whites assuming that black lives are only defensive reactions to white actions" (Gates, 2006, p. 199). This book focuses on the effects of white racism on African American families, and that may reflect or foster such arrogance, but I hope that it offers a counter to that arrogance, arguing for the autonomy and complexity of African American families. Racism is brutally real, but African American life has been and is about vastly more than the influence of racism.

From another angle, African American authors may write in ways that protect their characters and stories from white criticism and misunderstanding. Meisenhelder (1999), for example, argued that Zora Neale Hurston's choice of voice, use of elements from traditional romance stories, and ways of having characters tell certain key things in *Their Eyes Were Watching God* might have been intended to prevent "white appropriation" (p. 89) (and black male appropriation) and misunderstanding of the story and of Janie, the central character.

I am suspicious of white people who claim to be free of racism and racist ignorance, and I am sure I have my limitations and biases. I work hard to combat racism and racist ignorance in myself, but in my efforts on this book, I may have overlooked or misunderstood crucial material in the novels. I may simplify in ways that make white people look more innocent or African Americans look less diverse than they are. And the focus on racism may make white people more important than they actually are in many of the novels and in the lives of many African Americans. On the other hand, the novels seem to me to be so full of insights and so rich in descriptive detail that I can hope that my analysis of the novels offers readers a great deal. Also, I quote extensively from the novels, so readers can see whether the quoted material seems consistent with the points I make about the material. And the novels on which this book is based are widely available, so anyone who wants to check the validity of my interpretations can check a quotation or explore the contexts of the passages I write about.

Chapter 3

When Family Members Are Forced by Racism to Separate

In the novels, there are a number of instances where racism separates family members. A family member flees from the threat of beating, sexual assault or possible death at the hands of white racists. A family member must move elsewhere to find a job because in a racist community there is no job or no adequate job for him or her. Unjust incarceration by a racist criminal justice system separates one family member from others. A family member leaves home to join the civil rights struggle. In the novels each racism-caused separation inevitably leads to difficulties as the family struggles to deal with the emotional and practical gaps resulting from the separation.

Family Separation Alters Family Connection, Support, and Functioning

When racism leads to separation, family patterns inevitably change. Even removing one person from the household alters much that goes on in the family, including who does what, who interacts in what ways with whom, and how well the family does what it has to do. So it is not just that somebody's leaving means people who are left behind are not so well connected with that person, that the person is missed, and that the person's absence is grieved, though these things occur and are extremely important. It is also that when one family member is no longer present, everything can change in the family, and that can be difficult for the people left behind. As can be seen from the examples developed in this chapter, the particulars of what changes will vary depending on the family members involved and where they are in life, who is separated from whom, and the family situation. To develop the line of thought about the importance of particularities, consider the following illustration from James Baldwin's *Go Tell It on the Mountain*. In this instance, how the family changes after the separation hinges on the roles the person who left was filling in the family, the poor health of one family member, the gender constellation of who was left, the maturity level of the younger person left behind, the fact that the two left behind are related as mother and son, the ideas in the family and community about what respectable people do, and of course the limits racism puts on African American families in that community. Now for the specifics. In *Go Tell It on the Mountain*, a racist event that led to family separation was the sexual propositioning of 26-year-old Florence by the white man at whose house she worked.

> She had been working as cook and serving-girl for a large white family ... and it was on the day her master proposed that she become his concubine that she knew that her life among these wretched had come to its destined end. She left her employment that same day ... and ... bought a railroad ticket to New York. (Baldwin, *Go Tell It on the Mountain*, pp. 81–2)

She had been living with her mother and brother. The separation would mean that the three of them would lose their mutual connection and support. Also, Florence's mother was quite ill and dependent on Florence's care. Given that an implicit rule of the family and quite possibly the local African American culture was that ill, infirm family elders should be taken care of by younger family members, once Florence left for New York, her mother would have to be cared for by Florence's ne'er-do-well brother, Gabriel. He was horrified at the prospect of having to care for his mother, partly because a son providing care for a mother risked inappropriate intimacies and the crossing of gender role lines. Also, Florence's leaving would mean that he and his mother would have to get along without Florence's intervention, translation, and cushioning. And her leaving would mean that the emotional debts the two adult children owed to their mother would be Gabriel's alone to pay. That would mean that he would have to change from a life of sin, a change he was reluctant to make.

> [Gabriel] could not endure the thought of being left alone with his mother ... With Florence gone ... <u>he</u>, then, must make amends for all the pain that she had borne. And his mother required of him one proof only, that he tarry no longer in sin. With Florence gone, his ... playing time, contracted with a bound to the sparest interrogative second, when he must stiffen himself, and answer to his mother, and all the host of Heaven ... 'You can't go,' he said. 'You can't go. You can't go and leave your mother thisaway. She need a woman, Florence, to help look after her.' (Baldwin, *Go Tell It on the Mountain*, pp. 84–5)

But Florence did leave. After she left, Gabriel was not only the one other person in his mother's home and so the person who must help her; he was also the only child she had left to mother. All her maternal energy, driven by dying fervency and religious hope, was focused on him. Perhaps it would have been that way even if Florence had not left, because Gabriel had long been seen by his mother as a sinner in need of salvation, but with Florence gone, their mother only had Gabriel to mother, to try to influence, change, and thereby rescue.

> All alone in the cabin his mother lay waiting ... for his surrender to the Lord. She lingered only for this ... She would not go to her rest until her son, the last of her children, he who would place her in the winding-sheet, should have entered the communion of the saints. (Baldwin, *Go Tell It on the Mountain*, p. 101)

So racism and Florence's unwillingness to be defined by her white employer as a concubine, a sexual object, and a person whose work included providing sexual favors led to family separation that had an immense impact on all three family members. There is no hint in the novel that the white man whose sexual advances were responsible for the separation had any thought about what he was doing to Florence's family or that he even thought that his advances would drive Florence away. The situation was difficult and sad, but as Florence, Gabriel, and their mother struggled with the family separation and changes that racism had forced on them, they had the resilience and energy to grow and change in ways that seemed good for them. Florence escaped the constraints of the Jim Crow world (and the definition it tried to impose on her as an African American woman who would willingly serve as a sexual object for a white man) to move to New York City, where economically and in terms of freedom from employer advances she was better-off. Gabriel did not like the changes brought about by his sister's leaving, but the changes led to him moving more quickly to something like responsible adulthood and to his eventually becoming a committed, active Christian and church member, which became central to his identity and place in the community. And Florence's leaving gave her mother the opportunity to do more of the mothering she hoped to do of Gabriel, pushing him toward salvation.

One can also see in the example how the particularities of the people involved, their relationships, and their context markedly shaped what happened as a result of the separation. Family systems theory leads us to expect that changes will typically happen when a person leaves the family (e.g. Rosenblatt and Barner, 2006), but in light of the diversity of people, families, and situations there is not a simple story about what will happen with separation. Thus, with separations caused by racism we can expect diverse family outcomes. The discussion that follows in this chapter focuses on several significant processes by which racism causes family separation, but the examples of what happens to families after the separation are diverse because of the diversity of the individuals, the families, and their situations.

Family Separation Due to Flight from Racist Violence

In some novels, family members are separated when someone leaves home in order to avoid becoming a victim of racist violence. For example, in Toni Morrison's *Song of Solomon* two children who have witnessed the murder of their father by white racist neighbors flee in order not to become the next victims of those neighbors, and they flee in separate directions. Another instance in which surviving family members flee for their lives after the murder of a family member occurs in Ernest J. Gaines' *The Autobiography of Miss Jane Pittman*. When Ned is murdered, his widow and their two young children flee to the north, becoming separated from Miss Jane Pittman, who is the mother-in-law to the widow and the grandmother to the children.

Family separations may have very substantial costs, because family is often central to people finding life meaning, support, safety, identity and much else that is good. In Morrison's *Song of Solomon*, the children who flee in separate directions, the second Macon Dead and Pilate, are all that each has left as family. Morrison does not write about what they lost by separating from each other, but one can imagine that they might have lost each other's support, sharing of memories, affection, and material help. And the abruptness of their flight coupled with them being children made it unlikely that they could talk through plans for reuniting or put words to what they were losing by separating.

Because their separation lasted for many years, Morrison's story is not one of a family dealing with one person leaving. It is the story of two separated children struggling to survive and growing up to create their own mostly separate-from-each-other family systems, systems that reflected what two orphaned children might grow up to do. The racist murder of his father, the separation from his sister, and the flight to save his life engendered in the adult Macon Dead the Second a hunger to own real estate (remember that his father died trying to save the land he owned). So the family system of Macon Dead the Second centered on his focus on real estate. Although Pilate and Macon Dead the Second spent years wandering far from each other, Pilate eventually settled in the same community as Macon Dead the Second, and she became a powerful woman in the community because of her wisdom and healing power, her ability to earn a living through selling bootleg liquor, and her almost magical power to influence people. Although she and Macon Dead the Second still had very little to do with each other, it was only through her magical intervention that the second Macon Dead was for a brief time sexually drawn to his wife and thus fathered his son. And clearly he valued the son, so the remnant of family connection between the two orphaned siblings made a difference for good.

Labor Migration and Family Separation

Joblessness and hiring discrimination can come home to African American families in ways that can make great difficulty in family interactions (Boyd-Franklin, 2003, pp. 98, 106–9; Feagin and McKinney, 2003, pp. 113–14). In several novels, a key element of the story is the way that joblessness and job denial affect a character, particularly a man. Men lose or are turned down for jobs that they could do well. For the African American families in the novels who are on the edge of survival economically, if an adult does not have a job, that can be very difficult for the family. Plus historically in African American families a man's identity was tied to his providing for his family (Hines and Boyd-Franklin, 1996). Sometimes, in the novels, men are doing their job competently but are laid off because white coworkers do not want to work with an African American. Here is a character, Jimboy, in the Langston Hughes novel, *Not Without Laughter*:

'Donahoe laid me off yesterday on account o' the white bricklayers said they couldn't lay bricks with a nigger.' (Hughes, *Not Without Laughter*, p. 71)

Jimboy is told that he cannot work because he is not in the union, but then as an African American he is not allowed to join the union.

'I said I'd join, but I knew they wouldn't let me … I told the guys there I was a bricklayer and asked 'em how I was gonna work if I couldn't be in the union. And the fellow who had the cards, secretary I guess he was, says kinder sharp, like he didn't want to be bothered: "That's your look-out, big boy, not mine."' (Hughes, *Not Without Laughter*, p. 87)

Jimboy faces a bleak employment future in his hometown of Stanton, with the only job possibilities being menial and ill-paying (hard work, low wages, and being defined constantly as less than white men).

What was there in Stanton anyhow for a young colored fellow to do except dig sewer ditches for a few cents an hour or maybe porter around a store for seven dollars a week. Colored men couldn't get many jobs in Stanton, and foreigners were coming in, taking away what little work they did have. No wonder he didn't stay home. Hadn't Annjee's father been in Stanton forty years and hadn't he died with Aunt Hager still taking in washings to help keep up the house? (Hughes, *Not Without Laughter*, p. 45)

So Jimboy leaves his wife Annjee, his son Sandy, and his mother-in-law, Aunt Hager, in search for a job elsewhere. They are no longer united as a family. The separation deprives Jimboy of interaction with his wife, son, and mother-in-law and them of interaction with him, and the separation is hard emotionally for Annjee and Sandy. On the other hand, the separation seems to make it even clearer than it was before to Annjee how much she loves Jimboy. And his move north puts him in a better situation in terms of job possibilities and perhaps relative freedom from racism. So once again racism causes separations that are difficult.

When family members migrate elsewhere for work (and to escape the local versions of racism and racism-driven poverty that are linked to joblessness and menial jobs), those left behind can understand their leaving but still miss them and feel sad and worried about them. Here are the thoughts and feelings of an adult, Jacob, thinking about his brothers who have fled the dreadful working situation of their home area in rural Maryland.

A hot tear crept down his face … Strong remembrance of his three brothers all gone off to … Baltimore to try and make something of themselves and singing and slaving the worse kind of paying jobs washed over Jacob. Little runty Levi … tugged the hardest at Jacob's heart. But he did, too, worry about big, tall Tom who Jacob knew good and well would be trying to act like some big city hustling man with his hair all slicked back with piles of grease ... Wasn't so much worried about Emerson. He ... had the most sense ... But still in all, Jacob ... couldn't help but want 'em home. Needed them so bad. (Wright, *This Child's Gonna Live*, p. 48)

As this quote illustrates, separation does not necessarily end emotional connection. Family members still care about one another. There is still a family system of sorts. So racism does not necessarily neutralize the power of family relationship. In fact separation may make it clearer than it was before how important family members are to one. The "Needed them so bad" at the end of the above quote can be taken to refer to many things, including missing mutual interaction, mutual support, and shared work efforts. Thus, in grieving for family members who have left to find jobs or better jobs there is the potential for a powerful awareness of family connection and interaction and the significance of that connection and interaction.

From another perspective, a case can be made that reality is talked into existence through couple and family interaction (see Berger and Kellner, 1964, for a pioneering theoretical statement). To the extent this is so, when racism separates family member from family member, among the many things they lose is the interaction that helped them to make sense of what goes on in their daily life. From that perspective, to the extent that racism separates family members it also in some sense undermines the relationships they had in place to make sense of things. They may turn to other relationships for sense-making, but if they do not, that can leave them unsure of what to make of things. And in any case not making sense of things together means that family members are not only separated physically but also can be separated in terms of developing different meanings for significant experiences and events.

Family Separation Due to Unjust Incarceration

In several novels, an important element of the story is family separation due to unjust incarceration by a racist criminal justice system. As might be expected from family systems theory analyses of how the incarceration of a family member can have a substantial impact on the family (e.g. Imber-Black, 2008), the instances in the novels in which incarceration of a family member occurs are in part stories of family change and sometimes great difficulty as a result of the incarceration. One example comes from Alice Walker's *The Color Purple*, when Sofia is imprisoned after a confrontation that began with Sofia refusing to work as a maid for the mayor's wife.

What she in jail for? ...
Sassing the [white] mayor's wife ...
[The mayor's wife] eye Sofia wristwatch. She say to Sofia, All your children so clean ... would you like to work for me, be my maid?

Sofia say, Hell no.

Mayor look at Sofia, push his wife out the way. Stick out his chest. Girl, what you say to Miss Millie?

Sofia say, I say, Hell no.

He slap her …

Sofia knock the man down.

The polices come, start slinging the children off the mayor, bang their heads together. Sofia really start to fight. They drag her to the ground. (Walker, *The Color Purple*, pp. 84–5)

Terrible things happen to Sofia, as the white police apply extra-judicial punishment to her.

When I see Sofia I don't know why she still alive. They crack her skull, they crack her ribs. They tear her nose loose on one side. They blind her in one eye. She swole from head to foot. Her tongue the size of my arm, it stick out tween her teef like a piece of rubber. She can't talk. (Walker, *The Color Purple*, pp. 86–7)

Squeak, the mistress of Sofia's husband Harpo, is suddenly burdened with taking care of the six children of Sofia and Harpo, with the help of Sofia's sisters. Family and friends talk about trying to get Sofia out of prison by appealing to one of their white relatives (because so many African Americans in the community have been fathered by white men). Squeak is elected because the prison warden is her uncle (his brother had fathered her), but then Sofia is sexually assaulted by the warden. Following the assault she returns home to Harpo, feeling ashamed and insecure.

She turned her face up to Harpo. Harpo, she say, do you really love me, or just my color?

Harpo say, I love you, Squeak. He kneel down and try to put his arm round her waist.

She stand up, My name Mary Agnes, she say. (Walker, *The Color Purple*, p. 97)

Sofia is subsequently moved out of prison and put to work, as a semi-slave, for the white mayor and his wife. As a semi-slave, and a person who is continually defined as much less that whites and deserving of terrible punishment for her initial resistance to working for the mayor's wife, Sofia is not allowed contact with her family.

They won't let me see my children … Well, after five years they let me see you once a year … Us pull into the yard and all the children come crowding round the car. Nobody told them I was coming, so they don't know who I is. Except the oldest two. They fall on me, and hug me. And then all the little ones start to hug me too. (Walker, *The Color Purple*, pp. 103–4)

After 11 1/2 years, Sofia is finally freed by the mayor and his wife. Sofia has missed years of opportunity to mother her children and the life she could have had with Harpo and the rest of her family. And they have missed what they could have had with her.

> Her bigger children married and gone, and her littlest children mad at her, don't know who she is. Think she act funny, look old and dote on that little white gal she raise [the child of the mayor and his wife]. Yesterday us all had dinner at Odessa's house. Odessa Sofia's sister. She raise the kids. Her and her husband Jack. Harpo's woman Squeak, and Harpo himself. Sofia sit down at the big table like there's not room for her. Children reach cross her like she not there. Harpo and Squeak act like a old married couple. Children call Odessa mama. Call Squeak little mama. Call Sofia 'miss.' (Walker, *The Color Purple*, pp. 198–9)

So racism undermines Sofia's connection with her children and her husband. She is not there for her children, even though she lives nearby, because she is an enslaved worker in the mayor's house. Sofia's husband, Harpo, and the children found ways to get along without Sofia. They had followed patterns that are not uncommon in African American family systems of (a) opening family boundaries so as to allow people not in the nuclear family to provide help and (b) role flexibility in accommodating to the ways that racism blocks or undermines a family's customary and preferred pattern of carrying out roles (Pinderhughes, 1982). Harpo and the rest of the family had also found ways to make their realities in a Berger and Kellner (1964) sense without Sofia, so in that sense racism did not overwhelm them when it pulled her from the household. In fact, the family was already organized to be flexible in terms of who was with whom and who was carrying out what roles. Sofia had actually been away from home at an earlier time, before the incident with the mayor and his wife, so her sisters had already been a presence in the lives of her children and had important roles in caring for and raising them. Harpo had not been monogamous prior to the incident with the mayor. And more generally, the family had been functioning all along as an extended family with considerable contact, support, and mutuality within the larger family group, which gave it more capacity to deal with the absence of Sofia. So even though for everyone, particularly Sofia, there was a great deal of loss, change, and sadness resulting from the forced removal of Sofia from the household, one should not overstate the extent of individual and family devastation by racism due to Sofia's incarceration. In this story, as in the others already discussed in this chapter, the tragic costs of racism do not necessarily block individuals and families from making the best of things, from growing, and from finding ways to cope and to live their lives. But still, there are all those interactions that did not happen, all the realities not constructed together, and all those losses and the attendant sadness to deal with.

Family Blaming Resulting from Unjust Incarceration

Across the novels a number of individual and family problems arise from family separation due to unjust incarceration, including loneliness, economic difficulties, role overload, and grieving. In James Baldwin's *If Beale Street Could Talk*, one problem that arises as a result of unjust incarceration is family blaming. Fonny, the 21-year-old lover of 18-year-old Tish, is arrested and jailed for a rape he did not commit. The arrest hinges on police-coerced, police-coached, and police-manipulated testimony by the rape victim and on lies told by the white arresting officer. It also hinges on the fact that Fonny is the only black man in the police lineup when the victim, who said she was raped by a black man, is asked by the police whether anyone in the lineup looks like the man who raped her. Fonny was with Tish and a friend many miles away from the scene of the rape at the time when it occurred.

The arrest and jailing mean that Fonny is separated from Tish. Tish is three months pregnant with their child when Fonny is arrested. And as Tish's mother says,

'You and Fonny be together right now, married or not, wasn't for that … damn white man.' (Baldwin, *If Beale Street Could Talk*, p. 33)

The separation produces great difficulty in both Fonny's family and Tish's. A key difficulty is the blaming that arises as a result of Fonny being jailed. Here is part of a conversation between Fonny's father and Tish's father about blaming:

'The first thing we got to do … is to stop blaming each other, and stop blaming ourselves. If we can't do that, man, we'll never get the boy out because *we'll* be so fucked up.' (Baldwin, *If Beale Street Could Talk*, p. 124)

So the racist acts that led to the incarceration not only produce family separation in a physical sense, they also led to blaming that produces emotional separation and is thus an additional heavy burden on family relationships. In particular questions arise about whether if Fonny had been parented differently he would not have become a target for the racist police officer. There are perspectives from which the blaming is irrational. After all, the racist police officer acted with malice and dishonesty, and it was his actions, not Fonny's, that led to Fonny's incarceration. But there is a sense in a racist system in which self-blaming and blaming within the family may make psychological sense. Since family members know they live in a racist system, they might think that they should learn to act to avoid as many of the problems that can arise from that system as is possible, and children are typically raised to navigate the racist system in order to avoid problems (see Chapter 9). From that perspective, if someone is victimized by the racist system, family members may question what one or more of them did that made the problem arise. And from a broader perspective, blaming can be seen as connected to agency. That is, the blaming can be taken to mean that people are unwilling to be passive victims in a very dangerous social environment but that they see themselves as able to do things that can protect them in some ways from racism and can promote their own well-being. Blaming can be harmful in families, but it can be seen as connected to the faith that all is not lost, that there are things to do to navigate the racist environment with some safety. But then from another angle, blaming can be understood from a critical race theory perspective as a way for racism to define African American families as responsible for their own plight. And that is a heavy burden.

The story of the unjust incarceration of Fonny is tragic, but as in other instances discussed in this chapter, family members are not defeated. They use what they have individually and collectively to make the best of the situation. Fonny and Tish affirm their love for one another. They and their child in utero receive great, loving support from some of their family members, and the fathers of the two lovers find strength and affirming connection in their shared efforts to make sense of things and to raise the money necessary for Fonny's legal defense. Still, the racial system and the racist white police officer have exacted a terrible toll on family relationships in the novel.

Family Separation Because of Involvement in Civil Rights Work

In Marita Golden's *Long Distance Life*, a novel set during the Civil Rights Era, Esther leaves her lover Randolph, her son Logan, and her mother Naomi in Washington, DC, to go to Alabama to work for civil rights. For Esther it is a deeply meaningful thing to do. Naomi has been critical of Randolph, who is married to someone else while being Esther's lover and fathering Logan. But Esther's absence draws Naomi and Randolph closer together in their shared concern for Logan and perhaps in their shared feeling of loss. Esther's involvement in efforts to promote civil rights spurs Randolph and Naomi to have long conversations about the possibilities, the gains, and the potential problems with improvement in civil rights. Esther stays away four years. With the separation, Naomi, Randolph, and Logan are denied conversations with Esther, her company and love, and the co-construction of realities with her. They are denied information about her daily life, which means they are also denied a sense of how meaningful what she is doing is to her and potentially to them. And Esther is often not safe, and for a while she is even jailed in Alabama for her civil rights work. When Esther comes home, she and her son cannot get back the years they missed being with each other.

> Logan came and sat on the bed and asked Esther, 'Why did you come back?'
> Esther ... let her hand rest on Logan's cheek and said, 'I'd done as much as I could do.'

He hoped she would say, 'I came back to see you. Because I missed you more than I could stand.' But she had denied him those hallowed words, which had been the music of his dreams ...

'Was it worth it?' ...

'If I didn't think it was worth it, I could not have come back to face any of you. Not with the price I asked you to pay.' (Golden, *Long Distance Life*, pp. 188–9)

So another cost of the racial system can be that some family members separate from others in order to fight for the rights that are denied African Americans by the racial system. But when a person works to mitigate racial injustice and to make life better for African Americans, separation in order to do that work can seem from some angles to be meaningful, good, and laudable.

From another perspective, the Civil Rights Movement fight against racism could create emotional separation between older family members and younger ones because the younger family members so valued the work of the Civil Rights Movement while perhaps disparaging the work of earlier generations for civil rights. Here, for example, is an interaction between a mother and daughter who have strong differences about the work of the NAACP in the years before the Civil Rights Movement.

'You don't have to live in a slum to be concerned about social conditions ... Your father and I have been charter members of the NAACP for the last twenty-five years.'

'... That's being concerned? That middle-of-the-road, Uncle Tom dumping ground for black Republicans?'

'You can sneer all you want ... but that organization has been working for black people since the turn of the century.' (Naylor, *The Women of Brewster Place*, p. 85)

The generational distance can also come from family elders who assert that despite the changes brought by the Civil Rights Movement, racism persists.

'Mama ... how can you—a black woman—sit there and tell me that what we fought for during the Movement wasn't important ... ?'

'... I'm not saying it wasn't important. It was damned important to stand up and say that you were proud of what you were and to get the vote and other social opportunities for every person in this country who had it due. But you kids thought you were going to turn the world upside down, and it just wasn't so. When all the smoke had cleared, you found yourself with a fistful of new federal laws and a country still full of obstacles for black people to fight their way over—just because they're black. There was no revolution.' (Naylor, *The Women of Brewster Place*, p. 84)

So in the novels the brave and in part successful efforts to fight racism through civil rights activism could not only lead to physical separation in African American families, they could also lead to emotional separation. But here too, family members need not be defeated in their efforts to get along. Family connection persists. The fact that mother and daughter could have the conversation that they have in the Naylor novel means that they are drawn together both because they are talking and because there is underlying agreement about the value of resisting racism and working for all African Americans. That is, from a perspective that says that family conflict enables family members to know one another better and to air their differences, the Naylor passages are not only about family schisms that arise from racism but also about family members who work at coming together in their airing of differences, their agreement about basic values, and their underlying love.

Chapter 4

Racism and Relationship Commitment

In the novels, racism can lead to processes that undermine relationship commitment, but in their determination to make a go of things in the face of racism some characters in the novels do things that strengthen relationship commitment.

Racism Can Damage the Capacity to Have an Intimate, Committed Relationship

In some novels, racism causes such harm to an African American character that it undermines the person's capacity to have an intimate, committed relationship. The paths by which racism undermines relationships are diverse. In some novels young children are abandoned, orphaned, or otherwise cut off from parents and other caregivers, and this childhood history of loss may lead children, when adults, to have trouble committing to anyone. In the family systems literature, children with that kind of background may not trust others to be able to continue in a relationship or may not trust others at all, and thus may create relationship systems around them that close boundaries to potential help and emotional support (Pinderhughes, 1982). Adults with childhood loss of significant relationships may not have had the kinds of experiences that would lead them to be able to hold up their end of a committed relationship. They may fear that there is something about them that leads others to leave or die. What follows is an example from the novels of that kind of fear in someone who has experienced frequent losses. Guitar, a central character in Toni Morrison's *Song of Solomon*, talks about his fear that if he loves someone they will die.

> 'Everything I ever loved in my life left me. My father died when I was four. That was the first leaving I knew and the hardest. Then my mother. There were four of us and she just couldn't cut it when my father died. She ran away. Just ran away. My aunt took care of us until my grandmother could get there. Then my grandmother took care of us. Then Uncle Billy came. They're both close to dead now. So it was hard for me to latch onto a woman. Because I thought if I loved anything it would die.' (Morrison, *Song of Solomon*, p. 311)

Fear of killing someone with one's love would mean that the closer one came to loving someone the more one would want to hold back one's love because of fear of killing the person. That means one would avoid love relationships and could seem to someone with whom one might be moving toward a love relationship to be pulling away just as the relationship seems to be getting closer. So the problem is not only Guitar's but also that of anyone who comes close to being loved by Guitar.

One could read what Guitar said as meaning that people somehow die, without Guitar doing anything to make the death happen, when Guitar loves the person. But at the end of the novel Guitar sets out to assassinate Milkman, who has been a close friend, and who at one time he seemed to love. The ostensible motivation for trying to kill Milkman is that Guitar believes Milkman has cheated Guitar and a group with which he is associated out of treasure they deserve. But one could take that as a pretext, that the real reason Guitar wants to murder Milkman is that things would not feel right to Guitar if Milkman lived because everyone Guitar loves he loses. Although the specifics of how things develops in the novel are fanciful, there may be a core of truth that fits many people who have come to feel that their losses arising from racism are somehow their fault. That is, perhaps one can come to feel so strongly that it is something about one that leads to one's losses that one can feel so uncomfortable in a loving relationship that one will do things to end the relationship.

Another way in the novels in which racism can undermine the capacity for a committed relationship is through the effect of sexual assault by a white man on a woman's sexual and relationship capacities. In Baldwin's *Go Tell It on the Mountain*, Deborah, then a young girl, is raped by a group of white men. The rape affects her future as a possible wife, first of all by engendering in her a hatred of men that makes it difficult for her to bring herself to think about marrying. Also, having been raped makes her, in the eyes of most African American men in her community, an inappropriate wife, which makes it almost impossible for her to find a partner, even if she were able to bring herself to consider marrying.

> There was her legend, her history, which would have been enough, even had she not been so wholly unattractive, to put her forever beyond the gates of any honorable man's desire. This, indeed, in her silent, stolid fashion, she seemed to know … She contained only the shame that she had borne—shame, unless a miracle of human love delivered her, was all she had to give. (Baldwin, *Go Tell It on the Mountain*, p. 110)

However, her downfall becomes a basis of attraction for Gabriel. Gabriel carries his own burdens that are in part rooted in how racism had harmed him and his family (see, for example, the discussion in Chapter 3 of what happened when Gabriel's sister Florence flees to the north rather than acquiesce to the sexual advances of the white man for whom she works). Gabriel is drawn to Deborah and eventually marries her because he thinks that she can help him and he can help her.

> It came to him that, as the Lord had given him Deborah, to help him to stand, so the Lord had sent him to her, to raise her up, to release her from that dishonor which was hers in the eyes of men. (Baldwin, *Go Tell It on the Mountain*, p. 123)

But the rape leaves Deborah permanently limited as a sexual person, and that becomes a problem of relationship commitment between her and Gabriel.

> Gabriel saw, as though for the first time, how black and how bony was this wife of his, and how wholly undesirable ... He thought of the joyless groaning of their marriage bed; and he hated her. (Baldwin, *Go Tell It on the Mountain*, p. 135)

Also the rape may be responsible for Deborah being unable to bear a child, an inability that is part of what Gabriel comes to hate about her. So that too is a way that racism has undermined her capacity (and Gabriel's) to have an intimate, committed relationship.

A very different kind of example of the loss of capacity for committed relationship comes from Toni Morrison's *Song of Solomon*. In that novel, as is described in Chapter 3, when the second Macon Dead was a boy, his father, the first Macon Dead, was murdered. The father, who was parenting alone because his wife had died in childbirth several years before, worked hard to build up his farm and was a good father. The first horrible intrusion of racism was that he was cheated out of his farm.

> 'Papa couldn't read, couldn't even sign his name. Had a mark he used. They tricked him. He signed something, I don't know what, and they told him they owned his property ... Everything bad that ever happened to him happened because he couldn't read.' (Morrison, *Song of Solomon*, p. 53)

From a critical race theory perspective it is not an accident that whereas whites have the opportunity to become competent to read and understand legal documents through learning provided by the educational system, the fate of many African Americans in the past and even now in the educational system has been and is functional illiteracy (Baugh, 2001). That difference in opportunity enhances the power of whites relative to African Americans when it comes to understanding legal documents. Doomed to illiteracy, the first Macon Dead unintentionally signed away his farm. Because he subsequently resisted giving up the farm that he had been cheated out of, the first Macon Dead was murdered by the wealthy white neighbors who had cheated him.

Following the murder of his father, the second Macon Dead, still a boy, was on his own. He grew to manhood and eventually had a wife and children. But the murder of his father continued to haunt him. One expression of that haunting was his overwhelming ambition to be like what he perceived white men to be and have what they have in terms of control of property. The angry obsession to be economically powerful dominates his thinking and undermines his marriage, his parenting, and his relationship with his sister. He and his sister Pilate, who as an adult lives near the second Macon Dead, eventually have a falling out, driven in large part by his greed and economic insecurity. In addition, the fact that the second Macon Dead is haunted by the murder of his father leads to him demanding things of his wife and children and controlling them in ways that are harmful to them as individuals and to their relationships with him and each other. He refuses to have sexual intercourse with his wife. In this environment, his son, Milkman (the third Macon Dead) struggles to find himself, never knowing why his father is the way he is. Milkman's journey to learn about himself and his father eventually leads him to understand how scarred his father had been when, as a child, he had seen his own father murdered. That helps Milkman to understand why his father focuses so much on wealth and property and so little on his wife, children, and sister.

> His father [was] an old man now, who acquired things and used people to acquire more things. As the son of Macon Dead the first, he paid homage to his own father's life and death by loving what his father had loved: property, good solid property, the bountifulness of life. He loved these things to excess. Owning, building, acquiring—that was his life, his future, his present, and all the history he knew. That he distorted life, bent it, for the sake of gain, was a measure of his loss at his father's death. (Morrison, *Song of Solomon*, p. 304)

Milkman finally understands how racism has undermined his father's capacity to have committed, intimate relationships.

In another example of racism damaging the capacity to have committed relationships, racism induced poverty leads to a situation of sexual exploitation of a child which leads to the child's family disintegrating. That is, in Gloria Naylor's *The Women of Brewster Place*, Ben is a sharecropper whose family economic well-being is at the mercy of his landlord, a white man, Mr Clyde. Mr Clyde requests that Ben's young daughter do domestic work in his household, and Ben agrees. Mr Clyde then uses the daughter as a slave owner would, as an object of his sexual pleasure. Her being used that way takes a terrible toll on her, on Ben, and on Ben's relationship with his wife Elvira. Mr Clyde brings the daughter home on Saturday mornings, so she can stay with her parents part of the weekend. She tells her parents about the sexual assaults. Her mother, Elvira, calls her a liar and insists that the girl pay her way by working for Mr Clyde. Ben, her father, does not speak up, but he believes his daughter.

> He watched his daughter come through the gate with her eyes on the ground, and she slowly climbed up on the porch. She took each step at a time, and her shoes grated against the rough boards. She finally turned her beaten eyes into [Ben's] face, and what was left of his soul to crush was taken care of by the bell-like voice that greeted them, 'Mornin,' Daddy Ben. Mornin,' Mama.'

'Mornin,' baby,' Ben mumbled with his jaws tight. (Naylor, *The Women of Brewster Place*, p. 151)

Elvira continues to insist that the girl needs to pay her way by working for Mr Clyde.

Ben discovered that if he sat up drinking all night Friday, he could stand on the porch Saturday morning and smile at the man who whistled as he dropped his … daughter home. And he could look into her beaten eyes and believe that she had lied. (Naylor, *The Women of Brewster Place*, p. 154)

Eventually, the daughter is lost to her parents, leaving the area to make a living as a prostitute in Memphis, where the compensation for being exploited sexually is better than she receives from Mr Clyde.

The girl disappeared one day, leaving behind a note saying that she loved them very much, but she knew that she had been a burden and she understood why they had made her keep working at Mr. Clyde's house. But she felt that if she had to earn her keep that way, she might as well go to Memphis where the money was better. (Naylor, *The Women of Brewster Place*, p. 154)

After she leaves, Mr Clyde evicts Ben and Elvira. Ben knows his daughter is prostituting herself, and the money she sends home from Memphis (in envelopes without return addresses) is from prostitution. Ben constantly consumes alcohol to kill his emotional pain. Soon Elvira leaves Ben (perhaps because of his alcoholism, perhaps because of their loss of the meagre economic base they had in sharecropping, or perhaps just because, after all that has happened, there is not much left of their relationship). So racism has done much to shatter the commitment of the members of the family to one another and has shattered the family.

How racism undermines the capacity for relationship commitment is specific to contexts, the biographical particulars of the people harmed, and the specifics of the harm. The common story is abstract, but the specific stories are likely to be, as in the above examples from the novels, strikingly diverse. And one can take that as something about the human psyche and family relationships and the many ways they can be wounded, and one can also take that as about racism and how in its pervasiveness and durability it can do damage in so many different ways. But then there are some commonalities to the damage done to relationship capacity, Each person who holds back from commitment or who has lost a committed relationship loses the potential support, co-construction of reality (Berger and Kellner, 1964), practical help, and sharing of memories that would come from a committed relationship. And so for anyone who does not have a committed relationship there can be loneliness, isolation sadness, psychological pain, less confidence about reality, and a poorer material life.

Couple Commitment and Racist Job Denial, Joblessness, or Terrible Jobs

A racist environment can have a powerful influence on couple relationships. Sometimes it shapes the deep psychological needs that can be the foundation of couple relationship (see, for example, Dunham and Ellis, 2010). Related to this, joblessness, job denial, and low pay, demeaning jobs can undermine a man's confidence and sense of place in a couple relationship (Pinderhughes, 2002). In several novels, racist job denial has such an effect. One example comes from Toni Morrison's *Sula*, when Jude is denied a job.

> It was after he stood in lines for six days running and saw the gang boss pick out thin-armed white boys from the Virginia hills and the bull-necked Greeks and Italians and heard over and over, 'Nothing else today. Come back tomorrow,' that he got the message. So it was rage, rage and a determination to take on a man's role anyhow that made him press Nel about settling down. He needed some of his appetites filled, some posture of adulthood recognized, but mostly he wanted someone to care about his hurt, to care very deeply. Deep enough to hold him, deep enough to rock him, deep enough to ask, 'How you feel? You all right? Want some coffee?' And if he were to be a man, that someone could no longer be his mother. He chose the girl who had always been kind. (Morrison, *Sula*, p. 82)

What Jude gained from the relationship with Nel was not only sympathy and sex but also the role of "head of the household."

> In return he would shelter her, love her, grow old with her. Without that someone he was a waiter hanging around a kitchen like a woman. With her he was head of a household pinned to an unsatisfactory job out of necessity. The two of them together would make one Jude. (Morrison, *Sula*, p. 83)

The two of them together would make one Jude in the sense that with Nel as wife, Jude could be a whole man because he would have the job of head of the household. That would, of course, require that Nel accept him as head of the household as he chose to be head. And as it plays out in the novel, central to his healing through relationship with Nel is that she subordinates herself to him.

There is some evidence from qualitative interview research that some African American men who have been injured by racism crave a woman's understanding of how they have been hurt by racism and may have trouble staying in a relationship where they do not have that understanding (Carolan and Allen, 1999). In the novels some women gladly take on the role of healer for a man hurt by racism. So even though Jude worried about whether his inability to get a job would put Nel off, she was drawn to his neediness. She needed his pain in order to be who she wanted to be, a woman whose love and acceptance was soothing to a man. She needed to be needed.

His fears lest his burst dream of road building discourage her were never realized. Nel's indifference to the hints about marriage disappeared altogether when she discovered his pain. Jude could see himself taking shape in her eyes. She actually wanted to help, to soothe. (Morrison, *Sula*, p. 83)

Just as having a partner who could soothe Jude and make him the head of a household made Jude feel whole, having someone who needed her made Nel feel whole. It offered her an identity and a sense of importance that had been missing in her life.

Her parents had succeeded in rubbing down to a dull glow any sparkle or splutter she had ... During all of her girlhood the only respite Nel had had from her stern and undemonstrative parents was Sula. When Jude began to hover around, she was flattered ... Nel's response to Jude's shame and anger selected her away from Sula. And greater than her friendship [with Sula] was this new feeling of being needed by someone. (Morrison, *Sula*, pp. 83–4)

Implied in Nel's acceptance of a relationship in which she soothes Jude is a sense that racism has cost her the possibility of a relationship in which more of her self is present, acknowledged, respected, and served (Ready, 2000). Perhaps the fictional Jude only wanted to be cared for and to be the man in a comfortable heterosexual partnership, but as Ready (2000, p. 7) read *Sula*, the relationship Jude wanted with Nel was one in which he was the oppressor and she the oppressed, that for him marriage involved ownership and control of a wife (and eventually of children). And from a family systems theory perspective, it is common that familial relationships take forms that fit the model of relationships in the larger system (Rosenblatt, 1994, pp. 142–3). One can think of the larger system as establishing a culture that imposes itself on the thinking of individuals and models relationships in families and other systems. And the larger system provides a sense of what people with power and privilege seek, and that can become a model for what those who lack power and privilege think is valuable to achieve. Whatever the underlying dynamics, Jude's seeking to meet needs in a marriage with Nel might well have meant that there was not as much chance as there might have been, had he not been so needy, for her to have her needs met and for them to develop together and co-evolve as a couple with considerable give and take about whose needs are met how and when. So here is another kind of situation in which racism can be seen to do harm, although what people do, given the damage, can be understood to be good (two people finding in each other a way to deal with their needs and pain). Of course, it would be much better for both of them if racism had not created the neediness they turned to each other to deal with.

A different but related example of how job denial affects a couple's relationship comes from Ann Petry's *The Street*. In the following excerpt, Lutie Johnson's husband, Jim, expresses his rage at racist barriers to him finding employment:

> Jim couldn't get a job, though he hunted for one—desperately, eagerly, anxiously. Walking from one employment agency to another; spending long hours in the musty agency waiting-rooms, reading old newspapers. Waiting, waiting, waiting to be called up for a job. He would come home shivering from the cold, saying, 'God damn white people anyway. I don't want favors. All I want is a job. Just a job.' (Petry, *The Street*, p. 30)

His inability to bring in an income in a racial system rife with hiring discrimination, along with his neediness that came from not being able to provide for his family and to have the self-respect that came with that, are central to creating the situation where Lutie is eventually on her own as a single mother in very difficult circumstances. Because Jim cannot find a job, Lutie takes a job as a domestic in Connecticut, leaving Jim at home in New York City, caring for their son Bub. The couple's separation and Jim's need for something to soothe the pain of not being able to work to support his family and to do something to at least briefly drive away the dreary monotony of unemployment leads him to another woman.

> When [Lutie] and Jim got married it looked as though it should have been a happy, successful marriage. They were young enough and enough in love to have made a go of it. It always came back to the same thing. Jim couldn't find a job. So day by day, month by month, big broad-shouldered Jim Johnson went to pieces because there wasn't any work for him and he couldn't earn anything at all. He got used to facing the fact that he couldn't support his wife and child. It ate into him. Slowly, bit by bit, it undermined his belief in himself until he could no longer bear it. And he got himself a woman so that in those moments when he clutched her close to him in bed he could prove that he was still needed, wanted. His self-respect was momentarily restored through the woman's desire for him. Then, too, he escaped from the dreary monotony of his existence. (Petry, *The Street*, pp. 168–9)

If the man is married and the woman he turns to is not his wife, his turning to that woman can end his marriage.

> [Lutie] had taken the job in Connecticut so they could keep the house. While she was gone, Jim got himself a slim dark girl whose thighs made him believe in himself again and momentarily released him from his humdrum life. She had never seen him since the day she had gone [home] and found that other woman there. (Petry, *The Street*, p. 183)

The day she comes home and finds Jim with another woman, Lutie moves Bub and herself out of the house, to stay with her father.

Jude in *Sula*, Jim in *The Street*, and Selina's father in *Brown Girl, Brownstones*, after having been denied jobs, go outside their marital relationship, turning to other women for sex and distraction. It seems that part of the story about these three men is that they each need from the woman they turn to a nurturance and caring they cannot provide for themselves. Why go outside the marital relationship? A difference between a wife and a mistress might be that there are reminders from a wife (in her actions if not her words) and from the dwelling they share, that the man has economic obligations that he is not meeting. If there are stereotypes of African American men in difficult economic situations that make them seem like irresponsible sexual players, one can see in the novels a different picture, a picture of men who are hurting and needy and doing what they can to try to get some soothing and self-esteem. Related to this, in one story there is clearly something like shame that can go with joblessness. Marita Golden had this to say about jobless men:

> The other fathers Esther knew seemed to always be hunting hungrily for work, ashamed to live face-to-face with families they could not feed and so were afraid to love. (Golden, *Long Distance Life*, p. 62)

So joblessness can, in this view, lead to a man not living with his family because he is too ashamed. There is something of this in Terry McMillan's *A Day Late and a Dollar Short*, where Lewis avoids the son he fathered in part because he had not been able to keep up child support to his ex-wife. But when he gets on his feet economically and in terms of self-esteem he becomes actively involved in his son's life and makes peace with his ex-wife.

In some novels, job denial changes a man permanently, and that affects his functioning as partner and parent. In the worlds of the novels, a man may not be able to keep on believing in himself when he cannot find a job and cannot provide at least some share of what the family needs economically. Here is what Selina (in Paule Marshall's *Brown Girl, Brownstones*) sees when her father comes home after a day of fruitless job searching.

> Despite his bitterness, there was a nuance, a shading of something else. A frightening acceptance, it seemed to be, which sprang, perhaps, from a conviction hidden deep within him that it was only right that he should be rejected. (Marshall, *Brown Girl, Brownstones*, p. 81)

Being so beaten down by job denial that he comes to accept job denial as appropriate could lead a man to be in some ways less for his family, less of a model and moral authority for his children, less of a partner to his wife, and less a person who holds up his end of things in the household.

Once job denial becomes part of a person's life, where can the person go for satisfaction, sustenance, achievement? In *The Street*, Lutie wondered if the inability of her father, Pop, to find a job was key to understanding why he had entered into a series of sexual conquests.

> Lutie found herself wondering if Pop would have been different if ... he had been able to find a decent job that would have forced him to use all of his energy and latent ability. There wasn't anything stupid about Pop. Life just seemed to have reacted on him until he turned sly and a little dishonest. Perhaps that was one way of fighting back. Even the succession of girl friends that started shortly after her mother died could have been the result of his frustration—a way he had of proving to himself that there was one area of achievement in which he was the equal of any man. (Petry, *The Street*, p. 81)

Pop's joblessness leads to his womanizing and his drinking and selling alcohol, and that leads to his harming his relationship with Lutie and costing Lutie and Jim their main source of income while they are still together as a couple. Lutie, with the help of Jim, had been bringing foster children into their house, and there was an income from that. But Pop, who was living with them, was using the house as a place to serve alcoholic drinks—partly for entertainment and life meaning and partly to bring in an income. When the child welfare authorities discover what Pop is doing, Lutie and Jim lose their right to be foster care providers. Because of this, Lutie takes the job in Connecticut, which sets up the situation with Jim turning to another woman, which destroys Lutie and Jim's marital relationship. And after Lutie and Jim break up, Pop's womanizing, though it may have been good for his morale, makes it less feasible for Lutie and her son Bub to live with Pop. So Pop's attempts to make a life for himself in the face of joblessness undermines the part of his family that centers on Lutie, and then undermines his relationship with her. And from a family systems theory perspective it is plausible that an adaptation to deal with one problem may unintentionally create other problems that will call for adaptations that unintentionally create still other problems (Bateson, 1979). So once racism creates one problem, it can start a cascade of other problems.

In a few novels there are men who are jobless because they cannot stand working at the only jobs that are available to them, jobs that are far beneath their abilities, jobs in which they are frequently humiliated, jobs then that make them seem and feel to be much less than they are or could be.

> 'Jimboy's all right, but he's just too smart to do this heavy ditch-digging labor, and that's all white folks give the colored a chance at here ... so he had to leave.' (Hughes, *Not Without Laughter*, p. 142)

He leaves for distant places, hoping to find a job that pays well enough and is appropriate for his abilities. His wife Annjee and son Sandy intensely grieve his leaving. His mother-in-law, Aunt Hager, rails against him because he has left, because he has not had a job, and because she never thought he was worth much. Thus, although he has left, he is still very much a presence in their conversation, thoughts, and feelings. And that makes sense, that people who grieve for a separation from a loved one continue to think about and leave psychological room for the person from whom they are separated (Rosenblatt, 1983). A family member who is not physically present is typically still very much a presence in the family. Eventually Jimboy settles in Detroit, and Annjee makes plans to join him. As she tells her mother:

> 'I got to go where it ain't lonesome and where I ain't unhappy—and that's where Jimboy is!' (Hughes, *Not Without Laughter*, p. 173)

Hence joblessness resulting from refusal to take the menial jobs that are available can come home to a family by leading to someone moving far from family in search of work. It can lead to further splits in the family as some family members leave to join the person who left in search of work. And this is a family system cascade of events set off by racism.

Grueling, demeaning, menial low-paying jobs have consequences for many characters in the novels and their families. The physical exhaustion, sore back, aching feet, and depressed mood can come home to family. Also, for women doing maid work and their family members there are extra burdens. The demands of maid work can affect how a woman interacts with her family and how much she can do for them. Working as a maid, caring for the house and children of white people, a woman is not doing these things for her own family, and that can create ongoing upsetness for her because she is not providing care for her own family. The following is a reflection by Lutie about herself and women like her, working as maids for white people.

> She'd been washing someone else's dishes when she should have been home with Jim and Bub. Instead she'd cleaned another woman's house and looked after another woman's child, while her own marriage went to pot, breaking up into so many little pieces it couldn't be put back together again. (Petry, *The Street*, p. 30)

Lutie sees the experience of her family as a common pattern for African American couples, a pattern that leads to many single mother households where it is difficult for children to get what children need.

> It wasn't just this city. It was any … place where the women had to work to support the families because the men couldn't get jobs and the men got bored and pulled out and the kids were left without proper homes because there was nobody around to put a heart into it … It all added up to the same thing, she decided—white people. She hated them. (Petry, *The Street*, p. 206)

If Jim had a job, she would not have had to go far away from him and their son to do maid work. The family effects of joblessness for Jim and for men/husbands/fathers in general that results from racism can lead to a cascade of problems. Lutie thinks about the low rent Harlem street she is forced to live on with her son because she has so little money.

Streets like the one she lived on were no accident. They were the North's lynch mobs, she thought bitterly; the method the big cities used to keep Negroes in their place. And she began thinking of [her father] unable to get a job; of Jim slowly disintegrating because he, too, couldn't get a job, and of the subsequent wreck of their marriage; of [her son] left to his own devices after school. (Petry, *The Street*, p. 323)

One thing this last quote highlights is that racism in the South and the North are not so different, that both do horrible harm, and both are designed to diminish and control African Americans and to terrorize African American men. In the novels, what is done to African Americans in the South is more obviously barbaric and unfair, but the novels also describe a powerful and damaging racial system in the North. And a key to the operation of the system in the North is the denial of jobs to African American men.

Conflict between Family Commitment and Obligations to the Black Community

In some novels racism sets up conflict between commitment to one's family and commitment to the African American community struggle against racism. One expression of that conflict is that sometimes, in the novels, racists set up situations in which a person who wants to help a family member must act in ways that hurt many other African Americans outside the family who have joined together to fight racism. In the Ernest J. Gaines novel, *In My Father's House*, Reverend Phillip Martin, who has been the leader in his community's civil rights efforts, learns that a son he has not seen for years is in town and has been jailed. Reverend Martin negotiates with the sheriff to have his son released to his custody. The sheriff will not take bail money but insists that Reverend Martin block African American community members from holding a planned confrontation with Chenal, the bigoted store owner who pays African American employees next to nothing and who treats them very badly. So the sheriff (and presumably Chenal) use Reverend Martin's family commitment as a weapon to undermine organized African American community efforts to change terrible things that Chenal does to African Americans. Reverend Martin agrees, and he sabotages the demonstration, sacrificing the community's efforts to help all for his personal desire to have his son released from jail. Other leaders in the African American community confront Reverend Martin. As they see it, his interest in caring for a member of his family has undermined everyone else's family.

'Every last man in here is a father, except for Jonathan over there ... And one day he'll be one too. But till we get rid of people like Chenal, change people like Chenal, Jonathan son'll have to go through the same thing mine did. His son'll have to work for Chenal for nothing—or, worse yet, leave home. We want Jonathan son to stay home, Phillip.' (Gaines, *In My Father's House*, p. 128)

From a family systems theory perspective, there seems to be a family and cultural rule that one care about and take care of family members. This plus the fact that in the novels African American family systems are vulnerable through the operation of the white-run criminal justice system gives whites leverage to use members of African American families who are influential in the African American community to act in ways that serve white racism and white economic interests. One would like to think that African American families are havens from white oppression, but in the example provides in Ernest J. Gaines' novel, *In My Father's House*, the family was not haven enough to shelter Reverend Martin and his son. And because they were not sheltered, the African American community was harmed.

In other novels that describe communal efforts to improve the situation of African Americans, one can see the conflict between working for the good of the African American community and working for the good of the family playing out in ways that might in some ways hurt the family. For example, in Marita Golden's *Long Distance Life*, as is discussed in Chapter 3, Esther leaves her son, her lover, and her mother (Naomi) in Washington, DC, to go south to work at voter registration and other activities of the Civil Rights Movement. She is gone for years, scarcely communicating with her son and mother, and not communicating at all with her lover. The cause is noble and vitally important, and she needs to do the civil rights work to find herself, but the family costs are high.

> Though she was only sixty-two, Naomi's hair was now ... solidly white. Awaiting Esther's return, praying for her safety had driven the rich black color from her hair. The sight of her mother's hair and the crevicelike worry lines across Naomi's forehead informed Esther, as did nothing else, of the price her family had paid for what she had chosen to do. (Golden, *Long Distance Life*, p. 185)

Esther's son Logan has suffered greatly in her absence. And when she returns, he has to deal with the ways she is not who he had imagined her to be and the ways their relationship is not what he had dreamed of during the years of separation.

> Logan had lived on the memory of his mother. And the glow of memory transformed Esther into an obedient cooperative phantom, too intangible to possess but too elusive to disappoint. Now Esther had returned and this real-life mother ... was more immune to his love than she had ever been ... in his memory. Esther had stolen five years of his life and Logan felt the absence of those years like an object he had hoarded and then lost. Logan felt he was owed an accounting. Had she squandered the years, frittered them away, lavished them on someone else now resident in her heart? Had those years been better to her than they were to him? What had she done with those years that were not only

hers but his as well? What had she done with their life? (Golden, *Long Distance Life*, pp. 189–90)

Esther's being gone had put the life of her lover, Randolph, on hold. As he says when he first sees Esther after their years of separation:

'Girl, I ain't done nothing since you left but wait for you to come back.' (Golden, *Long Distance Life*, p. 194)

What he says could be taken as the sweet talk of a lover. That is, it may not necessarily be honest but a way for Randolph to say that he cares about Esther and values her very highly. But at another level, there may be great honesty in what he says, that he has put his life on hold waiting for her to return. And in fact, each family member left behind by Esther had retained a commitment to Esther, another example of how a person who is absent from a family is still central to it. But for each of the family members left behind by Esther while she was in the south the commitment had a form not like the loud and taken for granted "yes" of an ongoing close relationships but more of a longing and hoping. The "yes" of commitment in an intimate relationship with daily interaction may be unspoken, but it can be nonetheless rich and vital. But after long separation, the commitment may often be more wistful, more of a longing for what was and a hoping for what might be. In this instance racism does not destroy family commitment, but it produces injuries and deprivations that change the commitment as Esther devotes years of her life (and in a sense the lives of the members of her family) to fight racism through work in the Civil Rights Movement.

Chapter 5
Racism-caused Grief, Rage, and Humiliation Come Home

Being a target of racism or having someone one cares about be targeted can be very upsetting. The novels are collectively rich in the complex and nuanced accounts of the emotional impacts of racism and how these emotional impacts show up in family life. This chapter focuses on the three emotions that were covered in the most detail in the novels (though each is only covered in a few novels). Focusing on only these three emotions seems to me to be appropriate because I think they provide a telling picture of the emotional impact of racism and of how the emotions set off by racism may affect families. The three emotions this chapter focuses on are grief, rage, and humiliation. I think that the three receive as much attention in the novels as they do because they have been common to African American experiences of racism. Also, the three emotions are not random or unrelated but are often linked aspects of what racism can set off in African American individuals and families. To take one example, James Baldwin talked about the links of rage and humiliation:

> One has got to consider ... the dilemma and the rage and the anguish of a Negro man who, in the first place, is forced to accept all kinds of humiliation in his working day, whose power in the world is so slight he can not really protect his home, his wife, his children, when he finds himself out of work. And then he watches his children growing up, menaced in exactly the same way he has been. (Terkel, 1961/1989, p. 9—the page cited is from the 1989 interview transcription)

In order to address the three emotions with clarity, this chapter is organized into separate sections on grief, rage, and humiliation, and the material in the novels supports that division, but at the same time it can be seen in some of the quotes about one of those feelings that it blends with one or both of the other two and with many other emotions.

Grief

For purposes of analyzing the novels, what I call "grief" includes chronic sadness, sorrow, feeling blue, feeling down, heartache, emotional pain, despondency, and depression. Grief as I see it in the novels is not a brief feeling but can go on or recur for weeks, months, even years following a specific loss resulting from racism. In many passages discussed throughout this book, one can see instances in which feelings of grief for a particular loss seem entangled in what is going on in relationships or in individual functioning. For example, one can argue that in the previous chapter Jude was grieving when he sought out Nel to soothe the pain of his being denied a job, and one can say that Lutie was grieving her separation from Jim as a result of his not being able to find a job, and one can then say that she grieved the breakup of their marriage. So commitment issues arising from racism were associated with grieving. There are also story lines in some of the novels in which grief resulting from racism seems a dominant reaction that intrudes into and shapes family life.

Grief and the Racist Murder of a Family Member

In several novels a family member is murdered by white racists in an act that is both allowed by the racial system in their time and place and reinforces the racial system. That is, murderous acts by whites targeting African Americans can be understood as acts of dominance, entitlement, and privilege in a racial system that even allows whites the freedom to take an African American life. And at the same time, those murderous acts can be a message to all African Americans to be very afraid of the consequences should they ever do anything to threaten white power and privilege. In one of the most striking examples from the novels, an event that is at the heart of Bebe Moore Campbell's *Your Blues Ain't Like Mine* begins when a 15-year-old boy, Armstrong Todd, is sent from Chicago to the Mississippi Delta to spend the summer with his grandmother. One day he speaks a few innocuous phrases of French in the presence of a white woman, and his speaking those words is perceived by the white woman's husband, his brother, and their father as a violation of the white-imposed Mississippi Delta code of interracial relations, and so they beat and then fatally shoot Armstrong. The impact of the killing and the subsequent acquittal of the killers in a racist Mississippi court profoundly change the lives of Armstrong's surviving family members. After testifying at the murder trial against the white killers, his grandmother flees for her life to Detroit, leaving home, family, and friends. Armstrong's parents, who live in Chicago, have been estranged and separated for years. After the death they are wracked with self-blame, and they also blame each other for the death. Armstrong's mother, Delotha, grieves so intensely that she cannot take care of herself, is cut off from others, cannot tolerate being near white people, and is so enraged that she considers killing the killer, her husband, and others. She bursts into rage at home, on the bus, in many places. She has no appetite, but she smokes incessantly. Armstrong's father, Wydell, who had a serious alcohol problem before the killing, sinks deeper into drunkenness and is pursued by feelings of guilt for not being a good father to Armstrong. He blames Delotha for sending Armstrong to Mississippi. One day at work he starts behaving in extremely strange ways and is taken to the psychiatric ward at the county hospital. When Wydell is hospitalized, Delotha is called. Though she has not seen him in years and has been thinking of killing him, she comes to visit him, and a process is started between them that brings them back together in their shared pain, their shared memories of Armstrong, and their memory of the love they once had. Wydell goes through a treatment program to gain control of his alcohol addiction. As they move forward into a renewed relationship, their grief does not go away, and Delotha's becomes transformed into yearning for a son.

> The longing for her son didn't disappear. When Delotha left the hospital [after each visit to Wydell], she mourned in her small apartment, overcome by loneliness and grief, so disconsolate she couldn't speak or even cry. What she wanted more than anything was a chance to begin again, to have a brand-new Armstrong filling her womb. (Campbell, *Your Blues Ain't Like Mine*, p. 209)

When Wydell finishes alcoholism treatment, the couple moves in together. Their sexual relationship is conflictful because Delotha wants to become pregnant and Wydell wants to use condoms, saying they cannot bring Armstrong back, they are too old to have a baby, and he does not know how to father. But eventually they have a daughter and then another one. Her grief for Armstrong haunts Delotha's parenting.

> The girls were a constant reminder of her past trauma and what it had taught her: She couldn't save them. They could be snatched away, stolen, brutalized, or killed at any time, and there was nothing she could do about it. Often when she tiptoed into their room at night to watch them sleep, she became angry, filled with a bone-chilling rage that rendered her body frigid and untouchable. Sometimes the only way she could bear to watch them walk away from her was to pretend that they weren't hers. (Campbell, *Your Blues Ain't Like Mine*, p. 280)

The couple eventually has a son, just what Delotha has been longing for and just what Wydell feared.

> He was filled with dread ... They kill boys ... Hang them by their necks and then torch their lifeless bodies. Throw them on the chain gang for nine hundred years ... He was good with girls; he could guide and protect them. What would it take to save his son? (Campbell, *Your Blues Ain't Like Mine*, p. 286)

Delotha is obsessed with and intensely possessive of their new son, W.T. She is so absorbed in mothering and protecting W.T. that she is unwilling to return to work. She does not want to share him with Wydell and effectively undermines Wydell's fathering of W.T. She recurrently makes the psychologically revealing error of addressing W.T. by the name of his murdered brother. She neglects her daughters, not even touching them, investing all her mothering and emotional energy in W.T. She continues to grieve for Armstrong and to think about what he would be like had he lived, and she remains intensely anxious about the possibility of W.T. being harmed. The estrangement the couple experiences over parenting W.T. pushes Delotha and Wydell far apart. Delotha's absolute insistence that they never discipline W.T. or doubt him, coupled with Wydell's passive acceptance of Delotha having her way, makes them extremely ineffective parents of W.T., and that makes enormous trouble for W.T. He is undisciplined and grows up to be a gang member and a hoodlum.

Wydell, feeling horribly alone and disconnected from Delotha and W.T., returns to drunkenness, and the couple separate. By then, their daughters are adults and out of the home, and they and Delotha have nothing to talk about. W.T. becomes involved in drug dealing, robbery, and violence. Had Armstrong not been murdered years before, perhaps Wydell and Delotha would never have been thrown together in their grief to produce W.T. and his sisters. But they were thrown together, and nightmarish issues with W.T. arose because of how their parenting was affected by their grief over Armstrong's death.

The murder of Armstrong produced long-lasting, intense grief, but in their grief his estranged parents found each other as they struggled with their neediness and shared loss. In their reconnection they were able to have some additional loving years, for a few years to have a successful business together, and to produce two daughters and a son. But they also continued to be profoundly affected by the loss. It shaped their sexual relationship and their parenting, eventually undermined their business, led to tragic outcomes for their son W.T., and led to circumstances that made their couple relationship unsustainable.

Sometimes a death of a family member by racism leaves a character in a novel without any other family relationship. In Alice Walker's *Meridian*, there is a side story of an African American father whose son is murdered by whites. The son's murder has dreadful consequences for the father's psychological functioning.

> When his son was killed he had gone temporarily insane ... He had wrecked his own house with an ax, swinging until, absolutely, profoundly silent and blank, he had been carried out of the state and placed in a sanatorium ... [Now] he lived peacefully in the ruins of his wrecked house, his sanity coming back— unwelcomed—for days at a time. Then he bellowed out his loss ... His martyred son was all the family he had. (Walker, *Meridian*, p. 215)

In the devastation of being family-less, the father lives alone and in deep grief. In a sense his relationship with his son continues, in the form of his ongoing pain and lamentation. They mark his continuing psychological links to his son and the continuing importance of his son to him. The wreckage of his house can be taken to symbolize what it means to the father to be without his son. His life is wrecked and cannot be repaired. He lives in the wreckage of his family and his house. Perhaps too, in the father's insanity there is a reflection of the insanity of the racist system that killed his son.

Any grief, including grief arising from racism, can lead to processes that cut one off from other family members. For example, in Bebe Moore Campbell's *Your*

Blues Ain't Like Mine, Delotha becomes an isolate in the months after her son's murder. One day she encounters a cousin, who chides her for being so unavailable to visits. She replies:

> "I don't know how to be around people no more." (Campbell, *Your Blues Ain't Like Mine*, p. 189)

And that is one of the dreadful consequences of the racist violence in her life. The violence leads to her grieving in a way that cuts her off from others who care about her and might be able to help. There is considerable evidence that grieving people may be rather isolated socially (Rosenblatt, 1990, 2000; Rosenblatt and Barner, 2006; Rosenblatt and Wallace, 2005a), even cut off from a spouse or other intimates. Thus, racist violence that takes the life of a family member may also divide family members from one another. How horrible it is that racism can set off emotional processes that can lead some people to be cut off from the support of others who might help and support them in their difficulties and might work with them in co-constructing realities (Berger and Kellner, 1964) about how the loss came about, the person who died, and what might be their future.

With deaths caused by racism, grieving can be entangled in fear. Fear might well be intended by whites who use violence to maintain the racial system, with the idea that people's fear of becoming victims or of loved ones becoming victims will control them. In Ernest J. Gaines' novel, *The Autobiography of Miss Jane Pittman*, Ned, the adult son of Miss Jane Pittman, is murdered by racist whites. He is murdered because he is building a school that whites in his community in Louisiana do not want built and because he urges African Americans to stand up against racism. With the murder of Ned, his wife Vivian grieves intensely. This, for example, is from the day Ned was murdered.

> Vivian was sitting in the chair just looking at the body. People all round her were crying, but she wasn't hearing a thing. Just looking at the body. I put my arms around her shoulders and I could feel her trembling. It was hot as it could be, but she was trembling like she had chill. I tried to say something to her, but she didn't hear me. I doubt if she even knowed I was there. (Gaines, *The Autobiography of Miss Jane Pittman*, p. 123)

Vivian wants to stay and continue Ned's work, but Miss Jane and others in the community send her back north to Kansas, because as Miss Jane said, "We were scared she could get herself killed just like Ned was killed" (Gaines, *The Autobiography of Miss Jane Pittman*, p. 125). It is not clear that Vivian thought that she and her children could become the next victims of racist murderers, but for her mother-in-law, Miss Jane Pittman, grief and fear were linked. Miss Jane Pittman, in her grief, feared additional losses and wanted to move her daughter-in-law and grandchildren to safety. Plus there might even be a possibility in Miss Jane Pittman's thinking that Vivian's grief could be seen as an act of resistance to the whites who worked together to murder Ned, and so there might be a rationality in the link of Miss Jane Pittman's grieving to her fear for Vivian and grandchildren.

From a family systems theory perspective, there is another way of thinking about Miss Jane Pittman's concerns about Vivian's grief and also her feeling that it was very important to send Vivian and her children north for their safety. That is that in some sense Vivian had become the carrier of family and community grief and anxiety about the possibility of further killings (see, for example, Fry, 1962, writing about individuals who bear the family's load of anxiety, and see Rosenblatt, 1994, p. 186). What fits in Gaines' account of the aftermath of Ned's death is that Miss Jane's loss is arguably as much as Vivian's, and Vivian gives no more hint that she would carry on Ned's work than does Miss Jane or anyone else, and yet it is Vivian who become the focus of grief support and anxiety about further killings. With Vivian as the carrier of family and community grief, people can focus their care on her, and by moving her to safety they can feel symbolically that they have been moved to safety and that something has been done to help assuage their grief.

In Grief Due to Job Denial a Person May Be Less Available to Others

Being turned down for a job for which one believes one is qualified, and quite possibly even better qualified than the white person given the job, can be devastating. One may grieve, and if one does, the grief can affect other family members and how one is as a member of the family. In Paule Marshall's, *Brown Girl, Brownstones*, Selina's father spends two years studying books about accounting, and when he feels that he is competent at accounting, he dresses to go out to apply for jobs at three big, white-run accounting firms. His wife ("the mother") warns him of the risk in looking for a job in the white business world.

> The mother has turned from the sink and said, her voice sharp with reproof yet strangely protective, 'But where are you going and you half studied that course? How can you be putting yourself up in these white people face asking for some big job …? You don want no job,' and turned to the children. 'Instead of him going to some small office where he might have a chance—no, he got to play like he's white.' (Marshall, *Brown Girl, Brownstones*, p. 80)

The mother sees the risk of failure and humiliation in her husband challenging employment racism, and she is right. Later that day Selina finds her father at home in the sun parlor:

> lying there on the cot as though he had been severely beaten and then flung there like his jacket. The floor around him was scattered with the accounting manuals … He whispered, 'They're all the same. They does scorn yuh 'cause yuh skin black.' (Marshall, *Brown Girl, Brownstones*, p. 81)

During the months that follow, his being denied employment continues to weigh on him. He no longer tries to find an accounting job, and takes up the trumpet with the fantasy that as a musician he will not have to depend on whites to hire him. But he is only a beginner at the trumpet. It is obvious to his daughter how wounded and sad he is because of having been turned down for accounting jobs, and so she tries to be supportive of him in his trumpet playing, although she can tell he is not at all talented. And in fact, the denial of an accounting job combined with his failure to bring in wages means that his spirit never recovers. In his dispirited state he is distant from his wife and children. Thus, in many ways he is lost to his family. So racist job denial can cause grieving, and one consequences of the grieving is that the victim may become distant from family members. And among the consequences of that distance is that the person is less able to work out with other family members (Berger and Kellner, 1964) realities about what to make of what has happened and what might be in the future. So not only does racism do damage by, among many things, causing grief, but it sets of processes that can produce secondary damage in the sense of cutting the grieving person off from potential family support and meaning making and cutting off family members from the person who is grieving.

The Way that a Conventional Understanding of Grief Does Not Fit

A conventional understanding of grief is based on the idea that a loss happens at some more or less specific point in time, and then grief follows that loss. For losses experienced by African Americans as a result of the workings of the racial system, it might not make so much sense to think of grief in the conventional way. The system continues, the losses continue, and there is an ongoing sense that there will be losses in the future (cf. Durrant, 2004. p. 83, writing about the novels of Toni Morrison). Consequently, there is not a specific time at which grief begins, and losses continue to pile up. Nor is there a time when losses stop. One can then think of the grief of Selina's father as not just about being denied a job but about the endless accumulation of losses resulting from racism.

Rage

By rage I mean violent or intense anger, wrath, or fury. Rage at racism is common in African American life (Boyd-Franklin and Karger, 2012), perhaps much more common in the experience of African Americans than many white people realize (Feagin and Sikes, 1994, p. 293). In quite a few of the novels there are stories of African American rage ignited by racism (see, for example, the examples of Jim and Jude in the preceding chapter). Victims of racism, both specific racist acts and the ongoing grind of daily life in the racial system, do not necessarily shrug it off or look at it with cool detachment. Feelings can run high, and the emotional reaction can extend over a long period of time, perhaps even a lifetime.

One reason for feelings being spread out over time is that the harm and damage caused by racism is so horrible, unjust, and damaging. Another reason is that the unfair, repressive, punishing system does not stop but continues day after day to abrade the individual. For example, if a woman works as a maid for white people who are recurrently demeaning and oppressive and who do not compensate her work fairly, she may feel renewed rage every day.

Based on their own encounters with racism, feelings of rage were part of the personal experience of at least some of the authors—for example, James Baldwin (Porter, 1996). For that reason, and because the 20 novelists were acute observers of African American life in the racial system, it is not surprising that a number of the novels describe such feelings.

In the novels, one of the problems with racism-caused rage is that directing the rage at the white racist harm-doers can be dangerous. There are circumstances nowadays in which African Americans motivated by rage, anger, indignation, and concerns about justice stand up to racism and effectively stop or at least mute racist offenses (for example, Tatum, 1999, writing about middle-class African American parents in California confronting white school officials and white parents about racist words and acts directed at African American children). However, those remedies are not necessarily available to contemporary African American families and were much less available, if they existed at all, in the past times in which many of the novels were set. In the world of many of the novels, African American who felt rage, anger, indignation, and concerns about injustice rarely had any recourse. In fact, expressing rage at racist whites, or even hinting that one felt it, could be risky. An example of the dangers of directing racism-caused rage at whites comes from James Baldwin's *Go Tell It on the Mountain*. Although a great deal of the critical commentary on James Baldwin's *Go Tell It on the Mountain* downplays the book's focus on the effects of white oppression and violence directed at African Americans (M'Baye, 2006), a case can be made that the effects of white injustice and cruelty on the characters in the novel are central to it (M'Baye, 2006). As is outlined in the previous chapter, Baldwin wrote about the rape of a main character in the novel, Deborah, by a group of white men. When her father learns about the rape, his rage leads to actions that puts his life in jeopardy.

> Deborah's father had gone to one of the white men's houses, and said that he would kill him and all the other white men he could find. They had beaten him and left him for dead. (Baldwin, *Go Tell It on the Mountain*, p. 74)

So the lesson for the family and the community is that rage arising from racism might not be safe to direct at white harm-doers (cf. Van Wormer, 2012, p. 183). Here is a related example from *Go Tell It on the Mountain*, where the family of a man murdered by white hooligans must keep their dreams of vengeance and even their grief behind closed doors, lest the hooligans take the life of other family members.

The streets were gray and empty—save here and there ... white men stood in groups of half a dozen ... There had been found that morning, just outside of town, the dead body of a soldier, his uniform shredded where he had been flogged, and, turned upward through the black skin, raw, red meat. He lay face downward at the base of a tree ... When he was turned over, his eyeballs stared in amazement and horror, his mouth was locked wide open, his trousers, soaked with blood, were torn open ... [revealing] the wound that seemed to be throbbing still. He had been carted home in silence and lay now behind locked doors, with his living kinsmen, who sat weeping and praying, and dreaming of vengeance. (Baldwin, *Go Tell It on the Mountain*, pp. 164–5)

Family Targets for Rage Arising from Racism

The rage ignited by racism and discrimination can come home to African American families (Boyd-Franklin and Karger, 2012; Feagin and McKinney, 2003; Putnam, 2011), and some of the time it can make unpleasant things happen among the people at home. For example, Lutie in Ann Petry's *The Street* is abrupt and distant with her eight-year-old son Bub because she is enraged by the racist barriers she is encountering and she is worried about how she and Bub can get enough money to have a better life and better housing despite the racist and sexist limitations she encounters (*The Street*, p. 316). And in Paule Marshall's *Brown Girl, Brownstones*, Selina comes to understand the links of her mother's sudden outbursts of rage at home to what happened to her mother as her mother worked in the white world. At home the rage can be expressed, perhaps often in ways that are not good for individual family members or for family relationships.

In Toni Morrison's *The Bluest Eye* a single racist act has profound effects on the family of Cholly Breedlove. As a teenager Cholly is caught by two white hunters while he was having a night-time sexual encounter with a young African American woman. Cholly is forced at gunpoint to continue having intercourse with her for the entertainment of the two white men. The rage and shame Cholly feels as a result of that encounter with the two white men is deep, but what to do with it? It is safer to direct the rage at Darlene, the young woman with whom he had intercourse, than to direct the rage at the white men.

Sullen, irritable, he cultivated his hatred of Darlene. Never did he once consider directing his hatred toward the hunters ... They were big, white, armed men. He was small, black, helpless. His subconscious knew what his conscious mind did not guess—that hating them would have consumed him, burned him up like a piece of soft coal, leaving only flakes of ash and a question mark of smoke. He was, in time, to discover that hatred of white men—but not now. Not in impotence, but later, when the hatred could find sweet expression. (Morrison, *The Bluest Eye*, p. 119)

Soon after the humiliating and enraging encounter, he flees the community.

His rage, shame and humiliation stay with him and are reinforced by other humiliating experiences at the hands of white people (Mayberry, 2007, pp. 25–6). So that first extreme experience of humiliation aimed at his masculinity engenders in him feelings of rage that grow as they are augmented by the humiliations, frustrations, deprivations, defeats, and other harsh experiences that come with being an African American man in a racist system, and one who was left at age 14 with nobody to take care of him and no home. What to do with the rage? As a young man he marries, and his wife becomes a readily available target for his rage, a much safer target than the racist society and the white people who humiliated, frustrated, and otherwise victimized him.

> She was one of the few things abhorrent to him that he could touch and therefore hurt. He poured out on her the sum of all his inarticulate fury and aborted desires. Hating her, he could leave himself intact ... Even a half-remembrance of [the] episode [with Darlene], along with myriad other humiliations, defeats, and emasculations could stir him into flights of depravity that surprised him. (Morrison, *The Bluest Eye*, p. 37)

In Cholly's battles with his wife Pauline, the couple is united in self-hatred, a self-hatred that is augmented by all the frustrations, limitations, diminishments, and deprivations of being African Americans in a racist society. And that self-hatred is transmitted to their children and pushes the children to despair (Wright, 1995, p. 82). Arguably, the tragedy of their family life is a result of many different forces, deprivations, and currents of racism, but one can make a case that had Cholly not brought so much rage into his marriage and parenting, things could have been different for him and his family. The rage in family conflict can be uniting in the sense that family members are drawn to the battle with each other and find important meanings in it (Simmel, 1955), but what a horrible kind of unity to have. So part of the collateral damage of racism-caused rage is what the rage may do what it comes home to a person's family.

Family Conflict over What to Do with the Rage

There is also the issue that people who are close to each other may differ enormously in what they do about how whites treat them and even whether it is appropriate to feel rage. In the novels, some characters see the good in some whites or just endure white racism in silence and with a sense that what really matters is a future in heaven, while others in the same family rage. In some novels those differences define an area for family conflict. The following, from Langston Hughes' *Not Without Laughter*, begins with a statement by Jimboy, followed by one by Harriett, his sister-in-law, followed by one by Hager, Jimboy's mother-in-law (and the mother of Harriett and Annjee).

'I know white folks … I lived in the South'

'And I ain't never been South,' added Harriett … 'but I know 'em right here … and I hate 'em!'

'De Lawd hears you,' said Hager.

'I don't care if He does hear me, mama! You and Annjee are too easy. You just take whatever white folks give you—*coon* to your face, and *nigger* behind your backs—and don't say nothing. You run to some white person's back door for every job you get, and then they pay you one dollar for five dollars' worth of work, and fire you whenever they get ready.' (Hughes, *Not Without Laughter*, p. 86)

At one level, this dialogue is an example of the ways white people can intrude into African American family discussions (see Chapter 8). But at another level, the dialogue shows how family member differences in emotional reactions to racism can be divisive. That is another aspect of how the rage from racism comes home to families in ways that can make trouble among family members. They may struggle with one another about what feelings to have in reaction to racism and what to do with the feelings.

Replicating the Rage of the Larger White System

From a systems theory perspective, another way to think about African American rage in response to the racial system is to note that what happens in larger systems is often replicated in smaller systems embedded in or linked to the larger systems (Rosenblatt, 1994, pp. 142–3). The larger system sets up, in a sense, rules for how power is used and what emotionality goes with that usage of power, and those rules are transmitted to the family systems that are linked to and dominated by the larger systems. Thus, every time that whites use power and domination in relationship to African Americans they are, among many things, transmitting ideas about how to use power in relationship to those who have less power. So when an African American man is rageful and bullying in relationship to his woman partner, or an African American parent is rageful or bullying in relationship to a child, that may be an expression of the carryover of larger system rules into the rule system of the family. For example, when Cholly in Toni Morrison's *The Bluest Eye* repeatedly attacks his wife and eventually rapes his daughter, one way to understand those actions is that he is working with implicit but well learned rules stemming from his experiences with and observations of whites. White rage, white bullying, white sexual assaults of African Americans have created the implicit rules that he is following. Similarly, Harriet's expression to her family of hatred of whites in *Not Without Laughter* by Langston Hughes can be understood as, among other things, a reflection of what she has learned about how whites refer to "the other" in their families (for whites the other is of course African Americans), and so she is importing the white system rule into her family.

Humiliation

Humiliation involves feeling bad about being reduced to a lower position in relationship to where one was before, where one would like to be, or in relationship to others. In humiliation one can be said to feel demeaned, chastened, made smaller, made less than, degraded, discredited, dishonoured, humbled, or shamed. Racism often seems intended to humiliate. And so it is not surprising that in some of the novels African Americans carry their feelings of humiliation home, feeling terrible, put down, and low in self-esteem, and that can influence other family members and family relationships. For example, earlier in this chapter, there was an account of how Cholly, in Toni Morrisons's *The Bluest Eye*, carried an early humiliation caused him by two white men into his adult years and his marriage. His humiliation eventually played out in violent encounters with his wife, but at the time of his humiliation Cholly had no family members who witnessed his humiliation and apparently none who were in a position to know about the humiliation and to try to comfort him. However, a few novels speak to issues of witnessing a family member's humiliation and the dilemmas people face when trying to comfort a humiliated family member.

Witnessing a Family Member's Humiliation

Family members may witness another family member's humiliation in an encounter with racism, and so a humiliating encounter can be punishing not only for the person experiencing the humiliation but also for the witnessing family members. For example, children witnessing a parent's humiliation may experience the situation with feelings of pain, anxiety, alarm, and insecurity. In one example, Sandy, the 10-year-old son of an African American woman who is working as a maid, is stung by the white employer's unfair criticism of his mother.

> Sandy stood near the sink with a burning face and eyes that had suddenly filled with angry tears. He couldn't help it—hearing his sweating mother reprimanded ... by this ... white woman ... Black, hard-working Anjee answered: 'Yes, ma'am,' and that was all—but Sandy cried. (Hughes, *Not Without Laughter*, p. 77)

Sandy's tears might have been partly a response to the unfairness and partly a sympathetic response to his mother. But I think also a child may have difficulty with white people humiliating a parent because a child so needs for the parent to be respected and counted on to show the way and to be strong for the child. If a person who one counts on to help one to grow up to have a good adult life is diminished, what hope is there for the child? The child may well fear that she or he too will have such experiences. But the child might also resolve to block such experiences from happening to herself or himself. Here is an example where a daughter, Nel, witnesses the humiliation of her mother, Helene.

The conductor let his eyes travel over the pale yellow woman ... 'What you think you doin', gal?'
Helene looked up at him. So soon. So soon. She hadn't even begun the trip back [South] ... and already she had been called 'gal.' All the old vulnerabilities, all the old fears of being somehow flawed gathered in her stomach and made her hands tremble. (Morrison, *Sula*, p. 20)

In 1919, the time of Helene's encounter with the conductor, there were, on trains in the south or going to the south, different passenger cars for whites and African Americans. In the quote, the conductor humiliates Helene by putting her in her place on the train and in the racial system. That interaction concludes with his sealing her in her place.

'We made a mistake, sir. You see, there wasn't no sign. We just got in the wrong car, that's all. Sir.'
'We don't 'low no mistakes on this train. Now git your butt on in there.'
He stood there staring at her until she realized that he wanted her to move aside. Pulling Nel by the arm, she pressed herself and her daughter into the foot space in front of a wooden seat. There for no earthly reason ... certainly no reason that Nel understood then or later, she smiled. Like a street pup that wags its tail at the very doorjamb of the butcher shop he has been kicked away from only moments before, Helene smiled. Smiled dazzlingly and coquettishly at ... the conductor. (Morrison, *Sula*, p. 21)

As Nel watches the encounter and watches the reactions of others on the car to the encounter, she comes to full realization of how humiliating the encounter with the conductor and her mother's meek, apologetic reaction were.

Nel looked away from the flash of pretty teeth to the other passengers. Two black soldiers, who had been watching the scene with what appeared to be indifference, now looked stricken ... As the door slammed on the conductor's exit, Helene walked down the aisle to a seat ... Nel sat opposite, facing both her mother and the soldiers, neither of whom she could look at. She felt both pleased and ashamed to sense that these men ... were bubbling with a hatred for her mother that had not been there in the beginning but had born with the dazzling smile. (Morrison, *Sula*, pp. 21–2)

Helene's humiliation did not overwhelm Nel but gave her a determination to never let what happened to her mother happen to her.

She resolved to be on guard—always. She wanted to make certain that no man ever looked at her that way. That no midnight eyes or marbled flesh would ever accost her and turn her into jelly. (Morrison, *Sula*, p. 22)

One way humiliation of the mother became a family system matter is that it became a lesson to the child about the potential of the racial system to humiliate and that leads to her resolving not to allow herself to be humiliated. And in that resolve there is a distancing from the mother, so with Nel's strength comes a psychological schism between herself and her mother. To the extent that that means they henceforth interact about a narrower range of experiences, they have to some extent lost each other as co-constructors of realities (Berger and Kellner, 1964). Their relationship system has less of whatever comes with relationship closeness and higher frequency of interaction, which means they may be, as individuals, less sure of things because they no longer have each other to interact with in ways that solidify realities. And it also means that in the future they will be less likely to see things in the same way, because they will be less likely to talk things through to agreement and mutual understanding. Also, if there is a thread of contempt and humiliation in Nel's distancing of her mother, that may be a reflection of the system dynamics discussed earlier in this chapter regarding rage. Nel's contempt and perhaps implicit humiliation of her mother may be an importation into their family system of the very obvious humiliation and contempt that was there in the larger system during the incident with the train conductor. From that perspective, Nel is not only reacting to a mother who embarrasses her and who has become in her eyes less of a model of strength in the larger world. Nel is also, in a sense, bringing the rules of interaction in the larger system into her family, and quite possibly her mother is also doing that by accepting the expression of contempt that Nel provides and allowing Nel to implicitly humiliate her.

Empathy with a Humiliated Family Member

There are times when a humiliating encounter, in all its unpleasantness, is dreadful and nothing more. Sometimes, however, the experience of humiliation helps one to better understand a family member who had experienced rather the same thing. Maud Martha, for example, has a humiliating day as a maid for a white woman and the white woman's mother-in-law. The experience helps Maud to understand her husband Paul.

> For the first time she understood what Paul endured daily … His boss … wished to underline Paul's lacks … As his boss looked at Paul, so these people looked at her. As though she were a child, a ridiculous one, and one that ought to be given a little shaking. (Brooks, *Maud Martha*, p. 162)

Similarly, a young woman's experiences of racist humiliation helped her to empathize in retrospect with what her mother must have felt. Her experience was in a very different kind of situation than her mother's, but she could see, in her experience, the system of white stereotyping, diminishment, and obliviousness that would have been part of her mother's daily experience as a maid for white people.

She remembered the mother striding home through Fulton Park ... bearing the throw-offs under her arm as she must have borne the day's humiliations inside. How had the mother contained her swift rage? (Marshall, *Brown Girl, Brownstones*, p. 287)

Thus, part of life in the racial system can be the experience of humiliation and perhaps learning to empathize with loved ones who have been humiliated in the racial system. Hence, whereas some of the time humiliation pushes family members apart or sets off processes that create schisms, there are other times where an experience of humiliation may bring one closer to family members who have had similar experiences.

Feelings Rules

In a systems theory perspective, human systems can be said to have feelings rules, rules about what feelings are appropriate in what situations and about how to express feelings (Rosenblatt, 2012). Among the many ways that the racial system has historically constrained African Americans is with rules about what feelings African Americans can express or not express in the presence of whites. As can be seen in many quotations from the novels, there were many situations in which African Americans had to suppress their anger and rage, and perhaps any other feelings in front of whites—for example, looking at excerpts earlier in this chapter, Cholly not expressing feelings at the white hunters in Toni Morrison's *The Bluest Eye* or Helen in Morrison's *Sula* being so meek with the train conductor. A failure to observe the racial system feeling rules could be very dangerous—consider the quote near the beginning of this chapter from James Baldwin's *Go Tell It on the Mountain* about the terrible beating Deborah's father received from white men. By contrast, as can be seen in these passages and others in this chapter and book, whites could freely express contempt, amusement, rage, and other feelings toward African Americans. This created a situation in which African Americans had to bottle up feelings, and then had to bottle up feelings about bottling up feelings, until in the safety of the home or in some other exclusively African American social situation. So some of what might go on in some household situations when someone came home from a difficult encounter with whites could be understood as the releasing of bottled up feelings. Similarly, one could understood Cholly's physical battles with his wife in Morrison's *The Bluest Eye* as a release of feelings fueled by the encounter with the hunters and all the other humiliations, frustrations, and deprivations he encountered in his dealings with whites and the racial system.

Families also can be said to have rules about what feelings to express when and how to express the feelings that are appropriate to express (Rosenblatt, 1994, p. 129). There may be different rules for women and men or for adults and children. However, among African American characters in the novels, one difference that is striking is that between those who are devoutly Christian in a way that stands for peace and acceptance of one's situation versus those who do not believe in that way and hence do not act according to the religious rules. One example in this chapter is the interaction between Harriett and Aunt Hager, in a passage from Langston Hughes' *Not Without Laughter*. Their disagreement can be taken as family conflict arising from harm done by the racial system, but it can also be understood as something of a struggle about what the family's feeling rules should be regarding hatred and related feelings arising from encounters with racism.

Chapter 6

The Economic Costs of Racism for African American Families

In the majority of the novels, most or all African American families live in very poor economic circumstances. These circumstances can be measured by the poor quality of their housing, how little and what they have to eat, their meager possessions, how little money they have for even minor purchases, and how much they talk and worry about economic issues. Most families in many of the novels are not doing well economically in an absolute sense and in comparison to white people. And whereas some forms of racism, for example insults directed at an individual or the racist denial of a job to an individual, may or may not affect a whole household, the members of a household experience the deprivations of poverty together.

In Sarah E. Wright's *This Child's Gonna Live*, the central characters are living 65 years after the end of slavery in a dilapidated cabin that housed slaves before emancipation. They are close to starving. They are always sick—worm diseases, colds that never end, possibly tuberculosis. They lack land on which to grow food. They lack adequate fuel for their stove and lamps, adequate transportation, adequate medical care, easy-to-get water, and much else. These deprivations are forced on them by the local white oligarchs, who use terrorism to take land from African American families and pay African Americans next to nothing for the back-breaking menial labor that is all that is available to them.

In some novels the things done by whites to keep African Americans poor are not explicitly stated, but in some they are. Here is a passage from Bebe Moore Campbell's *Your Blues Ain't Like Mine* about the actions of the white political and economic elite of a Mississippi county.

> Their great-grandfathers had made the family fortunes with blacks and cotton, and both had continued to enrich them. And not by chance. The Honorable Men of Hopewell had blood on their hands ... They had manipulated relief benefits so that poor whites were ... pushed out of the county in order to keep in blacks who would work for starvation wages ... [They] manipulated higher property taxes for the colored and lower ones for themselves, so that ... poor blacks wound up paying for both the white schools that their children couldn't attend and the dilapidated colored schools that were in session only after the cotton crop was harvested. Years before, these men had shut down several fledgling enterprises owned by colored when the competition threatened the economic

health of white businesses. The would-be entrepreneurs were sent fleeing for their lives. (Campbell, *Your Blues Ain't Like Mine*, pp. 108–9)

Thus, it is clear that African Americans of Hopewell are poor in large part because of decisions by whites in power to keep African Americans poor. It is also clear that to the extent that African Americans are kept in poverty, whites are enriched; that is, whites gain economically from their strategies for keeping African Americans poor. From a critical race theory perspective, the racial system of Hopewell was operated by whites who used their power to their advantage and to keep African Americans from getting ahead economically, educationally, and in other ways.

The white stereotypical image of African American poverty may be one of adults with little or nothing to do during the day, but in fact in many of the novels adults who are poor are far from being idle. For example, early in Ann Petry's *The Street*, Lutie works long, grueling hours to support her husband and their son Bub, and to some extent her father and his current woman friend. And then when Lutie and her husband break up and she also separates from her father and his woman friend, Lutie works hard to support herself and her son. The situation is similar for characters in many of the novels, people working hard or trying to work hard, in order to support themselves and family members at a poverty level. Racism limits options for earning a decent living, and thus it impoverishes families. But since racism is often about exploitation, the limitations and impoverishment of racism are often accompanied in the novels by opportunities to work hard in order to barely get by, and so it should not be surprising that many of the novels show families coping with racism in the ways that racism allows, particularly through the hard work of individual family members. But then, of course, being limited to hard work also means that the racial system limits what other family members can hope to get from a family member who works hard in order to earn a living. The family members who work long, demanding hours and come home exhausted have limited resources of time and energy to give to the family.

To some extent in the novels working hard is gendered. In the racial system in which African American families in the novels try to survive, women more than men find work or relatively reliable work. And so it is more often they than men who work hard at paid jobs. The fact that women can find work more than men is a central issue in some of the novels—for example, Lutie finding work when her husband Jim could not in Ann Petry's *The Street* or Angie finding work but Jimboy her husband not finding work he could tolerate in Langston Hughes' *Not Without Laughter*. Thus, while efforts to find work and willingness to work hard may not be gendered, the reality in quite a few of the novels is that it is more women's hard work at paid jobs than men's that enables a family to eke out a living. Moreover, it is not just the long, hard hours of paid employment through which a woman helps to sustain her family but in almost all the novels, women who work hard to bring in wages also work hard at home—food preparation, cleaning, childcare, laundry, and the like—to sustain the family. Although some men in the novels who were unemployed are described as helping a wife—for example, Jim in Ann Petry's *The*

Street helps with laundry, going to the market, and house cleaning—in none of the novels is a man described as engaging in a double day of hard work as many of the women are described.

Poverty, Health, and the Work One Can Do for One's Family

Poverty can undermine physical health and strength in ways that can block one from earning as much money as one might for one's family.

> Robert was only a handyman. There was in him a weakness from the years of slow hunger that would never let him be a strong-bodied man able to work for a strong man's wages. (West, *The Living Is Easy*, p. 162)

In fact, in West's *The Living Is Easy* Robert's history of poverty means that he is not only physically weak but he is almost illiterate and very unconfident. He cannot provide adequately for his wife Serena, their infant son Tim, and his father-in-law, in whose house they live. The day comes when Serena's rich sister Cleo, who has for years been helping them financially, sends money for transportation and a request for Serena to join Cleo in Boston. Having grown up in dreadful, humiliating poverty and being unconfident and only a marginal provider, Robert can fear that Serena will discover there is nothing to him and that she will leave him and never return. But he cannot offer anything economically to hold her, and the reality is that her going would mean there would be more food for the family members left behind. Had Robert not been so weakened physically by many years of racism-imposed poverty, he might have had the self-confidence and perhaps even the financial resources to make staying home with him attractive to Serena and to provide adequate support for her and the family.

Poverty and Family Conflict

When people live in poverty they can be pushed to an emotional limit where the next difficulty can be more than they can handle. Couple conflict can be a sign that the partners are dealing with more than they can handle. The background for the following example of such conflict, from Ann Petry's *The Street*, is that Lutie and her husband Jim have long been in dire economic circumstances. Jim has been unable to find a job, and they have used up the $1000 of life insurance money he received when his mother died. They face the possibility of not having enough money to feed themselves and their son Bub and to make payments on their house. However, they have found a way to continue to pay their living expenses by taking in foster children, who come with government support money. But Lutie has invited her father, Pop, to come to live with them because he has been evicted from his apartment. The fact that Pop is a heavy user of alcohol and will hold drinking parties wherever he lives alarms Jim because for the government foster care authorities and for Jim it is totally unacceptable for there to be such drinking in a house with foster children. Lutie sees things differently. In her thinking Pop is her father and needs a place to live and freedom to be himself. So Lutie and Jim argue about Lutie's invitation to Pop to move in with them.

> They were both shouting. The small room vibrated with the sound of their anger. They had lived on the edge of nothing for so long that they had finally reached the point where neither of them could brook opposition in the other, could not or would not tolerate even the suggestion of being in the wrong. (Petry, *The Street*, pp. 173–4)

It can be difficult for two partners to support one another psychologically and feel supported when they live in poverty. The frustrations, tensions, limitations, needs not met, physical exhaustion, health problems, and the compromises they must make in order to barely get by drag them down. From a family systems theory perspective, poverty may, among many things, lead to conflict over family rules by setting up circumstances and needs that provide a justification to someone in the family for violating the rules. "The right thing to do is X, but we are in desperate circumstances, so I say we should violate the rule about doing X." The X may be almost anything, for example, to eat healthful foods. In Lutie and Jim's case, X was being careful not to do things that jeopardize their income from foster care. Poverty may increase the likelihood of conflict over family rules because poverty puts a family into a nonsteady state. A steady state, where things flow along rather smoothly from week to week makes it easy to go with the rules. But with poverty, things arise that disrupt the steady state and demand efforts to problem solve that can make breaking rules make sense, partly because the rule breaking can be seen as supporting a higher order rule like "survive" or "honor your parents." One can imagine someone saying, "We have to eat, and bad food is what we can afford" or one can imagine Lutie saying, "My father needs a home and we can make room for him." Rule violation can set off intense family conflict, which at the extreme can make it challenging for the people to maintain their relationship. And in fact for Lutie and Jim things spiral down to the point where they stop being a couple, and it is clear that they were driven apart by their poverty, which was rooted in racism.

> If they hadn't been so damn poor she and Jim might have stayed married. (Petry, *The Street*, p. 183)

Another potential family problem that comes with poverty is that there can be family conflict because the value of earning enough to get by may clash with the value of taking care of oneself physically. In some novels conflicts arise with one family member expressing one of the values and another expressing the other. In Marita Golden's *Long Distance Life*, Naomi talks about such conflict between her parents. When her mother would express sorrow about the damage she did to her hands while washing clothes for white people, her father would be upset because for him the highest priority was putting food on the table. In the quote that follows it seems to be a recurring conflict, but one that is limited because Naomi's father could be shamed into silence and confusion by what Naomi's mother would say about her hands.

> Washing clothes meant boilin' them over a fire. Washing clothes meant using lye soap that eat up your hands ... Sometimes, at the end of the day, my mama would look at her hands and ... sit there and cry. And she'd say, 'I used to have such pretty hands, such pretty hands.' And Daddy would start hollerin', 'You worried 'bout your hands, I'm worried 'bout getting food for y'all to eat.' And Mama'd tell him, 'A woman wants to be proud of something she came in the world with, wants to think some part of her is beautiful. Even a colored woman wants that.' And Daddy'd look all ashamed and confused and suck harder on his pipe and get up and go on the front porch. (Golden, *Long Distance Life*, p. 26)

A couple in poverty can enter into intense conflict about things that would not be matters of conflict if they were not in poverty. In Sarah E. Wright's *This Child's Gonna Live*, a married couple, Mariah and Jacob, enter into intense conflict because she is thinking of taking their children north to try to find a way out of poverty. She is far along in pregnancy and working at digging potatoes for a white farmer to try to earn enough to pay to give birth in a hospital, since the child she gave birth to before the current pregnancy died of an infection due to careless handling by the local midwife.

> 'Woman!' He shoved a swollen-jointed finger up to her eyes, 'Just lift one finger to take either one of my children out of Tangierneck, and I s'pect that'll be the last finger you'll ever lift ... And another thing, woman, child dies, gonna be your fault for lifting and lugging them potato baskets. Told you to stay out of them fields.' (Wright, *This Child's Gonna Live*, p. 17)

There would be no threat of separation and no risk to her health from doing heavy field work late into pregnancy had they not been deprived of their land by a wealthy and powerful white man, forced to pay the white man rent on the property he had taken from them, and forced to work for miserable wages on a white-owned farm.

Sometimes one of the underlying mechanisms of couple conflict and difficulty is that what one wants to spend money on, perhaps even needs to spend money on, is something the other does not approve. Differences in priorities for spending can arise with any couple. But when a couple is in poverty and hence there is not enough money to meet basic needs a partner can fear that spending money on what the other wants will get them in terrible trouble when they need desperately to buy something else. The couple conflict could conceivably break up the couple, but most of the time in the novels such conflict only makes things hard for the couple and, if they have children, for their children as well. Toni Morrison's *The*

Bluest Eye, for example, is rich in accounts of how the grim demands of poverty create harsh interactions in a couple (Mayberry, 2007, p. 17). In *The Bluest Eye*, the couple at the center of the book, the Breedloves, moved north, to a community where white people are more numerous and African Americans are not necessarily welcoming of strangers. In the new community the Breedloves have no family and are challenged economically. The social situation in which they find themselves and their lack of economic resources lead to increasing marital difficulty.

> In her loneliness, she turned to her husband for reassurance, entertainment, for things to fill the vacant places ... Cholly was kindness still, but began to resist her total dependence on him. They were beginning to have less and less to say to each other. He had no problem finding other people and other things to occupy him ... Pauline felt uncomfortable with the few black women she met ... Their goading glances and private snickers at her way of talking ... and dressing developed in her a desire for new clothes. When Cholly began to quarrel about the money she wanted, she decided to go to work. Taking jobs as a day worker helped with the clothes, and even a few things for the apartment, but it did not help with Cholly. He was not pleased with her purchases and began to tell her so. Their marriage was shredded with quarrels. (Morrison, *The Bluest Eye*, pp. 93–4)

Pauline's day labor brought in money that provided some help with their basic economic needs, but the Breedloves were still in economic difficulty, and eventually their conflicts about money spilled into her work in a way that led to her losing her job (and considerable income she had coming to her for work she had already done).

> 'I would have stayed on 'cepting for Cholly come over by where I was working ... He come there drunk wanting some money. When that white woman see him, she turned red. She tried to act strong-like, but she was scared bad. ... She told Cholly to get out or she would call the police. He cussed her and started pulling on me. I would have gone upside his head, but I don't want no dealings with the police. So I taken my things and left. I tried to get back, but she didn't want me no more if I was going to stay with Cholly. She said she would let me stay if I left him. I thought about that ... It didn't seem none too bright for a black woman to leave a black man for a white woman. She didn't never give me the eleven dollars she owed me.' (Morrison, *The Bluest Eye*, p. 95)

Also, for a family in poverty when some possession is not only precious in itself but represents many hours or even weeks of work, family conflict can bubble up if a family member harms it, even if the harm is unintentional. Here a mother rages at her daughter:

> 'I work two months to pay for that dress and you mess it up before I get a chance
> to wear it! Standin' on my feet in that shop all day and then when I get home—'
> (Hunter, *God Bless the Child*, p. 14)

With money scarce, even something as innocuous as a child drinking milk can lead
to harsh ranting at the children who are present when the milk is drunk, a ranting
that arises out of economic insecurity and an awareness that the family's precious
supply of milk is being depleted too quickly.

> 'I don't know what I'm supposed to be running here, a charity ward ... I guess I
> ain't sup*posed* to have nothing. I'm sup*posed* to end up in the poorhouse. Look
> like nothing I do is going to keep me out of there. Folks just spend all their time
> trying to figure out ways to send *me* to the poorhouse ... Don't *nobody* need
> *three* quarts of milk. Henry *Ford* don't need three quarts of milk.' (Morrison,
> *The Bluest Eye*, p. 23)

In the example just given, it is a neighbor child who drinks so much milk, but the
point remains valid, that the poverty imposed by racism creates family tensions over
how their limited economic resources are used. Related to this, there are findings
from a research study on parenting in which the majority of people studied were
African American that economic hardship makes for tense parenting and a lower
level of expression of affection (Mistry, Vandewater, Huston, and McLoyd, 2002).
That seems consistent with the following example, in which a mother is irritated
with her child for leaving the lights on while he sleeps, because she has to pay the
utility bill. She is on the edge of starting a long scolding of him, and then realizes
that it might not be good to always harp at him about money matters.

> 'How come you're not in bed?' she demanded.
> 'I fell asleep.'
> 'With your clothes on?' she said, and then added: 'With the lights on, too? You
> must be trying to make the bill bigger—' and she stopped abruptly. She was
> always talking to [him] about money. It wasn't good. He would be thinking
> about nothing else pretty soon. (Petry, *The Street*, pp. 188–9)

In fact, her constant talk with her son about money and her desperate need
to have rules followed that will help them deal with their difficult economic
circumstances eventually lead to a very serious problem when eight-year-old
Bub agrees to do something for the building superintendent to bring in income.
Unfortunately, what he agrees to do is illegal, and once he is arrested, the legal
system, and his mother's understanding of what she needs to do to get him out
of jail and to remain his mother, lead to disaster for them. At one point, Lutie
talks to herself about how her ongoing anxiety about money pushed her son to
get into such serious trouble.

'You helped push him because you talked to him about money. All the time money. And you wanted it because you wanted to move from this street.' (Petry, *The Street*, p. 389)

And what she says about herself fits research (Mistry, Vandewater, Huston, and McLoyd, 2002) reporting that economically distressed mothers experience a decreased sense of well-being, and that impacts their parenting.

In some novels, there are poignant discussions involving children who want something the adult or adults cannot afford.

When he went home, he described the sled minutely to [his mother] and [grandmother], Hager, and wondered aloud if that might be what he would get for Christmas. But Hager would say: 'Santa Claus are just like other folks. He don't work for nothin'!' And his mother would add … 'This is gonna be a slim Christmas, honey, but mama'll see what she can do.' (Hughes, *Not Without Laughter*, p. 149)

There is an interesting additional feature in this excerpt from the Hughes book. The two adults agree that money is tight, but they seem perhaps to disagree about how much they might try to satisfy the child's wish for a sled, so implicitly that may be another family conflict related to poverty.

To sum up, in many of the novels racism causes family poverty that then leads to family conflict and efforts to deal with the poverty that can make for very difficult relationship problems. The visual images of African American poverty may ordinarily be of inadequate housing, poorly furnished dwellings, and perhaps people who are ill fed and ill clothed, but missing from such visual images is the family conflict and other relationship difficulties that come with poverty. Judging by the novels that address poverty, the damage and immorality of racism-caused poverty is in part what it may do to family relationships.

Mixed Feelings about a Family Member Who Has Left Poverty

One might assume that if any family member finds a way out of poverty, others would be pleased. Somebody they care about has succeeded, and a family member who is economically better-off might be able and willing to provide economic assistance to family members who are less well-off. But paradoxically, other family members may be upset if one of them escapes poverty, because the success of one family member can make others feel worse about their situation. Here is an interaction, in the 1920s between a father from the South and his adult daughter who has moved to Washington, DC, and earned enough to buy a house, send money home, and bring her parents to Washington for a visit.

'You ain't said hardly nothin' to me since y'all got here,' I told him. 'Not even *Congratulations* or *Good job*. I worked hard for what I got, Daddy, and I want you to be proud.'

He took his pipe out of his mouth and said, 'I am proud of you, Naomi. Real proud. But you got to understand. I've worked another man's land for over twenty years and just barely kept my family from starvin'. My daughter comes North and gets so much it puts me to shame. Tell me how I'm s'posed to feel about me. Sure I'm proud of you. So proud I'm damn near ready to bust. But I look at all you done and feel like all my life's been a waste. You a landlord. I'm your daddy and I'm still a tenant.' (Golden, *Long Distance Life*, p. 39)

But then her being in the North during the economic depression that began in 1929 gives her extra resources to support her family back in North Carolina.

Folks down home were hit real hard. I was sending home not just money but clothes and food. And going down three or four times a year just to check for good measure. (Golden, *Long Distance Life*, p. 40)

Although her financial success is hard for her father, he and his household are better-off because of her success.

The issue of family feelings about others doing well comes up in a few other novels, for example, Terry McMillan's *A Day Late and a Dollar Short*, where when a sibling becomes very well-off financially other siblings feel uncomfortable about what the well-off sibling can do for their mother and other family members. The issue of family differences in economic well-being is important because African American families are not infrequently diverse in terms of economic standing (Chiteji and Hamilton, 2002), and the differences can make for family relationship difficulty.

Poverty and Wanting a Homeplace

Families on the edge economically may be on the edge of being put out of where they live, with no place else to live, being put into what Toni Morrison, in *The Bluest Eye*, called 'the outdoors.'

Knowing that there was such a thing as outdoors bred in us a hunger for property, for ownership. The firm possession of a yard, a porch, a grape arbor. Propertied black people spent all their energies, all their love, on their nests. Like frenzied, desperate birds, they overdecorated everything; fussed and fidgeted over their hard-won homes … Renting blacks cast furtive glances at these owned yards and porches, and made firmer commitments to buy themselves 'some nice little old place.' … They saved, and scratched, and piled away what they could in the rented hovels, looking forward to the day of property. (Morrison, *The Bluest Eye*, p. 18)

Having a homeplace is thus about a family having decent, affordable, ongoing, trustworthy, secure shelter that allows for a feeling of rootedness (Burton, Winn, Stevenson, and Clark, 2004). It can be about wanting enough space for the family not to feel too crowded (Hannerz, 1969, p. 45), and the crowding may be partly about some families taking in people (relatives or not) who do not have a place of their own to stay (Hannerz, 1969, p. 50). It can also be about being accepted rather than ostracized, being human as opposed to animal, and perhaps even feeling that one's housing allows one to be "like white people" (Yancy, 2004, p. 111). Thus, the hunger for a homeplace that can come with the insecure and inadequate housing of poverty may not just be for shelter but for security, belongingness, roots, personal and family renewal, a feeling of being fully human, and the satisfaction that may come from being at least at the economic level of poor white people.

In accord with the quote immediately above from Toni Morrison's *The Bluest Eye*, in some of the other novels it is clear that African Americans who establish a homeplace care about the homeplace intensely and work very hard at taking care of it. That is even clearly a part of the lives of some of the families in the novels who are better-off economically and have a homeplace. For example, in Terry McMillan's *A Day Late and a Dollar Short*, the two sisters who have their own home, Paris and Charlotte, constantly work at taking care of it. So out of the deprivation of decent, secure housing that is part of the legacy of racism comes, to some extent, a culture of wanting a homeplace and, for those with a homeplace, investing a great deal in caring for it.

Poverty and Family Ranking in African American Communities

The racial system pushes many African American families in the novels down, but some are pushed down farther than others, and some are less able than others to find a way to get by despite their poverty. Differences in how far down families have been pushed make for ranking in African American communities in a few of the novels, and one way that the ranking may show up is in parents wanting their children not to play with African American children from families that are less well-off. Not infrequently the African American families who are looked down upon are recent migrants to the north, people who come north with less education, fewer economic resources, and less knowledge of how to live in the north than the African Americans who have been in the north for a while and are relatively well-off.

'I ain't want you playing with them common low-class Southern niggers in this block, and I particularly ain't want them in my house.' (Killens, *The Cotillion or, One Good Bull Is Half the Herd*, p. 13)

There is social research evidence that neighbors may provide crucial economic and other help to neighbors in low income African American communities (Duck, 2012; Stack, 1974; Stewart, 2007). But from the perspective of some novels, the racial system does not necessarily unite African American families who are in poverty in their shared difficulty or in shared feelings about the white-controlled racial system that makes them impoverished. And in the world of the novels poverty can make an African American character acutely aware that some African American families are better-off than others and it would be preferable to be in one of the better-off families.

The Financial Costs to Families of Dealing with a Racist Criminal Justice System

The criminal justice system, as an arm of the racial system, can burden African American families economically. In several novels, this economic burden comes when a family member or lover is incarcerated. It can cost more money than family members, spouses, or lovers have to get decent legal help in an attempt to free the person who has been incarcerated. As was outlined in Chapter 3, in James Baldwin's, *If Beale Street Could Talk*, Fonny has been put in jail on trumped-up charges. His lover, Tish, her family, and Fonny's family have almost no money to pay for an attorney and a private investigator to help free Fonny. Jail is terrible for Fonny, and there is the fear that even if exonerated, he will be permanently harmed by his time in jail. Tish is terrified and distraught. Some in the two families struggle to do what they can do to help to get Fonny out of jail. In their efforts to raise money necessary for legal defense some become distant from others and some take chances that might lead to them losing their job or going to jail.

> Joseph is working overtime, double time, and so is Frank. Ernestine has to spend less time with her children because she has taken a job as part-time private secretary to a very rich and eccentric young actress, whose connections she intends to intimate, and use. Joseph is coldly, systematically, stealing from the docks, and Frank is stealing from the garment center and they sell the hot goods in Harlem or in Brooklyn. They don't tell us this, but we know it. They don't tell us because, if things go wrong, we can't be accused of being accomplices. (Baldwin, *If Beale Street Could Talk*, p. 128)

After a while the jail visits of Tish to see Fonny have to be cut back, though they desperately want to see each other, because she has to keep working to try to raise money for his legal defense. But then her father confronts her, saying that he will take responsibility for raising the money, that not only is her work to earn money blocking her support of Fonny but she is risking the life of her unborn child by pushing herself to work when she should be resting.

Within Fonny's family of origin, a terrible gulf develops. His father, Frank, is working very vigorously to save Fonny. This is connected to a schism developing between Frank on the one hand and his wife and daughters on the other. As things unfold, Frank loses his job because he was caught stealing in order to raise money for Fonny's defense. Devastated by everything— Fonny's continuing imprisonment, the emotional gulf within his family, the loss of his job—Frank commits suicide. The racial system, through its unjust and harsh treatment of Fonny, has created enormous economic difficulties that have harmed two families and claimed a life.

In a similar situation, in Baldwin's *Go Tell It on the Mountain*, Richard seems at one point to be doomed to a long prison sentence for a crime he did not commit, because neither he nor Elizabeth, his love, have money for a lawyer. The players in the legal system who prey on African Americans who have little or no money include lawyers and bailbondsmen. In Baldwin's *If Beale Street Could Talk*, there is this:

> If you cross the Sahara, and you fall, by and by vultures circle around you, smelling, sensing, your death. They circle lower and lower: they wait. They know. They know exactly when the flesh is ready, when the spirit cannot fight back. The poor are always crossing the Sahara. And the lawyers and bondsmen and all that crowd circle around the poor, exactly like vultures. (Baldwin, *If Beale Street Could Talk*, pp. 6–7)

Paying for legal help one cannot afford can make terrible trouble. In Ann Petry's *The Street*, Lutie eventually has to abandon her eight-year-old son Bub because she humiliates and endangers herself and then kills someone as she tries to raise funds for legal help she believes she needs in order to save Bub from jail. Lutie is not knowledgeable enough about the legal system to know that she does not need legal help to get Bub released. Or, to put her problem in another perspective, there are many white people (attorneys, magistrates, police officers) who could advise Lutie that she does not need legal help, but none of those people does that. And there are similar examples in other novels of African American characters who are not so knowledgeable about the legal system that they know that they can get someone off without expensive legal help. And none of the white people they encounter who are knowledgeable advises them that they do not need legal help. In fact, white lawyers who prey on African Americans almost always seem willing, in the novels, to charge heavy fees to African Americans instead of saying the few words that would help to deal with the legal system without an expensive lawyer. Perhaps it is not surprising that a white lawyer in a racist society who asks for a large sum of money from an African American family is unlikely to tell them that they do not need a lawyer or, as in Gloria Naylor's *The Women of Brewster Street*, they do not have to pay a lawyer but could use a public defender. In *The Women of Brewster Street*, Mattie hires a lawyer to defend her son Basil.

[The lawyer] wondered why she hadn't let the public defender take care of such a simple case. He would be receiving a huge fee ... Well, he sighed ... Thank God for ignorance of the law and frantic mothers. (Naylor, *The Women of Brewster Place*, pp. 47–8)

So in some of the novels there are white people who could help African Americans deal with the criminal justice system but who instead exploit them economically. Family members may have the satisfaction of trying to do good for someone they love, but in a fair and just system, as opposed to a racist system, people would not have to be oppressed and exploited as they try to do good for someone they love. And in a fair and just system, African Americans would not so often have to worry about bail and legal help for family members.

The Financial Cost to Families of White Extra-legal Punishment

In some of the novels, African American families experience financial costs because whites want to punish them (outside of the legal system) for not allowing whites to exploit or harm them. That is, in a system in which some white people use African Americans and the assets of African Americans to their advantage, African American resistance may be punished in ways that have economic costs for African American families. Here is an example involving a young woman's flight from a white man who wants to force himself sexually on her. She and her family pay the emotional and social cost of becoming separated and losing their closeness and mutual support. But then there is a concrete financial cost to her family for the woman's flight, white revenge-taking on her family's property.

Rutherford County wasn't ready for Etta's blooming independence, and so she left one rainy summer night about three hours ahead of dawn and Johnny Brick's furious pursuing relatives. Mattie wrote and told her they had waited in ambush for two days on the county line, and then had returned and burned down her father's barn. The sheriff told Mr. Johnson he had gotten off mighty light— considering. Mr. Johnson thought so, too. After reading Mattie's letter, Etta was sorry she hadn't killed the horny white bastard when she had the chance. (Naylor, *Women of Brewster Place*, p. 60)

A racial system that condones institutionalized extra-legal economic punishment by whites who feel wronged adds to the economic burdens of African American families and pushes some families, like Etta Johnson's, deeper into poverty. The economic punishment can be understood as part of a more extensive system of terror, so the poverty is not only a consequence of economic exploitation but of a system of terrorizing African Americans into compliance, with one of the many threats to keep African Americans compliant being extra-legal economic punishment. For families, this could make family members into agents of the system in that if any family member seems inclined to resist the system in some way other family members may try to block the resistance out of fear not only for the resistor's safety and their own but for the economic consequences of the resistance.

Chapter 7

Skin Color and Other Racialized Features as Family Issues

•

As critical race theories argue, colorism, discrimination based on skin color, is an important element of the racial system (Burton et al., 2010). Colorism is linked, in the racial system, to racist ideology, racist insult practices, discrimination practices involving knowing nothing more about a person than how a person looks, a privilege system which valorizes whiteness, and whiteness as an asset. Colorism in the racial system is so significant and powerful that historically it has been an important matter of status differentiation and contention among African Americans. And the importance that the racial system has given to color over the years has made for a very rich color vocabulary among African Americans. In fact, every one of the 27 novels analyzed for this book describes African American characters in terms of skin color, and the color vocabulary is rich and varied—for example, in Bebe Moore Campbell's *Your Blues Ain't Like Mine*, the skin color of Armstrong Todd is described as matching "a lemon wafer" (p. 9), and in Bernice L. McFadden's *Nowhere Is a Place*, one character is described as having "toasted almond colored skin" (p. 10). Related to the rich attention to skin color in the description of African American characters in these novels, in some of the novels there are skin color issues in the community that play out in families or even skin color issues within a family. In fact, skin color issues are at the heart of two of the novels, John Oliver Killens' *The Cotillion* and Wallace Thurman's *The Blacker the Berry*.

In many of the novels, skin color (and to a lesser extent other racially marked physical features, like hair texture and the shape of nose and lips) matter to some characters. One way to think about that is that African Americans who are lighter-skinned and who have other physical features that are more like what is considered "white" have in many eras and social ecologies been considered by themselves and by other African Americans to be elite and deserving of more privilege and power than African Americans with darker skin and other features that are considered less "white" (see, for example, Boyd-Franklin, 2003, pp. 28–51; Glenn, 2009; Hunter, 2002, 2004; Jones, 2002, p. 94; Russell, Wilson, and Hall, 1992, who marshaled considerable evidence, including some of the novels discussed in this book, to provide examples; Tate, 2009; Wilder and Cain, 2011). Since skin color (as opposed to other physical features) is what is emphasized in the novels and in the literature on the sociology of racialized features, my language in this chapter is primarily about skin color. But to the extent that the novels address other physical features that have meaning in the racial system, for example, hair texture and the shape of lips, those other features have the same meanings, impact, power and so on for individuals in the novels and for their families in the context of the racial system.

Skin color has been part of African American culture for a long time. But then, African American culture aside, there is considerable evidence that lighter-skinned African Americans are treated better than darker-skinned African Americans by whites and white dominated institutions (Hochschild, 2006; Hochschild and Weaver, 2007). Reflecting the higher status of light-skinned African Americans in white culture, Keith (2009) cited evidence that lighter-skinned African Americans receive more formal education, have greater personal and family income, and are more likely to have higher status jobs than darker-skinned African Americans. So skin color issues in the African American community and in African American families are related to experiences and status in the larger, white-dominated society.

Skin Color Issues in African American Families

There is reason to think that some African American families socialize lighter-skinned children differently than darker-skinned children (Burton, Bonilla-Silva, et al., 2010). Given that, and given that skin color and color caste have been important in African American life (e.g. Boyd-Franklin, 2003; S.L. Jones, 2002, p. 121), it is not surprising that in some novels, white standards concerning skin color and beauty have a powerful effect on family relationships. For example, in Toni Morrison's *Song of Solomon*, Macon Dead the Second had this to say to his darker-skinned son Milkman about his father-in-law (Milkman's grandfather), who had been a physician:

> He delivered both your sisters himself and each time all he was interested in was the color of their skin. He would have disowned you [because your skin color is so dark]. (Morrison, *Song of Solomon*, p. 71)

A mother or grandmother whose daughter or granddaughter has darker skin can feel concerned, protective, or worried about the darker skin.

> Her ... friends had taught her to feel defensive because [her daughter] was the [darker] color of her father. (West, *The Living Is Easy*, p. 42)

A child who is "a bit too dark" might, in parental or grandparental thinking, have to be a fighter or in some other way compensate for the darker skin. And a young woman with darker skin could be seen as needing to be careful with lighter-skinned men, lest they take advantage of her.

> 'I ain't never seen a yaller dude yet that meant a dark woman no good—an' [my daughter] is dark!' (Hughes, *Not Without Laughter*, p. 32)

A child with darker skin could wonder if her mother's seeming rejection of her has something to do with her skin color.

> It was, perhaps, her mother's disquieting color that, whenever she was held in her mother's arms, made Elizabeth think of milk. Her mother did not, however, hold Elizabeth in her arms very often. Elizabeth very quickly suspected that this was because she was so very much darker than her mother and not nearly, of course, so beautiful. (Baldwin, *Go Tell It on the Mountain*, p. 179)

In discussing *Go Tell It on the Mountain*, May (1996) pointed out that the "of course" in the last sentence of the quote immediately above shows how much the oppressive skin color standards that are part of the ideology of racism can be internalized by people who are hurt by those standards. It is another aspect of the insidious power of racism that African Americans may internalize racist standards about skin color even though those standards harm them and their loved ones. Why might they do this? Judging by accounts in some of the novels, the standards are transmitted intergenerationally in families and communities, so partly the internalization is a matter of accepting what family and community inculcate. But there is also the white societal context that holds up and enforces those standards, and that means that to pretend the standards do not exist in the larger society is a mistake. If the larger society's racial system operates on certain standards, in some ways it is adaptive to live as though those standards are real and possibly important, because they are. And from another perspective, family systems are generally captured by the systems of the larger society, so from a family rules perspective (e.g. Hare-Mustin, 1987; Rosenblatt, 1994, pp. 129–35) it is difficult for a family to have implicit rules that more or less govern what goes on in the family that are inconsistent with rules in the larger societal systems in which the family is embedded. As was laid out in Chapter 1, the racial system may well drive certain (typically implicit) family rules in African American families. And so if the rule in the larger society is that white physical features confer benefit, it is not surprising that African American families in the novels either have those rules or struggle to resist them.

Given that skin color standards are part of the story in a number of the novels and how important those standards are in African American communities, it is not surprising that in some novels a woman with darker skin could find herself disparaged or pitied by her own family.

> She should have been a boy, then color of skin wouldn't have mattered so much, for wasn't her mother always saying that a black boy could get along, but that a black girl would never know anything but sorrow and disappointment? (Thurman, *The Blacker the Berry*, p. 22)

> Felicia Kincaid was the daughter of the city's Black elite, descended on both sides of her family from mulattoes who had for generations inbred their white blood like a sacred inheritance. Felicia was born with a light tan coloring that, nevertheless, made her the darkest member of her family, a fact for which she was secretly pitied by aunts and openly chided by cousins. (Golden, *Long Distance Life*, pp. 234–5)

A parent or grandparent might express concern about the darkness of a man who a daughter or granddaughter was seeing, though the evaluation was qualified if the daughter or granddaughter was relatively dark-skinned.

> 'He is a bit dark, but you can't have everything.'
> 'Specially bein' the color you are … Just try not to have no children, that's all. Black children has a hard time in this world.' (Hunter, *God Bless the Child*, p. 117)

In the novels, the valuing of light skin could even threaten to divide husband from wife and parent from child when there was a difference between them in skin color. In some of the novels it is hard for a man who is dark-skinned to live comfortably with a light-skinned wife and child when they are in an extended family that values light skin highly and looks at dark skin with contempt. The following is about dark-skinned Victor who is married to light-skinned Lily who has gone to live with her light-skinned sister Cleo.

> This sister of hers had taught her to hate her dark husband … He was savagely conscious of Lily's white skin and the golden skin of her sister. Two goddamned color-struck hussies … God, let him get out of that house before his little honey-colored daughter … backed away from her own daddy because he was dark. (West, *The Living Is Easy*, p. 182)

Consistent with a literature on African American use of skin-lighteners (e.g. Glenn, 2009), in the novels a wife could try to lighten her skin to please her husband, even though he might talk as though such efforts were a waste of time and money. But then she might counter his seeming opposition to her efforts by asserting that she knows he cares about skin color.

> 'Don't know why you keep wasting all your time and my money on all them old skin whiteners. You as black now as you was the day you was born.'
> 'You wasn't there the day I was born. And I know you don't want a coal-black woman.' (Baldwin, *Go Tell it on the Mountain*, p. 100)

Thus, in some of the novels some African Americans clearly come to carry the oppressive standards that are a product of the racial system by disparaging darker skin. And this acceptance of white standards of attractiveness intrudes into family life by making some people critical of themselves or others in the family and by leading some to incur costs in time, money, materials, and personal comfort to try to lighten their skin. It makes family members in some sense agents of white standards.

Also, as was said earlier in the chapter, the oppressive standards are, in some novels, not only about skin color but about other features that have meaning in the racial system, such as hair texture, breadth of nose, and thickness of lips. Here is an example from a novel that was written in part to satirize the ways that some African Americans have been captured by white standards of appearance. In the example, a mother, Daphne, is looking at her teenage daughter.

> Daphne sweetly remembered … how she used to make the girl pull her lips in and keep them in when she was a baby, so they would grow thin … and how she used to put clothespins on the baby's nostrils just to pinch them into thin and slender. (Killens, *The Cotillion, or, One Good Bull Is Half the Herd*, p. 44)

Whiteness may not only be seen as representing physical attractiveness but also something like moral and spiritual goodness. Mariah, the central character in Sarah E. Wright's *This Child's Gonna Live*, remembered that when she was a child her mother cut pictures out from Christmas candy boxes of white girls to hang on the cedar tree and the walls.

> [Mamma] told Mariah, 'You got to be that good and pure before the Lord's gonna bless you.' (Wright, *This Child's Gonna Live*, p. 2)

So the skin color standards that intrude into African American families from the racial system might be not only about appearance but also, at least for one character in one novel, about goodness, purity, and God's blessings being assumed to be associated with lighter skin. What a powerful impact the racial system has had when that is the message an African American mother delivers to a child.

In some instances in the novels, the skin color standards and all that goes with them are deeply destructive to a family. For example, in Toni Morrison's *The Bluest Eye*, the Breedloves are weighed down in many ways by racism, and an important part of it is the weight of being considered physically unattractive by societal standards. As Valkeakari (2007, p. 79) wrote about it, "The Breedloves … have no one in their environment to assert blackness as a positive quality, or to call into question the rationale of attributing any ontological or existential significance to either whiteness or blackness. They therefore 'without question' take their imaginary blackness-derived 'ugliness in their hands, thr[o]w it as a mantle over them, and [go] about the world with it'" [The textual quotes Valkeakari provides are from Morrison, *The Bluest Eye*, p. 34—in the edition of the Morrison novel used for this book]. Valkeakari goes on to write (ibid.) that "Cholly and Pauline pass on this color-coded mode of thought and perception … to their two children … [so] 'Public fact becomes private reality' [Morrison, *The Bluest Eye*, p. 146—the page reference is to the edition of *The Bluest Eye* cited in this book] in Pecola's inner world as she falls prey to her family's and community's internalized racial self-hated." In that self-hatred described by Morrison and referred to by Valkeakari, terrible things happen in the Breedlove family, including the child Pecola being raped by her father. She bears a baby from that rape; her father dies in the work house. The story of the Breedloves and the title of Morrison's novel, *The Bluest Eye*, can be understood as messages about the ways that white standards of appearance can burden African Americans and, as in the case of Pecola, be central to the longings of African American children in families trapped in a cultural, social, and psychological world in which white standards of appearance are both destructive and valued.

Community and Family Resentment Regarding Skin Color Standards

In some novels African American feelings about skin color standards are sometimes mixed. The standards may be powerful in granting status and favor to lighter-skinned African Americans, but the standards are also resented and disparaged by some African American characters. Thus, another side to white beauty standards is that in some novels African American characters who most value such standards are resented, disliked, joked about, shunned, or otherwise made to seem not good people through the reactions of other African American characters. For example, a gossipy, judgmental, manipulative, and not-hard-working "milky skinned" woman in Hurston's *Their Eyes Were Watching God* was made by the author to seem shallow and unpleasant. The community so resented her love of herself, her contempt for darker-skinned African Americans, and her attempts to stop the protagonist, Janie, from partnering with the darker-skinned Tea Cake that they united to ruin her business. Tea Cake expressed his impatience with the woman who so idolized lighter skin, straighter hair, and more white facial features, so scorned African Americans without such features, and was so intent on undermining his relationship with Jamie.

> 'Don't make God look so foolish—findin' fault wid everything He made.'
> (Hurston, *Their Eyes Were Watching God*, p. 145)

Thus, Tea Cake expresses an important value countering the value being placed on whiteness, the idea that all humans are God's creations and are not to be disparaged. From that perspective, the woman in *Their Eyes Were Watching God* who so strongly speaks up for white standards of appearance is countered by religious ideas, and then it is not just that some African Americans are offended by the applications of white standards or see the harm done by those standards. It is also that for some it is an insult to God to accept and advocate for white standards.

Another side to rejection of and resentment about white beauty standards is that in some novels, some characters find white people physically repulsive, not at all the standard for how one should look, and are even concerned if a family member looks too white.

> Yoruba had been to Black happenings where the brothers and the sisters of the darkest complexion did violent putdowns on those unfortunates of the lighter hues ... She had even caught herself at evil moments, bugging her own mother because her mother's color had suddenly become unstylish ... 'You ought to get out in the sun more often Mother. You don't want to be mistaken for a hunkie ...'
> (Killens, *The Cotillion, or, One Good Bull Is Half the Herd*, p. 66)

Finding whites repulsive makes sense from several perspectives. One is that for some characters in many of the novels they are the enemy, which may underlie what Yoruba says to her mother. But another perspective is that if one has grown up surrounded by people who look like one, people who look different can seem strange and unattractive.

Related to this, an African American child given a white-skinned doll might resent the doll or feel repulsed by it. As one woman said, looking back at her own childhood:

> I destroyed white baby dolls. But the dismemberment of dolls was not the true horror. The truly horrifying thing was the transference of the same impulse to little white girls. The indifference with which I could have axed them was shaken only by my desire to do so. To discover what eluded me: the secret of the magic they weaved on others. What made people look at them and say, 'Awwwww,' but not for me? (Morrison, *The Bluest Eye*, p. 22)

African American children who were too light by African American community standards could be in danger from their many darker African American schoolmates and be thought poorly of by some in the community. They could need the protection of a parent just to get to and from school.

> Nel was the color of wet sandpaper—just dark enough to escape the blows of the pitch-black truebloods and the contempt of old women who worried about such things as bad blood mixtures ... Had she been any lighter-skinned she would have needed either her mother's protection on the way to school or a streak of mean to defend herself. (Morrison, *Sula*, p. 52)

And there could be reputational hazards in giving birth to a child whose skin was too light. Because of this, an African American woman with light skin might be glad that her child has darker skin.

> Her father may have left his mark on her, she thought, fingering her son's crinkly plaits, but nobody would ever call her son a half-white bastard or a high-yellow nigger. And nobody would tell him his mother was a white man's whore. She

wished her hair were nappy like [her son's] and that they shared the same rich pecan color. (Campbell, *Your Blues Ain't Like Mine*, p. 104)

In addition, there are in some of the novels characters for whom Black is beautiful in a child or a partner. May (1996), for example, pointed out that in Baldwin's *Go Tell It on the Mountain*, the father of dark-skinned Elizabeth saw her as beautiful ("the apples of his eye, that she was wound around his heartstrings, that she was surely the finest little lady in the land"—Baldwin, *Go Tell It on The Mountain*, p. 179). Similarly, May points out that in that same Baldwin book Frank desires and values his dark-skinned wife Florence.

On the other hand, in one novel lighter skin and other features more like those of whites count enough in terms of attractiveness that African American women who had lighter skin and hair more like white people's had trouble finding African American women friends, because some African American women feared that an African American husband might be drawn to a lighter-skinned, more white-like woman.

She didn't feel close to any of the women her age ... Most of them were married, and some didn't trust a high-yellow woman with good hair around their men. (Campbell, *Your Blues Ain't Like Mine*, p. 107)

In sum, there is not a simple picture from the novels about skin color and related physical features. Clearly they matter; clearly many African American characters in the novels pay attention to them, and part of it is that these things matter in the white world, but they also definitely matter, albeit in diverse and complex ways, in the African American world. So in the novels racism has an impact on African American families in this area, but it is a mix of accepting and even valuing the standards, taking the standards seriously, and working to do better by the standards but also disparaging the standards and African Americans who care about the standards and finding white features repulsive. The seemingly hegemonic system of colorism has cracks in it (Tate, 2009) or, from another perspective, is linked to a complex and rich pattern of cultural attitudes about skin color (Wilder, 2010). To some extent the negative reactions to the intrusion of white standards of attractiveness into the community and family can be understood as resistance (Patton, 2010; Tate, 2009), resistance to the influence of white culture and standards, resistance to the harm caused by endorsing standards by which many African Americans do not measure up well, and resistance to the undermining of self-esteem and feelings of self-worth for self, family members, friends, and others one cares about. But as the novels show, the white standards have been incorporated into a rich and complicated, context-sensitive system of African American beliefs and standards about skin color, how to talk about it, and even how to "wear" it (Wilder, 2010).

One can also address the issue of skin color from the perspective of the concept of boundaries in family systems theory (Rosenblatt, 1994, pp. 76–94). In the racial system of the United States, skin color and related physical features have been central to establishing and maintaining boundaries concerning who has the right to do what and who has what status. But as many of the novels richly show, the rules of the racial system have created problems for it by undermining the validity of skin color and related physical appearance markers as trustworthy indicators of what racism wants clearly established, distinct difference between whites and African Americans. That is, over the several centuries in which the racial system granted white men the right to have sexual intercourse with African American women whenever they pleased and without personal consequences, there are now many people who by some definition are African American but whose skin color and related physical features allow them to pass as white. That creates issues for those white people who value the system of classifying people by skin color, hair texture, and the like in ways that give them power, status, and other benefits. And since African American culture, though diverse, has also to a substantial extent adopted skin color and related physical features as markers of status, the interracial partnerings that have made pale skin, straight hair, etc. in some instances not the clear-cut boundary markers they once were have also created issues among African Americans. Then whites and African Americans who want the boundaries to be clear must find other ways to establish distinct boundaries.

Chapter 8

Family Conversations about White People

In some novels, white people and encounters with racism are not topics of family conversation. For the novelist and hence for the characters there are higher conversational priorities than white people. Or perhaps what is depicted in some cases could be taken as a defensive turning away from what is too unpleasant or frightening to talk about (Li, 2009). The characters in some novels may be so effectively silenced by the forces of racism from talking in public places about racism that they are silenced in the privacy of their relationships with family and friends and perhaps even in their own interior dialogue (DeLamotte, 1998, pp. 10–40, writing about Paule Marshall's *Brown Girl, Brownstones*). Then too the African American families in a few of the novels (particularly Zora Neale Hurston's *Their Eyes Were Watching God)* have little or no contact with white people. But one way that racism affects everyday family life in a number of the novels is that white people and the racial system are topics of conversation. That is not surprising, given that life in the racial system is difficult for African Americans characters in many of the novels. Many people in the novels have reason to talk about encounters with racism at work, in relationship to law enforcement, and elsewhere in the social environment. And that fits the findings of several research studies with data about African American conversation (e.g. Anderson, 1999, p. 59; St. Jean and Feagin, 1998).

To the extent that what family members talk and do not talk about is a matter of family system rules, one can say that for the families at the center of many of the novels there is an implicit (or maybe even explicit) family rule that says it is acceptable or even important to talk about at least some encounters with racism. The conversation family members have concerning racism might involve talk about unpleasant experiences with white people or fear of white people. It might involve trying to understand white people and the racial system. It might involve trying to make sense of what might or might not be racism or the ways that racism and the racial system block them from a good life or make things difficult for them.

Navigating a World Made Difficult and Dangerous by White People

In some novels there is family conversation about how to navigate a world made difficult and perhaps dangerous by white people. Some of the conversations about dealing with difficulty and danger are between parents and children and are discussed in the next chapter, which deals with parenting. In some novels there is quite a bit of adult conversation about what to do about difficulty and danger stemming from white people. In Sarah E. Wright's *This Child's Gonna Live*, Jacob and Mariah are riding in a car and have an exchange about whether to stop at a store where African Americans are treated with contempt.

> 'Stop this car soon as you get to a store so I can buy some meat and bread for to make these children some sandwiches.'
> Jacob said, 'Well, you know it's not a-many a store 'long this road that'll wait on colored.'
> 'Children's hungry, Jacob. Hear me when I tell you. Stop this car!'
> Jacob, he didn't say a neither 'nother word except, 'I ain't going into no place that act like they don't want me when I walk in.' (Wright, *This Child's Gonna Live*, p. 252)

In this exchange Jacob is uncomfortable with the diminishments he is sure he will experience if he enters the white operated store. But his discomfort may be about more than diminishment, because they live in a part of Maryland where at times whites terrorize, beat, and kill African Americans. So he may also be concerned about physical danger. The exchange between Mariah and Jacob also suggests that partner differences about how to find a safe path to meet basic needs in a racist world can lead to couple conflict. That means that racism can add to the conflict burden a couple must deal with, and at the extreme, the struggle to deal with racism may lead to very harsh and perhaps even relationship-threatening couple conflict. One can take that conflict as about competing preferences and values, differences in tolerance for various kinds of risk, or the struggle to establish family system rules about how to deal with whites and racism. One can also take the conflict as about family system processes when racism confronts a family with two or more undesirable or risky alternatives. When there is no good alternative, an individual might well feel ambivalent about any option, and at the family system level the ambivalence can be played out in conversation in which family members are in conflict with one another as they individually advocate for different options which for good reasons any adult in the family would think undesirable. That is, sometimes families in an environment of bad choices express the choice dilemmas through interpersonal conflict. And that is one of the family system costs that can arise from racism, family conflict as a family tries to navigate a path where all options are undesirable. For example, in the quote immediately above, stopping at the store and not stopping at the store are both undesirable options.

In some novels there is a character who speaks eloquently to others about an oppressive situation and what it takes to endure and survive it. In Ernest J. Gaines' *The Autobiography of Miss Jane Pittman*, Ned, the person who most strongly and publicly speaks up for resistance to racism, contrasts being "a nigger" with being a Black American. In the following passage, he is addressing school children, but many adults in the community are present, including his foster mother (Miss Jane Pittman) and his wife. His words are spoken with great courage because two menacing white men are within hearing distance and are understood by people in the community as likely to assassinate Ned if he keeps speaking up for the rights of African Americans.

> 'A nigger feels below anybody else on earth. He's been beaten so much by the white man, he don't care for himself, nor nobody else, and for nothing else. He talks a lot, but his words don't mean nothing ... There's a big difference between a nigger and a black American. A black American cares, and will always struggle. Every day that he get up he hopes that this day will be better. The nigger knows it won't.' (Gaines, *The Autobiography of Miss Jane Pittman*, p. 115)

Ned's words can be read as inspiring, uplifting, and strengthening, but they also put his life in danger. What a dilemma and burden to have to risk one's life in order to speak words of truth and inspiration to others. And what a strange and difficult thing it seems to be for Miss Jane Pittman and others who care about Ned to feel on the one hand that Ned is speaking truth and on the other hand that speaking truth puts his life at risk. In the time and place in which Ned risks his life, one racial system rule is something like, "no public conversation here, no words that whites can hear, about African American dignity and being a whole person." Had he been fostered by someone other than Miss Jane Pittman, Ned might have grown up with a family system rule that says it is best to go along with the rules of the racial system. But as I interpret the novel, Miss Jane Pittman, from her earliest times with Ned, took risks in the racial system in order to live a life like Ned was advocating. So in his life with Miss Jane Pittman there were family system rules about speaking something like the kinds of truths in public that Ned was speaking.

White-imposed Poverty and What Family Members Talk About

In some novels, the characters talk a great deal about their poverty and the ways that it is perpetrated by white racism. In Marita Golden's *Long Distance Life*, Naomi talks about growing up in a poor sharecropping family in the south and the active efforts by whites to keep African American families there poor.

> 'If you worked hard and made something of yourself, got a little store or some land, the white folks seem like they couldn't sleep nor rest easy till they took that away from you. Maybe they'd burn your store down or run you out of town ... My folks ... were sharecroppers. We lived in ... a shack ... All I ever saw my daddy do was work ... He worked hard. But not never seeing nothing for all his labor kinda took something out of him. There was many a year my daddy never saw a dollar to hold in his hand. By the time old man Cartwright, who Daddy rented the land from, charged us [for everything he] sold [us] on credit, the sale of [our crop] wasn't worth it ... I watched my daddy get old before he should've ... We *all* worked, every one of us ... All of us helped with

the 'bacca ... I know how it feels to be hungry. *Real* hungry.' (Golden, *Long Distance Life*, pp. 25–8)

Naomi's words are not only a statement of autobiographical fact; they also offer an explanation for how her parents and family were forced into poverty and how much she became who she is in an environment of white bullying and economic exploitation and African American poverty and powerlessness. So one reason in the novels for conversations about white people is to explain to younger family members the historical racial system context for how it is that the family is so poor and the way things now are with the family. The messages are things like, "Daddy wasn't lazy, but he could only do what he could do in a situation of white domination" and "I am who you know me as because of the demands of making it in a racist world." Similar explanations came up in research on African American grief (Rosenblatt and Wallace, 2005b), with some African Americans talking about family members who had the intelligence, energy, and other capacities to have gone far in life but were limited (for example, to a poor education and menial, low-income jobs) by racism.

White People as a Standard of Comparison in Family Conversation

In some novels, comparison with whites, who are almost invariably better-off financially, is part of family conversation about poverty. It is not merely that poverty weighs heavily on many African American couples and families in the novels, but for some their awareness of the better life of most white people adds to the burden. In the following quote, a boy notes the difference between the situation in his family and community and the situation for white families.

Sandy passed the windows of many white folks' houses where the curtains were up and warm floods of electric lights made bright the cozy rooms. In Negro shacks, too, there was the dim warmth of oil-lamps and Christmas candles glowing. But at home there wasn't even a holly wreath. (Hughes, *Not Without Laughter*, p. 152)

In the next quote a woman tells her mother how hard it is for her to listen to her mother talk about the housing, clothing, and other possessions of the wealthy white family for whom she is a domestic. An additional aspect of the situation is that the woman is speaking to her mother in front of her young daughter, so in part the message might be something like, "Don't torment my child (your grandchild) with these words that can make her feel bad about our housing, our clothing, and how hard we have to work to get so little." And in fact, as is discussed later in this chapter, the granddaughter grows up to be so determined to help her family to be well-off economically that she destroys her health and eventually works herself to death.

'Sometimes I get sick of hearin' how white folks live 'cause it makes me remember how I gotta live. Sometimes, just sometimes, I wish you'd stop.' (Hunter, *God Bless the Child*, p. 20)

In the novels, comparisons between what an African American family has and what white families have often come from African American women who are domestic workers for white families. For example, with regard to the quote immediately above from Kristin Hunter's *God Bless the Child*, Granny works for a white family whose material wealth she admires, and she has encouraged her granddaughter, Rosie, to admire the material wealth of well-off white people. In one conversation in which that comparison is made, Rosie, Mom, and Granny discuss how unpleasant the apartment in which they live is, and Granny says the following about the wealthy white family for whom she works:

'Everybody has their troubles ... rich and poor. 'Course the young ones don't care. Miss Emilie and her husband don't 'preciate that beautiful old house. They can't wait to chase after somethin' new and modern.' (Hunter, *God Bless the Child*, p. 73)

One can take what Granny says to simultaneously value the housing of wealthy white people while acknowledging that if one had their wealth one still might not be satisfied. That could be a lesson to Rosie, but she does not heed it. So years later, as a young adult, she works two demanding full-time jobs and dares to take numbers bets on her own, rather than lay off the bets and the economic risk on well financed representatives of the gambling syndicate. She constantly buys on credit, overdraws her checking account, and starves herself in order to acquire things for herself, her mother, and Granny. Her overwork, self-neglect, and life at the extreme eventually kill her. So her efforts to make a life for her family that is economically like that of well-off whites means that ultimately she and the support she offers are lost to her family. That was something that her mother, her lover, and her best friend saw coming and tried to stop through conversation with her. They warned her that she was killing herself by trying to achieve what cannot be achieved in a racist society. In this regard, Rosie's best friend, Dolly, said to Rosie:

'Why don't you stop killing yourself, Rosie? There aren't any colored millionaires. There never will be.' (Hunter, *God Bless the Child*, p. 208)

Dolly summarizes a view of the racial system that rather echoes what Naomi said above. Hard work will not get an African American much in the racial system. The system is designed to benefit whites, and to make it impossible for African Americans ever to get far economically and to show up or do better than whites.

Talk about the Racial System

African American families exist in a racial system in which, for the families in many of the novels, there is so much harm, injustice, threat, diminishment, frustration, and impoverishment that it is something to talk about. Sometimes the racial system has done terrible things to the family or to a specific family member. Here is an excerpt of a couple's conversation concerning whites in general and the whites who murdered their son:

> They talked about white people in low intense voices. 'I don't even think they're human ... They ain't never gon' be happy until they put colored people back in slavery.' 'They so scared of colored men. That's why they killed [our son]—scared he was good as them.' (Campbell, *Your Blues Ain't Like Mine*, pp. 208–9)

And here is a woman and her lover in Mississippi during the Civil Rights Era addressing the shame she felt about having had a white father.

> 'Where'd you get this white-girl hair? You part white, ain't you?'
> She nodded, lowering her eyes ... 'My real daddy is white, but that's all I know.'
> ... 'Ain't nothing to be ashamed of ... It ain't your shame. And it ain't your mama's, either.'
> She started crying. 'Thank you. That's the best thing anybody ever told me.'
> (Campbell, *Your Blues Ain't Like Mine*, p. 269)

Both of the excerpts of conversation immediately above are about a system designed to benefit whites, to give them more than African Americans, and to let them get away with whatever they choose to do to African Americans.

And then there is Sofia who is discussed in Chapter 3, a woman who, many years after the end of slavery, was sentenced by a court to be in effect the slave of a white couple for whom she had refused to work.

> They got me in a little storeroom up under the house, hardly bigger than Odessa's porch, and just about as warm in the winter time. I'm at they beck and call all night and all day. They won't let me see my children. They won't let me see no mens. Well, after five years they let me see you [my family] once a year. I'm a slave. (Walker, *The Color Purple*, p. 103)

The words Walker wrote for Sofia can be taken as a statement that the end of slavery did not end enslavement of African Americans, with the continuing versions of enslavement giving whites the power to, among many things, undermine African American family relationships.

In some novels, some people try to make sense of the system, try to find safety and a good life in the context of that system, and try to prevent or heal wounds caused by that system. Echoing what bell hooks wrote in her essay

"The Representation of Whiteness in the Black Imagination" (1992), an African American maid might be treated by the white people for whom she works as though she cannot hear them talk. That could put her in a position to hear what they have to say about African Americans and to tell family and friends what she heard. Here is something Aunt Hager says to her neighbor, Sister Johnson, as the two women work in Aunt Hager's house, ironing clothes for white people:

> 'You oughter hear de way white folks talks 'bout niggers. Says dey's lazy, an' says dey stinks, an' all.' (Hughes, *Not Without Laughter*, p. 140)

In this quote Aunt Hager not only provides information about the nasty things that white people say about African Americans, she also provides a sense of whites putting themselves at a higher status than African Americans and something of the justification whites feel they have for treating African Americans so badly. For example, people who are lazy need not be paid much and do not deserve much, and people who stink should be kept at a distance and not given the respect that people who are clean merit.

In Langston Hughes' *Not Without Laughter*, an experience Harriett had in childhood with racist teasing and torment stays with her to shape her later life and what happens to her family. Presumably all African American characters in the Hughes novel had unpleasant childhood experiences with whites, but Hughes singles out Harriett's experience I think to flesh out a story of how early childhood experiences with racism are a foundation on which each succeeding unpleasantness with white people makes clear what is going on and adds to the burden. The following passage is a partial explanation for why Harriett, at age 16, speaks so bitterly to her family about white people.

> Her first surprising and unpleasantly lasting impression of the pale world had come when, at the age of five, she had gone alone one day to play in a friendly white family's yard. Some mischievous small boys there, for the fun of it, had taken hold of her short kinky braids and pulled them, dancing round and round her and yelling: 'Blackie! Blackie! Blackie!' while she screamed and tried to run away. But they held her and pulled her hair terribly, and her friends laughed because she *was* black and she *did* look funny. So from that time on, Harriett had been uncomfortable in the presence of whiteness, and that early hurt had grown with each new incident into a rancor that she could not hide and a dislike that had become pain. (Hughes, *Not Without Laughter*, p. 88)

This passage provides a framework for what Harriett subsequently says about white people.

> 'So that's the way white people feel,' Harriett said to Aunt Hager and Sister Johnson and Jimboy, while the two children listened. 'They wouldn't have a single one of us around if they could help it. It don't matter to them if we're

shut out of a job. It don't matter to them if niggers have only the back row at the movies. It don't matter to them when they hurt our feelings … and treat us like slaves down South and like beggars up North … White folks run the world, and the only thing colored folks are expected to do is work and grin … as though it don't matter.' (Hughes, *Not Without Laughter*, p. 90)

One could interpret what Harriett says as simply speaking truth about an unpleasant, frightening, and dangerous environment. At another level, saying what she said is a way for Harriett to use the supportive presence of family and neighbors to air what is so hurtful, upsetting, unpleasant and worrisome for her about white people. The hearing she receives for her words provides support for her perspective and acknowledgment of how hard things are with whites. At still another level, what she says can be taken as her struggling to make sense of the horribly unjust and oppressive system in which they live.

The paths characters in various novels say they are following in order to find their way in a white dominated system explicitly take into account the demands of the racial system. Here is what Pa, in Alice Walker's *The Color Purple*, says to his stepdaughter, Celie, and to Shug (who is the former lover of Celie's husband and current lover of Celie), about allowing whites to have an advantage if one wants to survive and get along.

I know how they is. The key to all of 'em is money. The trouble with our people is as soon as they got out of slavery they didn't want to give the white man nothing else. But the fact is, you got to give 'em something. Either your money, your land, your woman or your ass. So what I did was just right off offer to give 'em money. Before I planted a seed, I made sure this one and that one knowed one seed out of three was planted for *him.* Before I ground a grain of wheat the same thing. And when I opened up your daddy's old store in town, I bought me my own white boy to run it. (Walker, *The Color Purple*, p. 182)

Thus, according to him one way to navigate the racist world in comparative safety is to be sure to give whites benefits from one's efforts. But then here is an alternative in the words a mother says to her daughter about how the mother overcame racism at work:

'When I first came they wun put me to work on the lathe. Just because your skin black some these white people does think you can't function like them. But when they finally decide to try me out I had already learn it by watching the others.' (Marshall, *Brown Girl, Brownstones*, p. 99)

The message in these words is that, despite the racism, persist, be resilient, and be prepared.

Later in the novel the mother says the following in an argument with her husband about his commitment to a new spiritual leader ("Father Peace") and church:

'Lemme tell you, life ain up in no Father Peace kingdom,' she said gently. 'It out here scuffling to get by. And having little something so you can keep your head up and not have these white people push you 'bout like you's cattle.' (Marshall, *Brown Girl, Brownstones*, p. 168)

In both the above quotes from *Brown Girl, Brownstones* the family interaction is about making it in a world where white people are a challenging, difficult, and demeaning force against making it. And the mother's message (to daughter and husband) is not to let the racists get the best of one, not to give up, and to do what one can to get along.

Talk about the Past: Slavery and Jim Crow

African American oral history includes stories passed down in families about life under slavery and Jim Crow (e.g. Valk and Brown, 2010). Thus, it is not surprising that in some novels set in more recent times family members talk about slavery or the Jim Crow era. One can see such family talk as a way to establish family identity, to explain how things got to be the way they were and are, or to underline the sacrifices of older relatives and ancestors in ways that inspire and perhaps obligate other family members. Here is an example of a character reflecting on what she had heard in family conversation about ancestors who were enslaved.

This was her mother's history as Meridian knew it: Her mother's great-great-grandmother had been a slave whose two children were sold away from her when they were toddlers. For days she had followed the man who bought them, until she was able to steal them back. The third time—after her owner had exhausted one of his field hands whipping her, and glints of bone began to show through the muscles on her back—she was allowed to keep them on the condition that they would eat no food she did not provide herself. (Walker, *Meridian*, p. 128)

One can read Meridian's summary of what she heard in family conversation as establishing a principle of family resistance to white oppression and a sense of why Meridian's mother might be fiercely caring for and concerned about Meridian. So in accounts of the past there are lines of thought that seem to define individuals and the family in the present in relationship to white oppression and in relationship to one another. This is not to say that people necessarily get a message about racism in the words they hear about their forebears. For example, what Meridian learned about her mother and her mother's mother was, at least for a while, not about life in a racist society as her mother and grandmother might have thought they were telling her.

It never occurred to [Meridian] that her mother's and her grandmother's extreme purity of life was compelled by necessity. They had not lived in an age of choice. (Walker, *Meridian*, p. 130)

Family stories about events in slavery or Jim Crow times not only provide an explanation for more recent family ways of acting, they can also be reminders of how much those now alive owe to their ancestors. One of the themes in those stories in several novels is that the family has an ancestor who lived under slavery and who was very strong and special and had gone through extreme difficulty in order to do good for her or his family.

> 'My daddy's name was Jonah. And there was six brothers born before him ... All them was born in slavery time, but they lived as free men 'cause their mama will it so. She became such a legend that black folks, white folks, and even red folks in my time would only whisper the name Sapphira.' (Naylor, *Mama Day*, p. 151)

Stories like these can be understood to a way for characters in the novels to say to younger family members that even in slavery times, members of their family were so strong and resourceful that they could rise above terrible oppression. The implication is that the contemporary members of the family must face racism with strength, the capacity to survive pain, and devotion to family. They have the ability, and they owe it to their ancestors. This theme in some novels of standing up to and resisting racist difficulties is congruent with research that shows that strength in the face of difficulties is an important value in some African American families (e.g. Rosenblatt and Wallace, 2005a, pp. 123–32) and that the strong black woman is an iconic resource for African American families (e.g. Falk, 2004, pp. 51–72). Family can be a crucial resource for survival and well-being for African Americans (Byerman, 2005, p. 125), and one way the family can be a resource is by providing models for surviving and succeeding.

Some characters in the novels are inspired and sustained by the history of their family (Byerman, 2005, p. 125). Also, to the extent that African Americans were, for much of history, blocked from developing many social institutions alternative to the family, it is not surprising that the story of how racism affects African American relationships would be to a substantial extent the story of racism affecting African American family life (cf. Byerman, 2005, p. 69, writing about Gloria Naylor's novel, *Mama Day*).

Then too, a novelist's choice to have characters talk about slavery resists forces in contemporary society that push to make slavery and its impact on families a secret and uses the powerful symbols and realities of slavery to illuminate contemporary issues concerning race and family (Rushdy, 2001).

Words in the Family about Affirming and Supporting One Another

The talk of some family members in the novels about the racial system affirms the experience of others in the family with racism and offers them support. If we consider lovers to be family to each other, here is one example. In Paule Marshall's *Brown Girl, Brownstones*, the central character, Selina, and her lover, Clive, compare painful experiences each has had with white people who saw them as not fully human and who attached negative meanings to blackness (*Brown Girl, Brownstones*, pp. 248–50). When Selina has an intensely painful and diminishing encounter with a racist white woman and is filled with disgust and despair for how she let it happen, Clive reassures her by talking about his own experiences.

> 'It happens. I took that same crap all through the army ... And every time I tried to sell a painting or get a showing somebody slapped me down with a smile. It happens, and whether it's a rope or a kick in the butt, a word that slipped out or a phony smile, it's the same damn thing.' (Marshall, *Brown Girl, Brownstones*, pp. 289–90)

Clive's message is that Selina is not alone and her experience with racism is of a piece with how the racist system operates in other areas of life than the one in which she encountered racism.

At times African Americans in the novels find amusement in talking about white representations of slavery and white abilities when compared to those of African Americans. What follows, part of a letter written by Celie to God, is about how Sofia, who is married to Celie's stepson, amuses other members of the household by the way she talks about white people.

> Sofia would make a dog laugh, talking about those [white] people she work for. They have the nerve to try to make us think slavery fell through because of us ... Like us didn't have sense enough to handle it. All the time breaking hoe handles and letting the mules loose in the wheat. But how anything they build can last a day is a wonder to me. They backward, she say. Clumsy, and unlucky. (Walker, *The Color Purple*, p. 102)

One can see in the things Sofia allegedly says a way to vent some of the rage and other pent up feelings stemming from dealings with white people, a way to elevate African Americans in relationship to white people, and a critical and insightful commentary about Sofia's white employers/enslavers and whites in general.

In some novels, making sense of the ways that white people are judgmental and critical of African Americans is done conversationally among African Americans with humor or with a mix of humor and seriousness. Rather than accept the harsh and demeaning judgments of white people, some characters choose to laugh at them while perhaps also trying to make sense of the judgments. Moreover, such laughter can be a defense against pain, humiliation, and feelings of defeat (cf. Feagin and Sikes, 1994, pp. 301–2).

Making light of difficult circumstances might be good for one's health and well-being. But making emotional light of pain may be about denial and repression, tuning out one's pain or pretending the pain is not there, is not grinding into one's personal and social life, and is not burdening one day in and day out. As Victoria Burrows (2004, p. 115) wrote about Toni Morrison's *Sula*, "repression of pain masked by laughter acting as solace is a recurrent trope." And arguably repression is not good for a person's emotional well-being.

To put the amusement at white people in perspective, in some novels, especially those set in the South before and during the Civil Rights Era, family members could acknowledge to each other their fear of white people.

> 'We all scared, William. You tell me a time when we ain't been scared.'
> (Campbell, *Your Blues Ain't Like Mine*, p. 129)

So laughter can only take one so far in the face of the real threats coming from white people. Related to that, sometimes African American characters support one another by acknowledging how difficult white people are.

> White folks is a miracle of affliction, say Sofia. (Walker, *The Color Purple*, p. 106)

Putting the difficulties that all in the family and African American community face into words can be understood as a way for all to have their personal experiences acknowledged and to feel the comfort and support of others who are in the same boat.

Words in the Family about God and Jesus

From slavery times to the present, religion and the Black church have been vitally important to many African Americans in finding support, meaning, affirmation, hope, and self-worth in a racially oppressive environment (e.g. Giggie, 2008). So it is not surprising that in some novels, the story of the children of Israel in bondage has important family meanings. Just like the Israelites in the Bible, just like ancestors who were slaves at the time of emancipation, one may someday be freed from the bondage of racism. The following was written by James Baldwin in *Go Tell It on the Mountain* as something in the thinking of Florence's mother in relationship to the world of slavery in which she had grown up and spent her young adult years. It was an aspect of her thinking that she had transmitted to her children, ideas that could help them deal with the ways that racism put them in bondage.

> For it had been the will of God that they should hear, and pass thereafter, one to another, the story of the Hebrew children who had been held in bondage in the land of Egypt; and how the Lord had heard their groaning, and how His heart was moved; and how He bid them wait but a little season till he should send deliverance. (Baldwin *Go Tell It on the Mountain*, p. 75)

> One had 'only to endure and trust in God.' (Baldwin, *ibid.*)

From another perspective on religion, if the racial system cannot change on earth, if the Lord will not change it on earth, there might still be hope for a system in heaven that is fair and equitable. Here is what a young woman says to her 10-year-old son Sandy.

'White folks sure is a case! ... So spoiled with colored folks waiting on 'em all their days! Don't know what they'll do in heaven, 'cause I'm gonna sit down up there myself.' (Hughes, *Not Without Laughter*, pp. 74–5)

And later Sister Johnson, a friend and neighbor of Aunt Hager, Sandy's grandmother says something similar in a front porch conversation overheard by Sandy.

'If de gates o' heaven shuts in white folkses' faces like de do's o' dey church in us niggers' faces, it'll be too bad! Yes sir! One thing sho, de Lawd ain't prejudiced!' (Hughes, *Not Without Laughter*, p. 81)

But then, when Sandy reaches his middle teens, he has the insight that the emphasis on a future in heaven with Jesus has much to do with the hopelessness of what there is for African Americans on earth.

He understood then why many old Negroes said: 'Take all this world and give me Jesus!' It was because they couldn't get this world anyway—it belonged to the white folks. (Hughes, *Not Without Laughter*, p. 260)

This quote points to what could be a tension at times within a family about whether to be wholeheartedly committed to religion, God, and a future in heaven or to see religion as obscuring how much their problems come from white people. Here, for example, is what one woman thinks about saying to her husband about his finding solace in religion and the belief that everything is God's will.

'Jacob, everything ain't the Lord's will. Some of these things happening is these ... white people's will. I don't care how much they go to the church, they ain't living by the word of the Lord. They living by their greedy pocketbooks.' (Wright, *This Child's Gonna Live*, p. 6)

However, even though she has reservations about finding solace in religious thinking like her husband's, she is depicted in the novel as still often speaking in her mind to God.

Words in the Family about Learning to Accept

Some characters in the novels, particularly older ones, decide that they paid such a high cost for living with anger and hatred directed at white people that it is best to try not to be upset by racism and racial injustice. Here is Aunt Hager talking with her grandson Sandy:

> 'These young ones what's comin' up now, they calls us ole fogies, an' handkerchief heads, an' white folks' niggers 'cause we don't get mad an' rar' up in arms like they does 'cause things is kinder hard, but ... when you gets old, you knows they ain't no sense in gettin' mad an' sourin' you' soul with hatin' peoples. White folks is white folks ... When you starts hatin' people, you gets uglier than they is.' (Hughes, *Not Without Laughter*, p. 179)

Thus, in the novels, choosing not to be upset sometimes is about adopting a religious sense of an ultimate future in heaven.

Talk about Restoring Justice in an Unjust System

Some conversations turn to issues of how to restore justice in the unjust racial system. In James Baldwin's *If Beale Street Could Talk* there is a conversation between the father of Fonny and the father of Tish (about the challenge of raising money for Fonny's legal defense) that frames theft by African Americans in the context of the injustices of the racial system. This is not exactly a family conversation by a strict definition of "family," but the two men are family in the sense of being in effect co-fathers-in-law, and they are working together to get Fonny out of jail and Tish and Fonny together again to prepare for Tish giving birth to the baby she conceived with Fonny. As the two men talk about white people, they conceptualize what white people are up to in pushing African Americans to be impoverished. In highlighting the unfairness of the economic system they see the justification of breaking the law to restore a modicum of justice.

> 'The white man ... he *want* you to be worried about the money. That's his whole game ... I ain't worried about they money—they ain't got no right to it anyhow, they made it from us—they ain't never met nobody they didn't lie to and steal from. Well, I can steal, too. *And* rob. How you think I raised my daughters?' (Baldwin, *If Beale Street Could Talk*, p. 125)

On the other hand, there are family conversations in some novels in which white people are seen as the model of what not to be, that it is best not to be immoral the way they are.

> 'White folks get rich lyin' and stealin' ... but I don't need money if I got to get it dishonest, with a lot of lies trailing behind me, and can't look folks in the face. It makes you feel dirty!' (Hughes, *Not Without Laughter*, p. 127)

In the Civil Rights Era, family members might talk about the horror and also the hopefulness of what is in the news concerning efforts to eliminate racist practices and about the changes that might occur. The conversations are often intense. Among many reasons for the intensity in the following conversation between Naomi, who is Esther's mother, and Randolph, who is Esther's lover, is that Esther has left them to risk her life in the South to fight for civil rights.

> 'She's acting like she's a leader, a Martin Luther King or somebody. She's a woman.' Randolph got so mad he could hardly sit still. 'Down there, going to jail to integrate. Hell, intergration'll put me outta business. Once Negroes start going downtown, the Eden Bar and Grill won't last a year. We begging for a gun to kill ourselves with and can't even see it. Now, this Malcolm X, he's kinda way-out, but he's talking my talk.'
>
> 'You *would* follow those old hate-filled Muslims. Like hating the white man is the answer.'
>
> 'Naomi, they don't hate the white man. They love the Negro ... You just like most Negroes, scared of freedom.' (Golden, *Long Distance Life*, pp. 160–61)

The exchange between Naomi and Randolph draws its intensity partly because of concern about Esther's safety, but there are also layers of concern about how the current ways of making it in the racial system could become ineffective if the system changes. For example, Randolph may lose the black clientele who go to his restaurant. So reducing the power of racism may actually, in Randolph's thinking, be costly to him. But then it is he, rather than Naomi, who accuses the other of fear of freedom. That kind of paradox, being fearful and yet accusing someone else of fearfulness, is not surprising in any circumstances but especially not in times of potentially great change. Coming to terms with great change may often put one in a situation of believing and saying contradictory things.

Randolph and Naomi were talking about changes that might be brought about in the system through nonviolent means, but people's words in some of the novels about changing the racial system are not consistently about peaceful efforts to change the system. At an extreme are instances where a family member fantasizes aloud about killing white people.

> Sofia say to me today, I just can't understand it.
> What that? I ast.
> Why we ain't already kill them off. (Walker, *The Color Purple*, p. 100)

Such words can be taken as an expression of the terrible pain, injustice, and loss that comes from the white-created racial system. But they also reflect underlying thoughts and feelings that make nonviolent protest not the only path people might think about.

Costs of Making White People a Topic of Conversation

If African American families talk about white people, they have less time to talk about other matters that would be good to talk about. Talking about racism might cut into talking about family relationships, health, shared values, and other potentially important topics. Among the many costs of racism then is that it cuts into the time available to talk about other matters. One can frame this in a line of systems theory thought developed by Gregory Bateson (1979, pp. 191–3), that any adaptation has its costs, so adaptations are also, from some perspectives, mal-adaptations. By talking more about whites, the racial system, and racism, there is less time to address other problems that become lower conversational priorities— for example, what to do about the child's shoes that don't fit well or how to deal with the rain leak.

One could argue that dealing with white racism is enough of a challenge in many families in the novels that talking about it seems necessary. There can be costs to ignoring what threatens and does great harm. But then white racism makes life painful, stressful, and difficult, and so talking about it can be stressful for everyone in the family, and the stress of talking about racism would have its costs.

Conversations about White People as a Device for Describing the Racial System

This chapter has up to this point emphasized that family conversations in the novels represent the sociology and psychology of African Americans figuring out and personally and collectively dealing with a racial system that is not good for African Americans. But another way of thinking about African American family conversations in the novels about whites is that they are devices for teaching white readers about the racial system. That is, to the extent that African American authors can assume they will have a substantial white readership and that whites are often oblivious to and ignorant of the racial system, family conversations in the novels are rhetorical devices for overcoming white reader obliviousness and ignorance. Then, for example, the first quote in the chapter from Sarah E. Wright's *This Child's Gonna Live*, about the challenge of buying groceries from white racist storekeepers can be read as, among other things, a way of saying to white readers that in the racial system even buying groceries can be difficult. And, in fact, one can read every conversational excerpt in this chapter as in part an authorial teaching device.

Although the novels were mostly written before there was a critical race theory, and none of the novels mentions critical race theory, one could take most of the novels as in a sense offering education to whites about what critical race theory says. Included in that would be educating whites about the pervasiveness of racism in US society, its institutionalization, the centrality of colorism in the racial system, the ways that the racial system impact African American families, and the social construction of race and racial identities. Perhaps some or many of the novelists did not write with any intention of educating white readers, but still, the words the novelists offered through family conversations in the novels are potentially quite an education.

Chapter 9

Parenting

Parents and parent figures in many novels are depicted as socializing children to survive, get along, and do as well as they can in a racist society. In accord with the vast literature showing past and current harmfulness of the racial system to African Americans, raising an African American child to be able to get along in the system is of obvious importance. One might say it is part of the rule system in many African American families in the novels to raise children to know the etiquette of relating to whites that is required by the local version of the racial system (Ritterhouse, 2006), and, in the process, to follow that etiquette. In fact, some would argue that a major impact of the racial system on African American families has to do with child rearing (e.g. Lasane-Brown, 2006).

That children in many of the novels are socialized to get along in the racial system connects with a very substantial academic literature that asserts that many African American parents socialize their children to deal with racism (for example, Banks-Wallace and Parks, 2001; Boyd-Franklin, 2003, pp. 28–39; Coard and Sellers, 2005; Feagin and McKinney, 2003, pp. 173–6; Hughes and Chen, 1997; Lasane-Brown, 2006; Mosley Howard and Evans, 2000; Peters, 1997; Suizzo, Robinson, and Pahlke, 2008; Thomas and Dettlaff, 2011; Valk and Brown, 2010; Vines and Baird, 2009; Willie and Lane, 2010). The socialization might include help developing positive racial/ethnic identity, recognizing racist situations, and the courage and self-esteem to face difficulties caused by racism. The socialization often is founded in part on the idea that an African American should learn about how to protect him or herself not only against racist whites and institutions but also against internalized racism (see especially Banks-Wallace and Parks, 2001).

Racism Directed at Children

In some novels, racism injures African American children. The children are humiliated, degraded, and attacked in racist encounters.

> … the white man across the street who spit at the colored children because he had woke up one day and found his neighborhood swarming with brown faces. (McFadden, *Nowhere Is a Place*, p. 226)

> 'Say, little coon, let's see you hit a step for the boys! … Down where I live … all our niggers can dance! … Come on, boy, snap it up!'

> 'I can't,' Sandy said, frowning instead of smiling, and growing warm as he stood
> there in the smoky circle of grinning white men. 'I don't know how to dance.'
> 'O, you're one of them stubborn Kansas coons, heh? … You Northern darkies
> are dumb as hell … Boy! I want to see you dance!' … The Southerner rose
> and grabbed him roughly by the arm … 'Com'ere, you little—' (Hughes, *Not
> Without Laughter*, pp. 214–15)

With the centrality of colorism in racism and with racism such a powerful force in
the lives of African American children it is not surprising that children in several
of the novels considered whether there were ways to stop being brown or black
and to become white instead.

> He wondered sometimes whether if he washed and washed his face and hands,
> he would ever be white … And would he ever have a big house with electric
> lights in it … it was mostly white people who had such fine things … He wanted
> to be a railroad engineer, but … there weren't any colored engineers. (Hughes,
> *Not Without Laughter*, pp. 174–5)

Similarly, here is an African American child's reaction to being shamed by white
boys who accused him of being "colored" and hence not someone who should be
living in Boston.

> In the bathroom he scrubbed his hands vigorously, but it was just as he had
> known it would be, there was no whiteness under the brown. (West, *The Living
> Is Easy*, p. 123)

The idea of removing the color from one's skin fits with sentiments and attitudes
described in the discussion in Chapter 7 of skin color. But the complexities of that
discussion suggest that simply making one's skin more white is not necessarily
protective, since many African Americans have lighter skin and are still targets
of racism.

In some novels, child thoughts about how to deal with the threats and insults
of racism go into other areas of concern than personal skin color. For example,
experiencing racist diminishment and seeing one's family ill-treated in a racist
world, one child wondered why God decided to make African Americans be what
they are in relationship to white people and whether an African American child
counts for anything.

> 'Daddy, how come God made us niggers? … Everybody calls us that … Ain't I
> something, Daddy?' (Wright, *This Child's Gonna Live*, p. 106)

Younger children do not necessarily recognize or understand the racism in their
environment. Thus, as accounts in some novels indicate, there can be quite a
shock when a young African American first comes to a realization about the racist

environment. Here is an example of an African American child who has suddenly become aware of the contradictions of the "the American Way of Life" as it relates to African Americans.

> Meridian was reciting a speech that extolled the virtues of the Constitution and praised the superiority of the American Way of Life … In the middle of her speech, Meridian had seemed to forget. She stumbled and then was silent on the stage. The audience urged her on but she would not continue. Instead she covered her face with her hands and had to be led away. Meridian's mother went out into the hallway where Meridian … [tried] to explain to her mother that for the first time she really listened to what she was saying, knew she didn't believe it, and was so distracted by this revelation that she could not make the rest of her speech. (Walker, *Meridian*, p. 126)

Meridian's mother took her daughter's situation as a teaching moment, and tried to tell Meridian about the mother's own reaction whenever something was not going well for her. In those situations the mother:

> simply trusted in God, raised her head a little higher than it already was, stared down whatever was in her path, never looked back. (ibid.)

But for Meridian the advice was not of immediate help, because she had discovered in the patriotic speech that glossed over the past and current pervasiveness of racism that there was hypocrisy everywhere that she had not grappled with. Nor did it help Meridian when her teacher empathized with her by saying that the hypocrisy in the speech Meridian had been required to give was long standing. She told her not to worry about the speech. "It's the same one they made me learn when I was here … and it's no more true now than it was then" (Walker, *Meridian*, p. 127). However, learning that the racial system, including its hypocritical disguises in terms of patriotism and other covers, was of long standing was not reassuring to Meridian.

To complicate the discussion, the racial system is not necessarily the same for women as for men, and so racial socialization ideally will be different depending on a child's gender (Lesane-Brown, 2006). For example, as was discussed in Chapter 6, in many of the novels racism made it easier for African American women to find jobs than for African American men, and all but one of the accounts of police brutality and arrests on trumped-up charges are about the victimization of African American men, not women. So there are special challenges in a racist world to raising an African American son to deal with job deprivation, police brutality, and arrests on trumped-up charges (Boyd-Franklin, Franklin, with Toussaint, 2000). And of course raising a girl to do well in the jobs available to African American woman would have its challenges—in part because in many of the novels those jobs involve accepting low-wage, humiliating drudgery cleaning up after and caring for white people. There are also special challenges referred to in some of the novels in raising an African American daughter in a world where white men are free to use African American girls and women sexually. And then there can be a double burden for African American women living in situations in which they may be burdened both by white men and African American men. To illustrate, here is a warning to a girl from her grandmother about African American women's double burden.

> 'De white man is de ruler of everything as fur as Ah been able tuh find out. So de white man throw down de load and tell de nigger man tuh pick it up. He pick it up because he have to, but he don't tote it. He hand it to his womenfolks. De nigger woman is de mule uh de world so fur as Ah can see. Ah been prayin' fuh it tuh be different wid you.' (Hurston, *Their Eyes Were Watching God*, p. 14)

The message to the granddaughter, like other quoted material in this section of this chapter, is testimony to the burdens African American children in the novels must carry and to the challenges of parenting African American children.

Parenting a Child to Be Better Able to Deal with Racism

Parenting is in part about raising a child to live safely and well in the situations in which the child now lives and in situations that seem possible or likely in the future. In the novels, parents generally care about their children and want things to go well for them. Thus, if something bad happens to an African American child as a result of racism, the child's parent may blame the racism but also blame herself or himself for not parenting the child better. The following is about a mother whose teenage son was murdered by whites.

> She couldn't stop crying or remembering the way Armstrong had wailed the day she sent him to Mississippi, the way he had pleaded in his letters that he wanted to come home. 'God is punishing me … He's punishing me for being a bad mother.' (Campbell, *Your Blues Ain't Like Mine*, p. 100)

Although so far in this chapter the implication has been that a child is socialized by its mother and father, children in some novels are parented not only by parents but also grandparents, older siblings, aunts and uncles, neighbors, extended family, friends, a church community, and others.

> She needed what most colored girls needed: a chorus of mamas, grandmamas, aunts, cousins, sisters, neighbors, Sunday school teachers, best girlfriends, and what all to give her the strength life demanded of her—and the humor with which to live it. (Morrison, *Song of Solomon*, p. 311)

This pattern of parenting by many is consistent with the literature on racial socialization in the African American community—for example, with the role of the church in racial socialization (Martin and McAdoo, 2007).

When does parenting begin? In a few novels, parental concerns begin before a child is conceived. For example, a parent may think that if her or his daughter or granddaughter partners with a man with lighter skin that will make it more likely that their children would have lighter skin and hence do somewhat better in the racial system. The following quote is from a grandmother.

> 'I want ... you to marry a fair-skin colored man, so your children will be lighter than you and have a better chance in life.' (Killens, *The Cotillion, or, One Good Bull Is Half the Herd*, p. 96)

African American parents employ many different strategies for parenting a child to do well in the face of racism (see, for example, Feagin and Sikes, 1994, pp. 311–16; Hill, 1999, pp. 81–102; hooks, 1989b; Hughes and Chen, 1997; Palmer, 2011; Ritterhouse, 2006). Davies (1985), writing about the representation of mothering in five African American novels (including two analyzed in this book), argued that being mothered well can free an African American from the wounding and suffocation of racism and sexual oppression. For example, in some of the novels analyzed for this book (including some Davis did not analyze), some parents tried to prepare a child for encounters with racism by teaching them African American history and fostering racial pride. Some parents talked explicitly about dealing with racism. Some did not shelter their children from learning about their own difficulties with white people, and some talked with their children about aspects of the racial system. Here is a mother talking to her 10-year-old son.

> 'Evening's the only time we niggers have to ourselves! ... Thank God for night ... 'cause all day you gives to white folks.' (Hughes, *Not Without Laughter*, p. 78)

But some, like the following parent, talk in more general terms as though they are parenting a child irrespective of racial issues, but implied in what they say is a great deal that addresses racism. For example, in the quote that follows, "the world" can be taken to include white racism and those who would "make them ashamed of what they were or how they looked" can be taken to be white people. So even if the last sentence in the following quote seems to deny that the mother is talking about racism, I think an appropriate reading is that she is talking about white people, but people of other races can be problems too.

> 'When I brought my babies home from the hospital ... I swore before whatever gods would listen ... that I would use everything I had and could ever get to see that my children were prepared to meet this world on its own terms, so that no one would sell them short and make them ashamed of what they were or how

they looked ... That's not being white or red or black—that's being a mother.'
(Naylor, *Women of Brewster Place*, p. 86)

Hughes and Chen (1997), in a study of African American parents in Chicago with children age 4–14, wrote that it is primarily with older children that parents actively prepare their children for experiences with racism and promote outgroup mistrust. In the novels, too, parents do not often talk with young children about racism or not trusting whites. And a young child might not yet have even been taught to pay attention to skin color.

> He hadn't had any inherent dislike of white children. He hadn't known there was anything special about them ... For [his sister] and his father were fair, his mother was very light. He had never noticed that he was darker. Nor had he known that their skin shades were preferable to darker ones. (West, *The Living Is Easy*, p. 121)

In fact, in some novels a parent of a young child works at sheltering the child from racism, deceiving the child into thinking that the world is benign (which is consistent with the findings of a number of racial socialization studies—Lasane-Brown, 2006). In Gwendolyn Brooks' *Maud Martha*, Maud insulates her young daughter Paulette from the obvious racism of a department store Santa Claus.

> Santa ... patted the children's cheeks, and if a curl was golden and sleek enough he gave it a bit of a tug, and sometimes he gave its owner a bit of a hug ... It was very merry and much as the children had dreamed. Now came little Paulette ...
> 'Hello!'
> Santa Claus rubbed his palms together and looked vaguely out across the Toy Department. He was unable to see either mother or child.
> 'I want,' said Paulette, 'a wagon, a doll, a big ball, a bear and a tricycle with a horn.'
> 'Mister,' said Maud Martha, 'my little girl is talking to you.'
> Santa Claus's neck turned with hard slowness, carrying his unwilling face with it.
> 'Mister' said Maud Martha.
> 'And what—do you want for Christmas.' No question mark at the end.
> 'I want a wagon, a doll, a bear, a big ball, and a tricycle with a horn.'
> Silence. Then, 'Oh.' Then, 'Um-hm.'
> Santa Claus had taken care of Paulette.
> 'And some candy and some nuts and a seesaw and bow and arrow.'
> 'Come on, baby.'
> 'But I'm not through, Mama'
> 'Santa Claus is through, hon ...'
> 'Why didn't Santa Clause like me?'
> 'Baby, of course he liked you.'
> 'He didn't like me. Why didn't he like me?'

'It maybe seemed that way to you. He has a lot on his mind ...'
'He liked the other children. He smiled at them and shook their hands.'
'He maybe got tired of smiling ...'
'He didn't look at me, he didn't shake *my* hand.'
'Listen, child. People don't have to kiss you to show they like you. Now you know Santa Claus liked you. What have I been telling you? Santa Claus loves every child, and on the night before Christmas he brings them swell presents. Don't you remember, when you told Santa Claus you wanted [those things] he said "Um-hm"? That meant he's going to bring you all those. You watch and see ... You'll wake up Christmas morning and find them and then you'll know Santa Claus loved *you too*.' (Brooks, *Maud Martha*, pp. 172–5)

For Maud Martha, deceiving her daughter is an act of kindness and also represents the hope that her daughter is still innocent enough to believe her mother's lies, to not, at such an early age, be struggling to understand racism and to find her way in a racist world.

Furtively, [Maud Martha] looked down at Paulette. Was Paulette believing her? Surely she was not yet going to begin to think tonight, to try to find out answers tonight. She hoped the little creature wasn't ready. She hoped there hadn't been enough for that. (Brooks, *Maud Martha*, p. 176)

Given such sheltering of younger children it should not be surprising that some children only start to struggle with racism when they are older (see, for example, the accounts earlier in this chapter of African American children trying to wash the color off themselves and of Meridian stopping in the middle of a speech she had been handed to deliver when she suddenly recognized the hypocrisy in it).

How do parents and others raise African American children to deal with racism? In some novels an African American parent teaches a child how to navigate a racist world indirectly, perhaps through providing an example to the child.

'Mama, you had no road map when you left down there and came up here and you found your way pretty good. I learned to read signs by watching you.' (Golden, *Long Distance Life*, p. 187)

Another example of a child learning about the hazards of the racial system through observing a parent was discussed in Chapter 5. Having observed her mother being humiliated by a white train conductor, Nel in Toni Morrison's *Sula* resolved never to get into a humiliating encounter with a white person.

Sometimes the indirect parenting involves children overhearing stories that include warnings about white people. Here is an example of two children playing on a porch who overhear an adult saying to other adults that whites cannot be trusted.

'Ain't I been knowin' crackers sixty-five years, an' ain't dey de cause o' me bein' ... in [this town] 'stead o' in ma home right today? De dirty buzzards! Ain't I nussed t'ree of 'em up from babies like ma own chillens, and ain't dem same t'ree boys done turned round an' helped run me an' Tom out o' town?' ... [The two children] stopped playing and sat down on the porch [to listen] as she began a tale they had all heard at least a dozen times. (Hughes, *Not Without Laughter*, pp. 82–3)

And here is an example of a daughter overhearing her parents talking about a difficult situation with a white man.

'How do you know he ain't a white man playing Indian?'
'Because I know. Grown-up white men don't want to pretend to be anything else. Not even for a minute.'
'They'll become anything for as long as it takes to steal some land.' (Walker, *Meridian*, p. 47)

Thus, in the novels, parenting that helps a child to deal with the racist world sometimes is done without parental intention. The parent, without intent to socialize at the moment, communicates stories, attitudes, and perspectives that may help the child to face and deal with racism. To add to the examples mentioned so far, Prince (2005, pp. 75–9, citing Grewal, 1998) pointed out how in Toni Morrison's *The Bluest Eye* Claudia is growing up in a home culture that resists the dominant racist culture. Her mother's blues singing and kitchen conversations with neighbors establish a sense of resistance to and autonomy from the white racist world. This is in striking contrast to the home life of Claudia's friend, Pecola, whose parents have been beaten down by racism and whose lives, as a consequence, are pervaded by self-hatred and by disappointment and anger directed at one another. Pecola's mother does not sing the blues, with its vocabulary and sentiments of resistance, does not have kitchen conversations of resistance with neighborhood women, and spends a great deal of time in the kitchen of a white family for whom she works. In the white family's kitchen, Pecola sees that her mother's priority is not parenting her own children, but caring for and doting on the child of the white family, and Pecola sees that her mother's energy and efforts go into giving the white family a higher quality of life. It is Pecola, whose desire to have blue eyes (and, hence, to escape the terrible difficulties of being a black child in the context of her family) provides the title for Morrison's novel. In fact, racial socialization in the novels is often indirect or unintended.

The racial socialization literature has developed a range of analytical categories for making sense of what African American parents might do in racially socializing a child, whether with intent to racially socialize or not (Lesane-Brown, 2006). The novels offer considerable riches about racial socialization, but they do not offer the range and depth of accounts of socialization that can match up with the range and depth of what is in the racial socialization literature. I think there are only five categories of what is in the racial socialization literature that appeared in at least a few of the novels and were written about in some detail. What follows is an exposition of those five categories.

White People Are Dangerous

In many novels there are accounts of African American children being taught directly to protect themselves and to survive encounters with racism. The overriding, common and important lesson is to beware of white people.

> His father said that all white people were wicked, and that God was going to bring them low. He said that white people were never to be trusted, and that they told nothing but lies, and that not one of them had ever loved a nigger. (Baldwin, *Go Tell It on the Mountain*, p. 34)

> How many times had Odessa told him ... that he couldn't say anything he felt like saying to these crazy crackers ... Mama told me never to trust crackers. (Campbell, *Your Blues Ain't Like Mine*, p. 36)

In some novels there are specific warnings to African American girls and young women about white men who might want to use them sexually.

> [Her] grandmother ... had said over and over ... 'Lutie, baby, don't you never let no white man put his hands on you. They ain't never willin' to let a black woman alone. Seems like they all got a itch and a urge to sleep with 'em. Don't you never let any of 'em touch you.' (Petry, *The Street*, p. 45)

Connecting to warnings about white people, here is a parental message in one novel that in relationships with white people an African American has to be in control of self, and covertly in control of the situation.

> 'A colored man can never afford to forget himself, no matter what the provocation. He must always be superior to a white man if he wants to be the white man's equal.' (West, *The Living Is Easy*, pp. 127–8, words said by a father to his son)

Parents in some novels accompany their warnings to children about white people with instruction about the etiquette the racial system demands of African Americans in relationship to whites. Such teaching is particularly clear in novels set in the South (cf. Ritterhouse, 2006).

> Armstrong remembered his grandmother's tutelage ... He would act polite and stupid. Wasn't that what white people wanted? (Campbell, *Your Blues Ain't Like Mine*, p. 40)

A child in one novel was also in a sense parented through his reading in that he had learned not to trust white people through what he read about them.

> John had read about the things white people did to colored people; how, in the South, where his parents came from, white people cheated them of their wages, and burned them, and shot them—and did worse things, said his father, which the tongue could not endure to utter. He had read about colored men being burned in the electric chair for things they had not done; how in riots they were beaten with clubs; how they were tortured in prisons; how they were the last to be hired and the first to be fired. (Baldwin, *Go Tell It on the Mountain*, pp. 34–5)

There can also be strikingly visible evidence of the harm caused by racism, evidence that adults can point to in educating children about the dangerousness of white people. For example, in Baldwin's *Go Tell It on the Mountain*, John's half-brother Roy comes home with a knife wound inflicted by a white youth, and Gabriel uses the wound to reinforce a warning previously given to John.

> '*This* is what white folks does to niggers. I been telling you, now you see.' (Baldwin, *Go Tell It on the Mountain*, p. 47)

Such teaching might help a child learn to be careful when dealing with white people, but it also can lead a child to think of white people as enemies in ways that might tempt the child to say or do something hostile in interaction with a white person. For example, in Ann Petry's *The Street*, eight-year-old Bub is standing in front of a white clerk in a candy store and thinks about directing his child's version of hostility at the clerk.

> He looked at her hard, remembering what Mom had said about white people wanting colored people to shine shoes. He would have liked to stick his tongue out at her to show her he wasn't going to be hurried. (Petry, *The Street*, p. 336)

When parents fear that their child has not learned adequately to recognize and deal with the dangers white people pose, for example, how not to keep a low profile in relationships with whites (Bowman and Howard, 1985), the parents might even send the child away or move the whole family to a place where the child might be safer.

> After the girl was whipped in the grocery store, in full view of her parents, her brother asked his father, 'Why you let that white man do that to her, Daddy?' ... The father's only answer was a lowering of his eyes. Nor did other Negro parents have a response to the persistent questions put to them by their children. More than one family packed up and boarded [a train heading north] because of the new, untameable spirit in their young. (Campbell, *Your Blues Ain't Like Mine*, p. 154)

Some research with a national probability sample of African-Americans (Brown and Lasane-Brown, 2006) indicates that in recent years African-American parents are less often than in the past emphasizing the dangerousness of whites and deference to white. So in this area the novels to some extent reflect earlier times. But as literature cited throughout this chapter suggests, many African American parents still act as though there are reasons to socialize their children to be careful around whites and to get along and do well in a racial system that benefits whites and makes things difficult for African Americans.

You Matter

Many of the African American children in the novels are valued by someone, most often by the person or persons who are raising them. That is, there is in quite a few novels a sense that no matter how difficult the circumstances in which a child arrived, the child matters to at least one person. That person does what she or he can do to nurture and protect the child. And that helps to build resilience in the child to being bruised by the racial system, because one way to help a child deal with racism is to give the child a sense that she or he is loved and worthwhile. In what follows, a father tells his son, who is quoted earlier in the chapter as being concerned about being labeled "nigger" and therefore not worthwhile, that his son can do good things and is definitely worthwhile.

> 'Sure you something. You my boy, ain't you? … Nigger ain't nothing but somebody who can't do no better. But you can do better … Better'n all who's gone before you. You can help build this Neck up to something. You's an Upshur. Upshur built this Neck up to what it is now.' (Wright, *This Child's Gonna Live*, p. 106)

Consistent with the social science and psychological literature on African American parents educating their children to get along in a racist society (e.g. Boyd-Franklin, 2003), one mother who worked at helping her children to think well of themselves focused her efforts partly on skin color.

> All my kids is taller than average, as good looking at they come and as dark as you can get, and I spent what I felt was a whole lotta unnecessary time and energy teaching em to appreciate the color of their skin. To not be ashamed of it. I used to tell 'em that the blacker the berry the sweeter the juice, 'cause everybody knows that back then being yellow with long wavy hair meant you was automatically fine, which was bullshit. (McMillan, *A Day Late and a Dollar Short*, p. 9)

She went on to say that her daughter Charlotte grew up despising her own skin color, so in the novels parent efforts to bolster a child's self-esteem in the face of racism do not always succeed. And then at another place in the novel her adult son says:

> Sometimes I wish I'da been born white. Things probably woulda been a helluva lot easier. (McMillan, *A Day Late and a Dollar Short*, p. 45)

We can take what he says to be not about self-esteem as much as about who has it easier in a racist society. But there can be a blurred line between self-esteem issues and awareness of how racism disadvantages one. That is, it is not always obvious if someone wishes he or she were white or feels discouraged at facing disadvantage due to racism whether self-esteem is implicated or it is just a way of talking about the racial system.

Sometimes the esteem-strengthening things that parents say to a child seem focused on the child's present and future as an individual pursuing personal well-being, but sometimes the words are also about what the child can do for the race.

> 'You's a 'dustrious chile; sho is! Gwine make a smart man ... Gwine get ahead an' do good fo' yo'self an' de race.' (Hughes, *Not Without Laughter*, p. 194)

Another way to prepare a child to deal with a racist world is to steep the child in knowledge about her or his cultural roots, about influential and brave African American leaders. Then the message is something like "You are a member of an illustrious group. Hold your head high."

> At bedtime [my husband would] tell Esther stories about folks like Harriet Tubman and Sojourner Truth. I asked him once why he was always pounding all that stuff in Esther's head all the time, why he couldn't just let her be a little girl. 'She'll find out she's a Negro soon enough' I told him. And he just said, 'But we got to let her know what it means.' (Golden, *Long Distance Life*, p. 50)

Then there are family roots that say that "you are somebody." They may be described in a way that places demands on a young person to take on a role of high responsibility, but they are also statements about the worth of the young person.

> 'You carry a legacy, all the things Grandad did, our father accomplished and Mom's work in the movement. It all gets passed on ... from them to me to you. We're expecting you to do your share.' (Golden, *Long Distance Life*, p. 247)

Each one of the self-esteem-raising things listed in this section of this chapter can be understood as empowering, and empowerment is arguably a key to an African American child's surviving, coping, and doing well in a racist world (O'Reilly, 2004, writing about the novels of Toni Morrison). Moreover, a parent's actions to empower a child in the face of racism can be empowering of the parent

(O'Reilly, 2004)—for example, with the parent taking to heart the words she or he says to the child.

Get an Education

Related to the idea that a child should think of himself or herself as somebody who matters is the idea in some novels that education is very important for an African American child. This emphasis is consistent with values that are described in scholarly writings about African American parenting (Barr and Neville, 2008; Bowman and Howard, 1985; Boyd-Franklin, Franklin, with Toussaint, 2000; Daniel and Effinger, 1996; Hines and Boyd-Franklin, 1996; Suizzo, Robinson, and Pahlke, 2008). Unfortunately, in some novels things happen that derail a child's path to education. Here is one example of that, in words a mother says to herself about her teenage son. He had done very well in high school academics and athletics and so he has great promise of going to a good college and doing well there. But now he has impregnated his girlfriend.

> Stressed time and time again the importance of getting a college education, especially for a black man. Instilled in him the importance of being honest, dependable, worthy. Strive to be the best even if he doesn't become the best ... How in the world is a baby supposed to fit into this picture? (McMillan, *A Day Late and a Dollar Short*, p. 252)

Education can be important for many reasons (Boyd-Franklin, Franklin, with Toussaint, 2000. It is a route to social status and economic security. It can help to neutralize racism in that it is an additional credential when seeking employment. Education can bolster a person's self-esteem and sense of self-worth. It can give a person knowledge and conceptual capacities for making sense of the world and making good choices. Also, education is not something that can be taken away from a person once the person has it by, for example, a Jim Crow legal system. And then what the mother quoted above says about education being especially important for a black man represents a belief that one way that racism works differently in the lives of African American men as compared to African American women is that in certain ways there are more barriers to African American men doing well. And presumably one reason she thinks that is her brother, who is very bright, has not ever been able to find a job that uses his intelligence, and as a consequence he has sunk into a life of poverty, alcoholism, and legal trouble.

Some characters in some novels see education for a child as a path not only to raise up the individual but also to raise up all African Americans.

> 'They's one mo got to go through school yet, an' that's ma little Sandy. If de Lawd lets me live I's gwine make a edicated man out o' him. He's gwine be another Booker T. Washington ... I wants this one ... to 'mount to something. I wants him to know all they is to know, so's he can help this black race o' our'n

to come up and see de light and take they places in de world. I wants him to be a Fred Douglass leadin' de people.' (Hughes, *Not Without Laughter*, p. 141)

'This boy's gotta get ahead—all of us niggers are too far back in this white man's country to let any brains go to waste ... You and me was foolish ... leaving school, but Sandy can't do like us. He's gotta be ... able to help the black race.' (Hughes, *Not Without Laughter*, p. 298)

In a novel set during the Civil Rights Era, efforts in support of civil rights added new meaning to an education. In Marita Golden's *Long Distance Life* Esther has been separated from her son Logan for four years while she worked in the Civil Rights Movement in Alabama. She returns as Logan is getting ready to enter Columbia University, and Esther says this to him.

'This education you're going off to get would be a wonder to most people I worked with in the South. There's still plenty of people can't read down there ... I taught a ninety-three-year-old woman on a tenant farm to read and write. She told me she wanted to learn so she could write with her own hands what she wanted put on her tombstone. We started out reading funeral home calendars, then moved to a church hymnal, then the Bible ... I got her to reading and writing pretty well and a few months later we sat up one night and she wrote her will and epitaph. She got in bed that night and she didn't say goodnight. She said goodbye. And when I came around the next day, the whole family was crying. She'd died in her sleep. I went into her room ... and that old woman had died with a small, crooked smile on her face. She hadn't had much say about her life, but she'd managed to have the last word about her death.'
Esther rested her arm on Logan's shoulder and said, 'Take that old lady's spirit with you in every classroom you go into.'
Logan had waited for a miracle. And it had arrived as miracles do, with so much simplicity that not until Esther removed her arm from his shoulder was he aware of what he had received. (Golden, *Long Distance Life*, pp. 197–8)

The miracle Logan has received is complex. The sense of how precious education can be to an African American elder who has been deprived of an education by racism is a powerful impetus to Logan's valuing his own education. Logan also gained a way to think about his mother having been away from him for so long that makes her absence from his life a blessing to some others. And one can argue too that the blessing is that his mother loves him and encourages him in a very powerful way to invest fully in his education.

You Have to Make Your Own Way

In a number of novels, children are socialized to make their own way in the world, often socialized to work hard and to recognize opportunity and seize it. In the world of the novels, some children are clearly taught that things will not be easy. Here is what teenage Rosie said to her two closest friends about that:

> 'My Mom says nobody never put down no bed of roses for her to lay on. She says I've got to make my own, same way she made hers ... I believe in "Mama may have and Papa may have, but God bless the child that's got his own."' (Hunter, *God Bless the Child*, p. 40)

Rosie and her two friends were close to high school graduation. Her friends urged her to stay in school, but Rosie wanted to leave school and work full time. For her, the value of making it economically was stronger than the value of education. And that tension between education and making your own way makes sense in the social world that many of the novels describe.

On Being or Not Being Like White People

Although much of what parents in the novels do in helping a child to deal with racism seems to be about helping the child navigate a world in which white people are a problem, in a few novels parents hope that a child will meet the standards they imagine white people hold for their own children.

> Yoruba said to her new friend, Pamela Jefferson, 'How come a white dance instructor? It doesn't make sense.'
> Pam laughed. 'Who's worried about making sense? All [our parents] want is for us to be like Mister Charlie's chillun.' (Killens, *The Cotillion, or, One Good Bull Is Half the Herd*, p. 102)

Sometimes efforts to be like white people are not about changing the inner self but about being able to show white people that one can look respectable by white standards, for example, by wearing nice clothing.

> 'I want white people to know that Negroes have a little taste; that's why I always trade at good shops.' (Hughes, *Not Without Laughter*, p. 235)

In novels set in more recent times, some middle-class African American children seem to have learned to fit into the white world so successfully that a parent whose generation had to face the sting of racism might find that trying to strengthen the child's racial awareness and capacity to deal with racism is difficult.

> Now his kids were growing up with whites, assuming an intimacy that he was not totally comfortable with. Logan worried that the white world would swallow them up. Their ... ease in that world bothered him ... Yet wasn't that what 'the struggle' had been about? He found himself ... questioning [them] about their teachers and classmates and friends. Listening closely to their accounts

for slights and insults their youth might blind them to. And it irritated him that when he gave them books on the lives of Black heroes they accepted them grudgingly ... Had the struggle been about this too? Feeding your kids their history like it was castor oil? (Golden, *Long Distance Life*, p. 252)

But it is also important for parents in some novels to teach a child to grow up Black or African American, not to grow up to be like a white person. Here are a father and son talking.

'I'd like to be rich one day,' Logan said wistfully.
'Long as you never say you want to be white.' (Golden, *Long Distance Life*, p. 167)

Efforts to try to bring up a child not to be like white people reflect realities for characters in a number of novels who hope to improve their situation in the racial system by finding ways to be more like whites because they feel that being that way will make them more acceptable to white people. So a character might try to look and act like it seems white people would approve of and push her or his children to meet the same standards. Reflecting discussions in Chapter 7, one expression of this for adults is trying to partner with someone of lighter skin. That would make the couple seem more like what white people might accept, and it would make for offspring whose skin color was closer to white.

All of the Negro leaders and members of the Negro upper class were either light skinned themselves or else had light-skinned wives. A wife of dark complexion was considered a handicap unless she was particularly charming, wealthy, or beautiful. An ordinary-looking dark woman was no suitable mate for a Negro man of prominence. The college youths on whom the future of the race depended practiced this precept of their elders religiously. (Thurman, *The Blacker the Berry*, p. 60)

However, as the irony in the quote immediately above suggests, there is not a sense in any novel that describes characters who try to emulate whites or become more like them that there is any hope of the emulation protecting characters from the harshness and oppression of the racial system.

In the novels, it is often middle-class African Americans who try to do better by white standards, and they are often objects of disgust, contempt, dislike, and ridicule for other African Americans. In fact, depictions of the African American middle class as objects of disgust are common in the writings of the Harlem Renaissance and the Black Arts Movement (Bernard, 2006). Moreover, black individuals, couples and families who try to do better by white standards are often depicted in African American fiction as creating additional problems for themselves, which is consistent with Bateson's (1979) point that systemic adaptation also leads to mal-adaptation. Jenkins (2007), for example, has suggested that black middle-class efforts to ward of white accusations of sexual and domestic deviance can lead to unsustainable and quite harmful efforts in pursuit of respectability. Thus, Jenkins (2007, pp. 47–59) makes a case for the problems of Lutie in Ann Petry's *The Street* as arising from Lutie ambitions for a decent social class standing that lead to her moving herself and her son out of her father's apartment in order to escape the image problems created by her father's beer drinking, immodest live-in girlfriend and the possible influence of the girlfriend on Lutie's son. Related to that, Lutie stops her son Bub from shining shoes and destroys his shoe shine kit, even though it represents his effort to help his mother deal with their poverty.

> 'I'm not going to let you begin at eight doing what white folks figure all eight-year-old colored boys ought to do. For if you're shining shoes at eight, you'll probably be doing the same thing when you're eighty. And I'm not going to have it.' (Petry, *The Street*, pp. 70–71)

Lutie does not want her son to be what white people want an African American boy to be, a person who starts at menial work and never gets beyond that. Her thinking is echoed in recent writings about the challenges of raising African American sons (e.g. Boyd-Franklin, Franklin, with Toussaint, 2000).

Similarly, in Marita Golden's *Long Distance Life*, Naomi wants her daughter Esther not to find a summer job doing the maid work or child care for white families that Naomi had experienced as diminishing and that she saw as central to how the racial system crushes African American women.

> Naomi told [Esther] she could get a job, as long as she wasn't cleaning anybody's house or watching someone's babies. Even though those jobs were considered respectable, sought after and the classifieds were filled with ads for COLORED GIRL WANTED, FAMILY NEEDS LIGHT-SKINNED COLORED GIRL or COLORED DOMESTIC SOUGHT, Naomi admonished Esther, 'If you want to work so bad, go on, but get a job where nobody can treat you like a mule or a slave. I swallowed enough pride for every woman in my family. I swore I'd save you from that.' (Golden, *Long Distance Life*, p. 58)

From another perspective, in Sarah E. Wright's *This Child's Gonna Live*, Jacob tries to neutralize the idea, for one of his sons, that Jesus was white, because in his thinking to the extent that whites persuade African Americans that Jesus was white, they elevate white people and diminish African Americans.

> 'Jesus a white man?'
> 'He ain't no such thing. He ain't no kind of color. People who painted his pictures just put him out to look like that.' (Wright, *This Child's Gonna Live*, p. 107)

Parenting Does Not Stop at Childhood's End

Some parents in the novels continue to parent in reference to racism after their children are grown because racism continues to be a problem and even a great danger. One form of such parenting involves telling adult children about parental or ancestral acts of resistance to racism. Such stories constitute a moral claim on the child. "Because I, or your grandmother, did this, you should do this and not that." Here is an example of a mother speaking out against her daughter's decision to change her name, because the daughter's original name had honored a grandmother who resisted racism.

> 'It broke my heart when you changed your name. I gave you my grandmother's name, a woman who bore nine children and educated them all, who held off six white men with a shotgun when they tried to drag one of her sons to jail for not knowing his place. Yet you needed to reach into an African dictionary to find a name to make you proud.' (Naylor, *Women of Brewster Place*, p. 86)

Among the messages this mother offers that illuminate parenting is that African American children may be given names at birth that honor family elders who have resisted racism, and so a name may symbolically strengthen a child to deal with the racist world.

Here is another example of parenting an adult child. A mother (Silla) is talking to her young adult daughter, Selina, who is planning to set off on her own in a racist world.

> 'Girl, so you know what it tis out there? How those white people does do yah?'
> At her solemn nod, at the sad knowing in her eyes, Silla's head slowly bowed.
> (Marshall, *Brown Girl, Brownstones*, p. 301)

I take Silla's head bowing to represent pain and sadness that her daughter has had to deal with racism, but it also may be a way of saying to her daughter that she cares deeply about her welfare, is there for her in facing racism, and hopes for the best in her daughter's dealing with racism.

Another kind of parenting issue arises when an adult child is threatened with racist violence. Then a parent is faced with the enormous challenge of trying to find a way to save the child from injury or even death. For example, in *The Autobiography of Miss Jane Pittman* by Ernest J. Gaines, Miss Jane Pittman is warned by a white man that her adult son is in danger of being murdered because of his ambition to educate local African American children.

> 'They talk 'bout your boy ... They don't want him build that school ... They say he just good to stir trouble munks niggers. They want him go back [north].'
> (Gaines, *The Autobiography of Miss Jane Pittman*, p. 110)

Jane then wants her son, Ned, to go back north, to flee for his life, and she talks to him, but he only says that he will go ahead with building the school. She goes to Ned's wife, Vivian, urging her to take the couple's children and flee to the North, because she is sure Ned will want to follow them if they leave. However, Vivian says that Ned knows what he is risking and that she has to stay with him. But there is another dimension to the situation, because what Ned is doing, which so risks his life reflects the ways that Miss Jane Pittman raised Ned to be strong in the face of racism.

Another issue in parenting an adult child is that parenting an adult child to deal with racism might go on even though the child resists and resents the parenting.

> 'You constantly live in a fantasy world—about going to extremes—turning butterflies into eagles, and life isn't about that. It's accepting what is and working from that ...'
> 'I'd rather be dead than be like you—a white man's nigger who's ashamed of being black.' (Naylor, *Women of Brewster Place*, p. 85)

In this encounter between Kiswana and her mother, the mother confronts Kiswana vigorously (including the passage quoted earlier in this chapter). Kiswana is an adult, but her mother is working hard to teach Kiswana things Kiswana has apparently not yet learned about the debt that is owed to her ancestors. Kiswana's reaction to her mother's outburst is to become mute, perhaps with shame or perhaps because she feels outgunned by her mother. And to that muteness her mother reacts in a way that lovingly encourages her daughter to stand up and be strong.

> Mrs. Browne lifted Kiswana's chin gently, 'And the one lesson I wanted you to learn is not to be afraid to face anyone, not even a crafty old lady like me who can outtalk you.' (Naylor, *Women of Brewster Place*, p. 86)

So the message an African American parent may offer an adult child may be consistent with the message that was offered the child before the child grew up, to have good self-esteem and to be strong.

Parents and others can provide an adult offspring with models for coping with racism. For example, Selina saw in her mother a model of endurance in the face of the enormous difficulty of living in a racist society.

> 'How had the mother endured, she who had not chosen death by water?'
> (Marshall, *Brown Girl, Brownstones*, p. 287)

There is a lot to this brief quote. First of all, the fact that Selina could ask the question implies that she and her mother may have talked little or perhaps none about her mother's dealing with racism. One implication of the quote is that endurance in dealing with racism is not necessarily something a mother would speak to her daughter about, so whatever parenting might be involved in this area is via modeling. Another implication of the brief quote is that Selina felt buoyed up by realizing she was not alone in her difficulties and that her mother, an older friend who was rather parental (Miss Thompson), and others had found ways to endure. Such role models give one not only patterns for how to act but the reassurance of not being alone in the racial system.

> She was one with Miss Thompson ... the whores, the flashy men ... She was one with ... the mother and the Bajan women, who lived each day what she had come to know. (Marshall, *Brown Girl, Brownstones*, p. 287)

Chapter 10

Racism Can Undermine Parenting by Mothers and Fathers

In some novels, one avenue by which racism harms African American families is that it undermines parenting by making parenting by a child's mother and/or father more difficult or less effective or even separates the child from mother and father.

Parents on the Edge of Survival

Racism can undermine parenting by pushing parents down to a level where they must put much of their focus, energy, time, and efforts into survival for themselves and their family (Jones, 2011). With parents working as hard as they can to put the next meager meal on the table and to have a minimally habitable place to live, a child may experience the parents as neglectful and emotionally distant. But if for the parents the struggle to provide for the child and themselves takes so much, the child is getting all that the parents can provide.

> 'Mamma, did you ever love us? … I know you fed us and all. I was talkin' 'bout something else. Like. Like. Playin' with us. Did you ever, you know, play with us?'
> 'Play? Wasn't nobody playin' in 1895. Just 'cause you got it good now you think it was always this good? 1895 was a killer, girl. Things was bad. Niggers was dying like flies … I set in that house five days with you and Pearl and Plum and three beets … What would I look like leapin' 'round that little old room playin' with youngins with three beets to my name? … Don't that count? Ain't that love? You want me to tinkle you under the jaw and forget 'bout them sores in your mouth? Pearl was shittin' worms and I was supposed to play rang-around-the-rosie?'
> 'But Mamma, they had to be some time when you wasn't thinkin' 'bout …'
> 'No time. They wasn't no time. Not none … With you all coughin' and me watchin' so TB wouldn't take you off and if you was sleepin' quiet I thought, O Lord, they dead and put my hand over your mouth to feel if the breath was comin'. What you talkin' 'bout did I love you girl. I stayed alive for you.'
> (Morrison, *Sula*, pp. 67–9)

In this passage from *Sula*, the message of Eva to her daughter Hannah is that where there is desperate poverty, parenting is stripped to its most basic level, survival. But in that survival the parent can care desperately about the well-being of her children. Central to loving in such a situation is keeping self and children alive. But then another layer of meaning in the passage from *Sula* is that in a time of high death rates and desperate poverty there may be a culture of survival in which adults maintain a demeanor that says they are completely serious and focused on survival. That is, Eva says in the passage that with survival so much in doubt for everyone that the community of African Americans would have judged her to be inappropriate had she been playful. But then with so many deaths maybe most if not all adults, including Eva, were grieving. And grief would have suppressed playfulness.

Although Eva says to Hannah something like "I did love you, but I loved you in the way I had to in that time and place," one can also take the entire passage from *Sula* to mean that when racism puts families into deepest poverty it deprives children of many aspects of what some would see as essential to parental love. In this there is an interesting question for family systems theory about whether it is best for children and families for a family system to fit local conditions and culture or to transcend local conditions and culture to meet standards that seem from other perspectives to be optimal for children and families. Who is to say that if parenting in a difficult situation does not seem loving by some standard that the parenting should change to fit that standard?

The novels offer many examples of appropriate and effective parenting (see the previous chapter), but they also offer many examples of what some might consider poor parenting. One form of what might be considered poor parenting involves parents treating children with contempt and not seeming interested in or aware of the children's thoughts and feelings. Although there are many ways to understand the appropriateness and value of parenting like that, one possibility is that racism so pushes a parent to pay attention to the parent's own life and so diminishes the parent that it leaves the parent constantly worried and without much capacity to tune in on the lives, needs, and words of children. That leads to parenting that is insensitive to a child's pain and diminishes the child, just as the parents are forced to live with their own pain and to tolerate diminishment every day. To illustrate, in Toni Morrison's *The Bluest Eye*, a child reflects on what she experiences from her parents.

> Adults do not talk to us—they give us directions. They issue orders without providing information. When we trip and fall down they glance at us; if we cut or bruise ourselves, they ask us are we crazy. When we catch colds, they shake their heads in disgust at our lack of consideration. How, they ask us, do you expect anybody to get anything done if you all are sick? We cannot answer them. Our illness is treated with contempt. (Morrison, *The Bluest Eye*, pp. 12–13)

At one level, the child is talking about what might be a culture of parenting. If that were so, that kind of parenting might go on even if parents are not struggling with economic and other problems stemming from racism. But another possibility is that, consistent with what Eva says in the first quote in this chapter, the parents are struggling with survival so much because of racism that they do not have time or energy to talk to children, provide information to children, offer sympathy to children, or even know their children. Then too, in desperate times, a parent may have contempt for a child who is sick because in the racial system in which the parent lives and works there is no sick leave and no sympathy or let up in work demands for an adult African American who is sick. From that perspective, parenting that diminishes a sick child may be understood as socializing the child to what will be part of adult life.

From another perspective, among things needed to parent effectively, one must have enough self-esteem and self-confidence to have a reasonable capacity to take care of children. That may be related to a research finding that African American caregivers who report experiencing greater discrimination have adolescents who have more symptoms of depression and other indications of poor psychological functioning (Ford, Hurd, Jagers, and Sellers, 2013). That is, caregivers beaten down by racism may reflect the harm that racism has done to them in their parenting. That caregiver damage may also help to explain why, in several novels, men do not step forward to create a couple life with the mother of their children and do not take an active role in parenting their children. Here is an example that is central to the novel *In My Father's House*, by Ernest J. Gaines. It begins with an adult son berating his father for an event years before, when his father let his wife and children leave town.

> 'You had a mouth, a voice. You had arms, you had legs. You coulda walked out that door. That's all [Mama] wanted. You to walk out that door and call her back. That's all she wanted.'
> 'You just don't understand,' Phillip said. He was not trying to control the tears that rolled down his face. Neither was he trying to control his voice now, it was choked with emotion. 'I couldn't bit more leave that room ... than I can right now carry this car here on my back. I was paralyzed. Paralyzed. Yes I had a mouth, but I didn't have a voice. I had legs, but I couldn't move. I had arms, but I couldn't lift them up to you. It took a man to do these things, and I wasn't a man. I was just some ... brutish animal who could cheat, steal, rob, kill—but not stand. Not be responsible. Not protect you or your mother. They had branded that in us from the time of slavery. That's what kept me on that bed. Not 'cause I didn't want to get up. I wanted to get up more than anything in the world. But I had to break the rules, rules we had lived by for so long, and I wasn't strong enough to break them.' (Gaines, *In My Father's House*, pp. 101–2)

Undermined by racism, undermined by generations of diminishment, Phillip was unable to call the mother of his children back to him, to ask her not to move away but to stay with him and to rely on him to be a caring, supportive, and nurturing husband and father. In the passage quoted, the son blames the father for not being a caring husband and father, but the father says that a lifetime of having his ego diminished by racism, and the diminishment that generations of men before him had experienced, prevented him from developing the part of self that would have enabled him to do that. But then we can see in the quote that the father has since that time years ago become a man who can speak about the old self as though he has become different, so in some ways, despite continuing to live in a racist world, he has become a more confident man. And in fact in the novel he is the leader in his community in fighting for the rights of African Americans. He has become that too late by decades to change what happened with the woman he loved and their three children. But there is still a message in the novel that the damage racism does to people may someday, at least to some extent, be overcome.

If one believes that proper parenting involves considerable attentiveness and demonstrations of love, the problems in parenting for African Americans in some of the novels are compounded intergenerationally when racism leads an African American adult to be a damaging or neglectful parent. As a result of parenting that way there is then a greater likelihood that the adult's children will grow up not having had a good model of how to parent. So if the adult children become parents, they might not parent well.

> 'What you asking me to do now—to be someone's father—I don't know how to do. You know how I was raised. What I'm saying is, the only father I ever had is not the kind I want to be.' He looked at her, his eyes brimming with tears, filled with the deepest sadness she'd ever seen. (Campbell, *Your Blues Ain't Like Mine*, p. 214)

In this quote from the Campbell book, a man endorses standards of loving, attentive, caring fathering and says that he knows that he does not know how to father in that way. That he is able to say that is meaningful. Being able to say what one does not know how to do represents some knowledge of what one does not know how to do. The sadness in the quote could be sadness that he cannot father or sadness at the fathering he had received. In either case, we can, on the basis of this quote and the previous one from the Gaines book, argue that one of the great damages done by racism is how it can undermine fathering. And then here is another example.

> The aspect of married life that dumbfounded [Cholly] and rendered him totally disfunctional was the appearance of children. Having no idea of how to raise children, and having never watched any parent raise himself, he could not even comprehend what such a relationship should be. (Morrison, *The Bluest Eye*, p. 126)

Cholly's incomprehension and lack of any sense of how to parent, combined with his frequent drunkenness, was at the root of a horrid family tragedy, his rape of his daughter. The assault began this way:

> Had [Cholly] not been alone in the world since he was thirteen, knowing only a dying old woman ... whose age, sex, and interests were so remote from his own, he might have felt a stable connection between himself and the children. As it was, he reacted to them, and his reactions were based on what he felt at the moment. So it was on a Saturday afternoon ... he staggered home reeling drunk and saw his daughter in the kitchen ... What could a burned-out black man say to the hunched back of his eleven-year-old daughter? (Morrison, *The Bluest Eye*, p. 127)

In a society where individuals are held by the legal system to be responsible for their own law breaking, Cholly's rape of his daughter leads to him being imprisoned. But with a broader view of the racial system one could say that perhaps many people had some responsibility for what Cholly did—for example, the racists whose actions deprived him of parents and the racists who in various ways undermined his self-esteem.

Parents Who Are Not There for Their Children

In many of the novels there are accounts of active, caring, effective parenting. But there are also stories in which racism and the poverty linked to racism lead to parents not being there for their children. Cholly Breedlove was abandoned by his mother when he was a newborn. His great aunt rescued him and cared for him into his teen years, but then she died. After she died he had the terrifying encounter with two white men that is discussed in Chapter 5, and that pushed him out of the community and into a search for the man who had allegedly fathered him. He eventually found the man, but the man would have nothing to do with him. At that point, Cholly had lost everything.

> Abandoned in a junk heap by his mother, rejected for a crap game by his father, there was nothing more to lose. (Morrison, *The Bluest Eye*, p. 126)

Sometimes the abandonment of a child is more subtle. As a parent struggles with the dilemmas created by poverty and the other problems of living in a racist society, the parent may frequently be distracted, upset, and angry. A parent who often has an angry facial expression in the presence of a child can make trouble for the child, even if the angry expression is about whites and what they have done to limit and diminish the parent. For example, in Ann Petry's *The Street*, Bub, Lutie Johnson's eight-year-old son, is recurrently concerned that his mother's appearance of anger is about him, even though it is about the situation the racial system has put her in. And her angry appearance silences him and prevents important things from being talked about.

> [Bub] started to tell her just what it was like to be alone in the dark. But her face was shut tight with anger and her voice was so hard and cold that he decided he'd better wait until some other time. (Petry, *The Street*, p. 316)

So racism can undermine parenting by instigating parent anger that in some ways can reduce child-parent communication and thus reduce the parenting that a child receives.

Years before, Lutie had been out of contact with Bub for weeks at a time while she worked as a maid. In fact, in several other novels as well it is clear that the long hours demanded of women working as maids could mean that a child was neglected who very much would have benefitted from receiving more of a mother's attention and care. For example:

> Harriett was the youngest ... of the three children. With [her father] dead going on ten years, [her mother] washing every day, [her oldest sister] married, and [her middle sister] herself out working, there had been nobody to take much care of the little sister as she grew up. Harriett had had no raising, even though she was smart and in high school. A female child needed care. (Hughes, *Not Without Laughter*, p. 45)

In this quote Hughes makes the case that at least some children need more parenting than they are likely to get with a mother doing washing or maid work, that in a society that demands long hours of strenuous work of many African American women, a child may receive less care than the child needs (VanWormer, 2012).

In some novels there are accounts of parents doing horrible things to children, and one can speculate that the parent brutality is in some ways rooted in generation after generation of African Americans experiencing racist brutality. But that is only speculation, because in those instances the authors write nothing about the racist roots of the brutality. Here is one example.

> One day last week I forgot that I hated my father, forgot that I had even thought of him as a monster, forget the blows he'd dealt my body over the years and the day he called me to him and demanded that I show him my hands. 'Are they clean?' he asked as I slowly raised my arms, 'Yes, sir,' I said and shook my head furiously up and down. They were clean, in fact still damp from my having washed them. 'Come closer,' he said. 'Come closer so I can see better,' he said. I moved closer and closer until my small hands were right beneath his chin. 'I see a speck of dirt,' he said and stifled a laugh. I smelled the whisky ... 'A speck of dirt ... hmmm ... right there,' he said, and smashed the hot tip of his cigarette

down in the soft middle of my eight-year-old palm. (McFadden, *The Warmest December*, p. 1)

In some novels, another way that racism affects parenting is that it leads to fathers moving far away to find work. For example, in Baldwin's *Go Tell It on the Mountain*, Gabriel's father abandoned Gabriel's mother, Gabriel, and his sister Florence shortly after Gabriel was born. Gabriel's father moved north, fleeing the racism and poverty of the South for what might be a better life (Baldwin, *Go Tell It on the Mountain*, p. 77). In part because of the undermining of fathers as men that was discussed earlier in this chapter and in part because of the lack of local jobs for African American men in the South and the greater number of jobs for African American men in the economically developing North, in the novels far more children are cared for by mothers alone than by fathers alone or by two parents.

'Every man I ever knew left his children.' (Morrison, *Sula*, p. 143)

Family Challenges When Children Are Created by White Sexual Assault

With the racial system giving white men in the times and places in which many of the novels are set the freedom to sexually exploit African American women without fear of repercussions, a number of African American women in the novels are impregnated by white men. There is historical evidence that in some families there was ongoing discomfort about a child having been fathered by a white man (VanWormer, 2012). But even if an African American family were completely accepting of a child fathered by a white man, the child might be burdened with discomfort about personal identity and with a need to know more about her or his origins than family members are willing or able to tell. For an African American child who has an unknown white father, there could be poignant exchanges with other family members as she or he tries to learn the identity of the biological father.

'Daddy. Tell me who my father was.'
He gave her a quick look, and to Ida's surprise there was pain on his face. 'Ain't I been a father to you?'
'Yes, and I love you, Daddy. I just want to know who the other blood half of me is. That's all.'
'Well, I done told you; I don't know. Now you let it rest. Leave it alone.'
(Campbell, *Your Blues Ain't Like Mine*, p. 106)

In this quote, the child has a father, the person she calls Daddy, and he loves her, but she still wants to know who her "blood" father is. Daddy is pained by her question, because he has been a good and loving father to her. And his evasiveness can be taken as coming from his defensiveness, but as the story unfolds, it seems more that he was protecting her from learning who her "blood" father was because that learning could make trouble for her. So here is another aspect to how racism can be said to undermine parenting, that in situations in which they lived, it could be safer for a parent not to answer a child's question honestly about who her biological father was. But then another view of the situation is that racism simply changes what is called for from a good and loving parent, that the Daddy in the quote above was doing good, loving parenting by the standards of his culture.

Surrogate Parents

In some novels, a child's parents disappear through abandonment, imprisonment, labor migration, or death. The absence of parents is very much about the racial system. Sometimes, because of the racial system, parents cannot take care of themselves, let alone a child. Or the system imprisons or kills one or both parents. Thus in some of the novels there are children who are parented by surrogates, which is consistent with informal adoption processes and family rules described in the social science and psychological literature about African Americans (e.g. Bertera and Crewe, 2013; Boyd-Franklin, 2003, pp. 52–72).

In the novels, when a child goes to a surrogate and the birth parent is alive, the birth parent might be unaware or indifferent, but sometimes the birth parent is aware and thinks the surrogate is best for the child. At the extreme, a child's going to a surrogate parent might be seen as saving the child's life.

> She might not have given him away to the people who wanted him. She might have murdered him instead. Then killed herself ... She might have done it that way except for one thing. One day she really looked at her child and loved him with as much love as she loved the moon or a tree, which was a considerable amount of impersonal love ... When she gave him away she did so with a light heart. She did not look back, believing she had saved a small person's life. (Walker, *Meridian*, p. 89)

Who the Surrogates Are

Novelist accounts of surrogate parenting fit social science and family therapy literature on the commonality and cultural appropriateness of grandmothers, aunts, other kin, and sometimes neighbors, family friends, or even strangers informally adopting or otherwise providing care for African American children (e.g. Anderson, 1999; Bertera and Crewe, 2013; Boyd-Franklin, 2003, pp. 52–72; Burton and DeVries, 1992; Davis-Sowers, 2012; Pinderhughes and Harden, 2005). As in the social science and family therapy literature, in the novels, most often a grandmother becomes a surrogate parent. Here are quotes from the novels, though not all that could be provided, to give a sense of how important surrogate parenting is in the novels. Of all the children in the novels who have lost their parents, only a few of them are left on their own. (So the racial system may undermine parenting by a child's birth parents, but in the novels African American family members or people in the community typically step in to care for a child if the birth parents do not or cannot.)

'That's my son's child. I've had her since she was six months old. Her parents went back to Tennessee and just left the baby. Neither of 'em are worth the spit it takes to cuss 'em.' (Naylor, *The Women of Brewster Place*, p. 34)

'I remember driving past the row houses where John French and Freeda French raised my mother and kept me a year or so when I was a baby.' (Wideman, *Sent for You Yesterday*, pp. 22–3)

Old Mr. and Mrs. Tate had raised half the orphans and strays in Homewood in that big house of theirs. No children of their own but always kept a houseful of kids. (Wideman, *Sent for You Yesterday*, pp. 38–9)

'Ah ain't never seen my papa … Mah mama neither. She was gone from round dere long before Ah wuz big enough tuh know. Mah grandma raised me. Mah grandma and de white folks she worked wid.' (Hurston, *Their Eyes Were Watching God*, p. 8)

'[Aunt] Helen saved us. Raised us like we were her own children.' (McFadden, *Nowhere Is a Place*, p. 278)

Among the tenants in the big house were the children Eva took in … . She sent … for children she had seen from the balcony of her bedroom or whose circumstances she had heard about … When her granddaughter Sula was eleven, Eva had three such children. They came with woolen caps and names given them by their mothers, or grandmothers, or somebody's best friend. (Morrison, *Sula*, p. 37)

'I done raised seven grandchillen 'sides eight o' ma own.' (Hughes, *Not Without Laughter*, p. 36)

Some children are abandoned at birth and are taken in by someone who not only gives them care but an identity. For example, Cholly Breedlove's aunt not only brings him into her house, she names him.

'[Your father] wasn't nowhere around when you were born. Your mama didn't name you nothing. The nine days wasn't up before she throwed you on the junk heap. When I got you I named you myself on the ninth day. You named after my dead brother, Charles Breedlove. A good man.' (*The Bluest Eye*, p. 106)

Possible Costs to Children of Surrogate Parenting

A surrogate parent may be loving and competent and make the difference between a child surviving and not surviving. But in some novels, surrogate parenting has its costs to a child.

Child loss of identity

In Toni Morrison's *Sula*, three boys who are apparently unrelated and who each arrive separately to live with and be cared for by Eva lose their unique individual identity because Eva gives each of them the same name, Dewey (pp. 37–8). In John Edgar Wideman's *Sent for You Yesterday*, Mrs. Tate at times cares for children whose names she does not know:

> All you cute little monkey-faced ones. That's the ones come to our door, that's the ones we took in. Days when this house full of children. Didn't know all they names. But loved all youall. (Wideman's *Sent for You Yesterday*, pp. 59–60)

So the children Mrs. Tate and her husband cared for are loved, but love is not the only thing a child needs. A child needs a firm identity, and that is hard to hold onto when the people taking care of one do not know one well enough to know one's name. But then, later in the Wideman novel, it becomes clear that some of the children who are with the Tates for a long time acquire a name ("Brother," for example) and acquire a last name identity as a Tate.

Issues with elderly surrogates

As is said above, grandmothers are the most common surrogates in the novels. The grandmothers in the novels seem typically to be loving, caring, and doing their best for the grandchildren under their care. Grandmothers have wisdom and knowledge. They offer stability. However, even though grandparents could conceivably be young, in the novels they are typically old. And their being old raises questions about their current and long-term capacity to nurture and support their grandchildren (cf. Burton and DeVries, 1992). In fact, in *Their Eyes Were Watching God*, a grandmother who is old and infirm forces her granddaughter, Janie, into early marriage, because the grandmother is afraid that she will not live long enough or have the energy to provide proper guidance. In the following quote 16-year-old Janie is pressured by her grandmother to get married.

> 'Ah'm ole now. Ah can't be always guidin' you' feet from harm and danger. Ah wants to see you married right away.' (Hurston *Their Eyes Were Watching God*, p. 13)

That marriage turns out to be a mistake for Janie, and soon she leaves her husband, not to return to her grandmother but to go off with another man. If one could generalize from Hurston's story about Janie's early launching, one of the costs of grandparent care is that children may be pushed prematurely into adult roles that they are not yet ready to assume.

Then too, grandparents have their own needs that they may want met by a grandchild. That might not be at all bad for the child. For example, helping a grandparent with farming and household chores may be character- and skill-building and may be good for a child's self-esteem and feelings of contributing to the grandparent and the household. And parents would, of course, also have their own neediness. But still a grandparent's neediness might be greater and bring more costs. For example, in Langston Hughes' *Not Without Laughter*, Sandy's grandmother, Aunt Hager, may have asked from Sandy more than was necessarily good for him to be asked to provide when Aunt Hager said to him:

> 'I thanks de Lawd you ain't gone too … You's ma standby. You's all I got, an' you ain't gwine leave yo' old grandma, is you?' Hager had turned to Sandy in those lonely days for comfort and companionship. (Hughes, *Not Without Laughter*, p. 178)

In this instance, Aunt Hager may be making it harder for Sandy to leave her to follow his mother to a distant city, but what might have been best for Sandy was to rejoin his mother.

When a caretaker who is old dies while the child is young, the child may be cared for by a relative who is not necessarily good for the child, as in Hughes' *Not Without Laughter*, where Sandy becomes the ward of his emotionally cold and distant aunt after his grandmother dies (pp. 232–3). At the extreme, a child whose elderly caretaker has died might have to head out on a possibly irrational and probably fruitless quest to find someone else who can care for him or her. For example, in Toni Morrison's *The Bluest Eye*, Cholly Breedlove is 14 when the aunt who has been taking care of him dies, and then he has nobody to care for him, and no home. Plus there is the possibility that he has made a girl pregnant. These were forces motivating him to leave town on a quest to find his father.

> Cholly knew that it was wrong to run out on a pregnant girl, and recalled, with sympathy, that his father had done just that. Now he understood. He knew what he must do—find his father. His father would understand … Running away from home for a Georgia black boy was not a great problem. You just sneaked away and started walking. When night came you slept in a barn … a cane field, or an empty sawmill. (Morrison, *The Bluest Eye*, p. 120)

Also, when somebody who is quite old raises one, they are not so likely to be alive when, as an adult, one would benefit from their wisdom, advice, help, and love (the parenting that continues into adulthood that is discussed in the preceding chapter). In Ann Petry's *The Street*, Granny, who cared for Lutie after her mother died, taught the young Lutie many old time (possibly African) ways of thinking and sensing (pp. 15–16). Granny provided security to Lutie (p. 404), morality (pp. 80–81), and wisdom. But Granny died when Lutie was a young adult, and then Lutie no longer had the possibility of receiving advice and help from Granny, and Lutie missed that.

> Granny would have told her what to do if she had lived. (Petry, *The Street*, p. 76)

And this quote is not simply a wistful longing, since Lutie gets into a number of situations where wise and knowledgeable advice might have saved her from difficult and even tragic circumstances.

Surrogates haunted by the fate of the child's parent

Some parent surrogates in the novels are concerned that a child will eventually have the same problems as the parent who could not take care of the child.

> The grandmother took Helene away from the soft lights and flowered carpets of the [brothel] and raised her under the dolesome eyes of a multicolored Virgin Mary, counseling her to be constantly on guard for any sign of her mother's wild blood. (Morrison, *Sula*, p. 17)

This kind of surrogate parenting might well be uncomfortably controlling, plus it is possible that it could have the unintended consequence of pushing the growing child in the very direction the parent fears the child will go.

Surrogates who do not care or who cannot be counted on

In the novels, some children are cared for by surrogates who cannot or will not nurture them well. A neighbor might reach out to a child who is cared for badly by surrogates, but that does not solve the basic problem.

> Aunt Hager ... told Sandy to ask Jimmy Lane in to dinner because, since his mother died, he wasn't faring so well and the people he was staying with didn't care much about him. (Hughes, *Not Without Laughter*, p. 137)

Some children love and appreciate their surrogate caregivers. But in retrospect, as adults, they could feel that the way they were treated was not good.

> Digging around inside of herself ... she found that she had no interest in that seldom-seen mother at all. She hated her grandmother and had hidden it from herself all these years under a cloak of pity ... She hated the old woman who had twisted her so in the name of love. (Hurston, *Their Eyes Were Watching God*, p. 89)

As was said earlier in this chapter, one part of the twisting that Janie experienced was being pushed into marriage before she was ready, and pushed into marrying a man who was not good for her.

Stepfathers who are not good to the child

In some novels, racism leads to a child's father being killed. If the mother subsequently partners with another man, that man might be a thoroughly good and present father, but sometimes he is not. In Alice Walker's *The Color Purple*, the lynching of the father of Celie and Nettie is kept a secret from them for many years, so they think the man married to their mother is their biological father. Unfortunately, he is a horrible replacement for the father who was lynched, because he makes frequent sexual advances toward the two girls, and fathers two children by Celie. The implication in the novel is that if the biological father had not been lynched, the daughters of the murdered man would have grown up without being tormented by sexual abuse and incest. Their lives would have been free of crushing terror, extreme emotional pain, and the grimness of sexual abuse.

In James Baldwin's *Go Tell It on the Mountain*, Richard's suicide after being unjustly jailed and being beaten and tormented by racist white police has an enormous impact on John, the child he and Elizabeth conceived together. Years after Richard's suicide, Elizabeth marries Gabriel. Gabriel makes a commitment to Elizabeth to be a father to John, but he is never an accepting and loving father. Instead, he is abusive and judgmental, and John grows up hating Gabriel. It seems that had Richard not been driven to suicide by brutal and unjust experiences with white police officers and jailers, John would have had a much more accepting and loving father in Richard than he had in Gabriel.

In Defense of Single and Surrogate Parents

Grandparents or other surrogates raising children may do a wonderful job. The idea that children should be raised by her or his birth parents comes out of a particular culture and set of values. It is inappropriate to assume that just because a child is not being raised by birth parents that something is wrong or the child is disadvantaged. Similarly, the value that says that a child being raised by a single parent is disadvantaged or that it would be better to be raised by two parents rather than one also comes out of a particular culture. There is nothing inherently wrong with a child being raised by a single parent. I think there is validity and insight to novels that depict the ways that racism forces children into situations where they are raised by single parents or surrogates, and that a novelist may depict that as an unfortunate and undesired outcome of a racist system makes perfect sense. But there also is validity and insight in depicting a child's experience of single parenting or surrogate parenting as healthy, beneficial, loving and totally appropriate. Also, as was discussed in Chapter 1, even though some people might see a child raised by grandparents, aunts, or other surrogates as somehow having lost her or his family, the child, the surrogates, and the community may not see things that way. Instead they may think of the child as a member of the grandparental family, the aunt's family or other families just as much as a member of her or his birth family. Arguably people are usually members of multiple social entities that could be labeled "family," so moving from one of one's families to another, one is still in one's family.

Children Without Family

In a few novels, the operations of the racial system that undermines families can lead to children being on their own, without family.

> 'My mama died when I was born. And my daddy, he weren't nowhere to be found. Ain't nobody never took care of me. I just moved from one place to another. When one set of folks got tired of me they sent me down the line.' (Baldwin, *Go Tell It on the Mountain*, p. 196)

> 'You know they ain't even got an orphanage in Jacksonville where colored babies can go? They have to put 'em in jail. I tell people … I was *raised* in jail …'
> 'I didn't know you were an orphan.'
> 'Well, not a regular orphan. I had people and all, but my mama died and nobody would take me in.' (Morrison, *The Song of Solomon*, p. 109)

Children without family must live and survive despite their inexperience, vulnerability, and limited resources. In the novels, some manage to grow up and do well enough. Then there are stories, like that in the quote that follows, that highlight how crucial family is for children and how damaging racism can be to children when it robs them of relationship with any kind of parental figure.

> The Wile Child was a young girl who had managed to live without parents, relatives or friends for all of her thirteen years … [She] was seen going through garbage cans and dragging off pieces of discarded furniture, her ashy black arms straining at the task. When a neighbor came out of her house to speak to her, Wile Chile bolted, not to be seen again for … weeks. (Walker, *Meridian*, p. 23)

In Toni Morrison's *Song of Solomon*, after their father is murdered by white neighbors, the second Macon Dead and his sister Pilate are hidden and cared for by the African American maid to the white family that murdered their father.

> After the first Macon Dead died, his children, a twelve-year-old Pilate and a sixteen-year-old Macon Dead, found themselves homeless. Bewildered and grieving, they went to the house of the closest colored person they knew: Circe, the midwife who had delivered them both and who was there when their mother died and when Pilate was named. She worked in a large house—a mansion— …
> for a family of what was then called gentlemen farmers. The orphans called to Circe from the vegetable garden early in the morning … Circe told them to stay

with her until they could all figure out what to do, someplace for them to go. She hid them in that house ... Circe would bring them food, water to wash in, and she would empty their slop jar ... Macon and Pilate stayed there two weeks. (Morrison, *The Song of Solomon*, pp. 166–7)

The children are not safe in that hiding place, so they leave and soon go their separate ways, each trying to get along without family help. They make it to adulthood, and by some standards they each do well as adults, but then tragic things happen in the lives of both of them, and one can wonder if their father had not been murdered by white neighbors and them thrown on their own, whether any of these tragic things would have happened.

Chapter 11

Conceptualizing

The 27 novels provide many accounts of racism coming home to African American families, often in ways that make family life very difficult. That racism has such a powerful effect on families in the novels does not mean that the families are passive in the face of racism. In fact the novels offer many accounts of families who find ways to fend off the worst that might happen or that make the best of their situation. One can see the family coping with the challenges, constraints, and horrible difficulties, and that coping can bring family members to places of love, wisdom, caring, mutual understanding, and mutual support. Consider, for example, the supportive conversations of Sandy's household in Langston's Hughes' *Not Without Laughter*. But even though family members do what they can to make the best of the situation, the impact of racism on African American families can be very negative. For example, racism leads to dreadful things happening to Lutie and her family in Ann Petry's *The Street* and to Mariah, Jacob, and their family in Sara E. Wright's *This Child's Gonna Live*.

Conceptualizing African American Families in the Racial System

The Value of Making "Family" the Focus

We have a vast accumulation of information on the harm to individual African Americans of racist discrimination, limitations, and injustices. Most national statistics that document racism are about (or rooted in) the experiences of individuals. But the discrimination, unfairness, injustice, and limitations often have family impacts. The person receiving poor medical attention has a family that carries extra burdens because of the poor medical care. The person who is profiled by the police has a family who might be profoundly affected by that profiling.

Government agencies and social scientists provide some data about African American families—particularly on family housing and family wealth. And that is reflected in the novels, where quite a few families struggle with sub-standard housing and have little financial wealth. But the novels provide a view of the influence of racism that I think is not as strongly represented in government data or the academic literature as it should be. If we want to understand the effects of racism, we need to have family data, family narratives, and views of family dynamics over time.

There are many paths by which racism aimed at one family member can spread to the family. One story line in that regard is about how racism directed at one family member includes sanctions that affect others in the person's family. For example, in Ernest J. *Gaines' The Autobiography of Miss Jane Pittman,* racist attempts to stop Miss Jane Pittman's foster son Ned from leading civil rights demonstrations result in her being evicted because of his participation in a civil rights demonstration.

Another story line is that some limitations on an individual affect the individual in ways that make the limitation have an impact on others in the family. For example, when Lutie in Ann Petry's *The Street* must work as a domestic for a white family living far away because there is no work that pays as well available to her close to home, that work deprives her son and husband of the work she would have done in their shared household and of her love, and it keeps her away from her husband so much that he turns to another woman. And later, when she is a single parent, her economic difficulties and preoccupation with those difficulties affect her parenting in ways that lead to great trouble for her and her son.

Another path by which racist harm to an individual becomes a family matter is that racism that diminishes the self of a person can come to affect the person's family. For example, as is discussed in Chapter 5, in Toni Morrison's *Sula* a humiliating interaction of an African American woman with a white person in the presence of her child affects the child's sense of self and her view of her mother in ways that are long-lasting and change the mother-child relationship. Similarly, individual pain can come home in ways that hurt or sadden other family members. Consider, for example, the impact on his daughter and wife of the pain of the father in Paule Marshall's *Brown Girl, Brownstones* when whites refuse to hire him. When the father/husband is denied a job in a situation where it seems that the job denial is based on racism, his misery and efforts to cope have an enormous influence on the whole family. The person who has experienced racism may have an emotional reaction to the racism (for example, rage or sorrow) that affects the family. Perhaps the individual does something in reaction to the racist event (for example, giving up on applying for jobs or turning to alcohol) that has long-term effects on the family. Perhaps the racism changes how the individual is in relationship to family members—for example, becoming needy or less communicative.

Theoretically it makes sense that the harm done to one family member can affect others in the family. Social science research on families has shown in many ways that an individual's experience may play out in ways that impact the person's family. For example, a person's mood resulting from what happened at work may affect the person's involvement in household tasks and how positive or negative the person is in interaction with a marital partner (Crouter, Perry-Jenkins, Huston, and Crawford, 1989). Similarly, more negative workdays may lead to anger or withdrawal in marital interactions (Schulz, Cowan, Pape Cowan, and Brennan, 2004).

Still another path by which racism targeting one family member may affect the entire family is that an individual experience of racism may come home to the family through the stories the person tells (e.g. Feagin and

McKinney, 2003, pp. 171–3; Rosenblatt and Wallace, 2005a, 2005b; St. Jean and Feagin, 1998). And as is illustrated in Chapter 8 these stories teach family members things, affect them emotionally, offer views of reality that may guide them, and otherwise affect them.

On the other hand, in the novels some diminishments of individuals draw family members closer together. For example, as is discussed in Chapter 5, sometimes the racist diminishment of one family member helps that person to understand another family member's struggles with racist diminishment. More generally, because family members share an environment of racism they may be able to feel empathy, sympathy, and understanding when one of them is wounded by racism.

However, family members do not necessarily pull together when one of them is diminished by racism. As is discussed in Chapter 8, there can be differences among family members about how to deal with diminishments, and those differences can create unpleasant family conflict. Related to this, as is discussed in Chapter 7, the diminishments of racism also are linked in the novels to issues in African American families of skin color and other physical features. Issues of so-called colorism can create discomfort in family relationships about who a person partners with, how other family members feel about a family member, and the future family members anticipate for a child based on the child's physical features.

When Poverty Stemming from Racism Harms the Family

The impact of poverty and racist processes intended to keep African Americans impoverished are described throughout this book but particularly in chapters 6 and 10. In poverty parents may work long, extremely hard hours to bring in a bare minimum of income, with the long hours and hard work depriving children of parental time and energy. Economic deprivation can lead to interpersonal difficulties in the family—unpleasant arguments over scarce resources, people too tired, hungry, or stressed to be good at resolving disagreements, people whose desperation can turn simple differences of opinion into raging conflict. In poverty, family members may sympathize, support, and give generously to one another, but they may also be too depleted to have much to give, or they may feel too much shame (for example, about their inability to bring in enough income) to be able to provide emotional support to other family members. At the extreme, poverty and hunger can narrow the focus of family members so that family relationships lack some of the playfulness, conversation, and other positive features they ideally should have.

Poverty is not only about food, housing and the basics of everyday life. As described particularly in Chapter 3, it can also be about getting a fair deal in the criminal justice system. In several novels, family members work desperately to raise funds to provide legal defense for a family member who has been arrested and imprisoned (often for a crime the person has not committed).

Effect of Racist Violence and Threats of Violence on Families

Families in some novels struggle to deal with the consequences of a racist beating or murder. As described particularly in chapters 5 and 8, sometimes the struggle is central to family life. And sometimes the violence is linked to racist efforts to deprive a family of their property or to run them out of town. The threat of violence is used by whites in some novels to stifle opposition to the racial system, and sometimes whites deliberately let family members know of a threat to a specific family member, using family anxiety about the person in danger to try to control him or her. From another perspective, the values of the white racist system may at times seem to become part of the implicit rule system of African American families. So, for example, white anger and bullying may create a template for anger and bullying interactions in an African American family. Similarly patterns of humiliation in white relationships with African Americans may lead to patterns of or interaction in African American families that mimic the racist patterns of humiliation.

Effects of Racist Sexual Assault and Sexual Exploitation on Families

As described particularly in chapters 4 and 10, racist sexual assault and exploitation of African American women can come home to families. An assault can affect a woman and those close to her for a lifetime. It can do terrible harm to sexuality in her marriage. It can lead to bad things happening to her immediate family if they protest or seek redress. It can spread shame, humiliation, and rage among the members of her family, and sometimes it leads to a family member using alcohol to deaden the personal pain or to another family member's denial that the assault happened. And denial of the assaulted woman's reality can push her away from her family.

A racial system that allows white men free sexual access to African American women, including rape without penalty, can lead to light-skinned babies being born, and the point is made in several of the novels that the wide range of skin color in African American families and communities is a record of sexual assault and exploitation by white men of African American women (see Chapter 7).

Effects of Legal System Racism on Families

Some novels speak to how the police and courts support the system of white racial advantage (see particularly chapters 3 and 6). The legal enforcement of racism may involve beating or even murder by the police. The police and the justice system may target a particular family member, for example, someone who was not deferential enough to white people or who protested a racial injustice, but the consequences of the enforcement may be great for every family member. There is anxiety and worry in a family about a member who is incarcerated and loss to them of companionship, emotional support, labor, and earnings of the family member.

There may also be threats to them from the police, and there can be extreme financial difficulty in covering the costs of a legal defense. The consequences of police brutality and arbitrary arrest may play out in a family for years as family members deal with the attendant financial, emotional, and relationship losses.

Effects of Job Denial and Menial Jobs on Families

In some novels, the racial system denies a man a job and keeps him jobless or only allows him a job that is so beneath him and belittling that he must quit, and then he is jobless (see particularly chapters 3 and 5). In some novels, joblessness or job denial leads a man to turn to a woman for tenderness and support, for distraction, and for an opportunity to enact an adult male role somewhere in his life by doing so in relationship to her. His neediness could be attractive to her and give her a sense of being useful, but it might also mean that some of her needs are not met. His not having work increases the economic burden on her to bring in income. And if her labors mean that she is separated from him for long periods of time, he might turn to another woman, and that and the inflexibilities and deprivations of their poverty might lead to an end to the couple's relationship. Plus, job denial and joblessness may change a man in ways that make him less than who he could have been in a couple's relationship.

Effects of the Racial System on Parenting

African American parents often do things to prepare their children to cope with racism (for example, Banks-Wallace and Parks 2001; Hughes and Chen, 1997). Although recent research shows that there are African Americans who say they have had no experiences of racism in the past year (Riina and McHale, 2010), judging by the novels (as summarized particularly in Chapter 9), children will experience racism and they will also know about it from observing adult experiences or hearing adults talk about their experiences. In the novels that address parenting, to deal with racism some parents shelter younger children from knowledge of racism but are less likely to hold back with older children. As is described in Chapter 9, parents may try to help a child to cope with racism by trying to strengthen the child's self-esteem, teaching the child to beware of white people, and teaching the child to understand the etiquette racism imposes on African Americans in encounters with white people. A few novels describe instances of family members teaching children about African American history and culture as a way to bolster the child in dealing with racism. A few novels illustrate the importance of learning communal values in the family, including the value of joining with other African Americans and of being a force for good among African Americans. There are parents in a few novels who try to teach children to be like white people or like what white people seem to want them to be, but other parents take the opposite approach, discouraging children from being like white people or like what white people seem to want them to be.

Although many novels include examples of good, caring, loving parenting (see Chapter 9), some novels tell how the racial system undermines parenting (see especially Chapter 10). Parents may struggle so hard to make a go of it financially and they may be so undermined in terms of self-esteem by racism that they cannot parent effectively. Some parents, men especially, move far away from their family to find a job, a decent-paying job, or what they hope will be a better life. Thus, children in a number of novels are raised by a single mother or someone other than a parent. Some parents in the novels did not receive adequate parenting when they were children, and so they do not know how to parent well. At the extreme, that can lead a parent to do terrible things to a child—for example, Cholly's rape of Pecola in Toni Morrison's *The Bluest Eye*.

Some children are orphaned or in some other way lose both their parents and are raised by surrogates, most often a grandmother (see Chapter 10). Surrogates may be loving and competent. But in some novels, there is considerable cost to being parented by a surrogate. For example, an elderly grandmother who is raising a child may become frail or die when the child is not ready to be launched. In a few novels, a child reaches a point where she or he has no parent and no parental surrogate and even though ill-prepared is on her or his own in finding sustenance, housing, and safety.

Effects of the Racial System on Family Conversation

In some novels, the racial system is a topic of family conversation (see particularly Chapter 8). The words said may be about a specific incident or experience, but they may also extend to the pervasiveness and general harmfulness of the racial system—for example, economic oppression, injustice, denial of rights, white bullying, white stereotyping, or the role of the police in maintaining the racial system. Characters in some novels talk about how white people seem less aware of the system than African Americans are and about the power of white greed and need for status and dominance in relationship to African Americans.

Most of the novels are in some ways about African American families enduring and surviving the racial system, and the family is often important in helping individual family members to deal with racism. The family may be a haven to come home to after the abrasions and struggle with the racial system (see particularly Chapter 8 and the section later in this chapter on families as havens). Some African Americans in the novels talk with family members about dealing with and resisting the oppression of the racial system. As part of that some share stories of ancestors enduring and surviving the racial system and about family members being strong. Some talk about stories in scripture, religious ideals, and racial uplift literature in ways that help them to endure and survive. A few struggle with how God can allow the terrors, deprivations, and diminishments of the racial system or what the value is of Christianity when Jesus is often depicted as white and whites are often their oppressors. Some characters in the novels talk with family members about learning to live with oppression, and sometimes that conversation seems to make life easier. And quite a few turn to each other for support and understanding in dealing with racism.

A Single Racist Event Can Profoundly Affect a Family

In the racial system of the United States, the experience of racism is an everyday occurrence for many African Americans. Workplace racism, racism in schools, discrimination in hiring, racial slurs, racist assumptions whites make about one, police profiling, medical racism, residential segregation, and the confusing ambiguities of the new (covert) racism can be part of everyday life. Thus, perhaps often the racism that comes home to an African American family has to do with the cumulative, ongoing burden of racism experienced day after day. But in six of the 27 novels, a single racist event that happens to a main character plays out in powerful ways in the person's family. Similarly, in the literature on slavery, Laurie and Neimeyer (2010) showed that many former Black slaves experienced a single event (a whipping, a rape, a sale of a relative) that profoundly affected them and their family for a lifetime. In more recent times, Rosenblatt and Wallace (2005b) found that the some narratives of bereaved African Americans about deceased loved ones were about single events that profoundly affected the life of the loved one and the entire family—for example, a stepfather in the military who challenged an officer's racist remarks and a few days later was assigned to extremely dangerous duty that profoundly changed his life and the lives of his family members.

But then it can be seen in some of the novels that to say that a single racist event profoundly affected a family involves a selective construction by the characters in the novels in the sense that the single event is surrounded by a web of racism. That web underlies, precedes, accompanies, and follows the specific event, so the apparent impact of the event is likely to be at least partly a result of that history and context, even if the characters in the novel do not seem to see it that way. Take, for example, two related events in Toni Morrison's *Song of Solomon*, whites cheating the first Macon Dead out of his farm and then murdering him. In the time and place in which Morrison placed the first Macon Dead, African Americans typically were not literate and hence could be tricked into signing legal documents they could not read. Also, in that time and place, African Americans had no standing in the legal system, so whites had entitlement to take land from African Americans by trickery and force and to get away with that. Whites even had the freedom to get away with murdering African Americans. In the phenomenology of the central characters in *Song of Solomon*, the single racist event of Macon Dead being cheated and then the single racist event of his murder stand out as having long-term family impact. However, one can say that the cheating and the murder occurred in a racist context with many elements, including racism-imposed illiteracy for African Americans and a lack of legal protection for them. As Morrison told the story, these contextual elements were present and are alluded to by one character or another, but it was the two very specific events, the cheating and the murder, that were central realities to the son of the murdered man and had an enormous impact on him and eventually on his family. So a comprehensive understanding of how racism comes home to African American families must be attentive to the power of single racist events, even though one can imagine ways that the surrounding racist system is entangled in those events.

Family as Haven from Racism

Family can be a haven for an African American (e.g. Feagin, 2006, p. 277; Feagin and Sikes, 1994, pp. 224–6; LaGrone, 2009), a place of peacefulness, safety, and renewal. Family members can help heal the wounds or find ways to reduce the harm that racism causes, and families can stop some aspects of racism at the door in that once one enters into the family space, the insults, white stares, and the like are excluded.

However, in the novels, family is not always a haven (LaGrone, 2009), because family members can be too needy, wounded, or depleted to help one another or because there are interpersonal or personal difficulties that make the home a battleground or a lonely place rather than a haven. In fact, in some novels, there is the message in the words said by a character that family members must stop harming one another. In some novels the issue of harm within the family is a tangle of alcoholism and drug use, malice, male violence and threats of violence, and interpersonal nastiness that potentially attacks and undermines the self-esteem of others. The harm that family members cause may be understood to arise out of the damage caused by racism, but characters in some novels are clear that that does not excuse the harm.

> All three of us, me and Lucy and Brother in that dope mess … You … wonder a second what I got to be feeling good about but that thought's gone before it gets hold to you and … you know you're feeling good … better than you ever thought you would … It was better than being nothing. World was a hurting trick and being high was being out the world … Who ever said you supposed to just stand still and suffer? … Being high was good. Bad part was you couldn't stay high. Bad part you still had to deal with that asskicking world to get high. You had to hurt people. Knew you hurting them just by being what you were. Stealing, turning tricks, lying. Taking from your family, messing over the people think they your friends. (Wideman, *Sent for You Yesterday*, pp. 152–4)

The hurting, taking from, and messing over referred to in this quote might be understood as ordinary family interaction processes. But one might wonder whether the cruelty, exploitation, disrespect, victimizing, etc. are only present in the family life or only take the form they have because of the pain, limitations, and examples of the racist system. That is what Guzzio (2011, pp. 131–2) seems to assert about the interactions of the characters in Wideman's book. But if Wideman thought that way he did not say it explicitly in the novel, and other authors did not necessarily say that either about instances of family members doing harm to family members in their novels. To take another example, in James Baldwin's *If Beale Street Could Talk*, Fonny's mother, Mrs. Hunt, says terrible things about Fonny and terrible things to Tish about her carrying Fonny's baby. One can imagine that the harsh judgments and the distancing that Mrs. Hunt engages in have their roots in the terrible things that the racial system has done to her. But Baldwin says nothing that warrants that view. Mrs. Hunt just comes across as a very nasty and difficult person. But then, perhaps the issue of whether racism is a source or the source of a family member's nastiness is irrelevant if one has to deal with the person's nastiness. No matter the origins, one must find ways to cope with it.

The novels also offer a number of examples of family being good for some people to come home to after being bruised by racism. For example, in Langston Hughes' *Not Without Laughter*, Sandy (returning from experiences of racism at school and in the community) and his mother (returning from her bruising job as a domestic worker for a white family) both find haven at home. In John Edgar Wideman's *Sent for You Yesterday*, the members of the French and the Tate families often find a haven at home with other family members from the bruising, racist world. In Ann Petry's *The Street*, Lutie finds in her son Bub the home and haven to which she can return each night.

An example of soothing the wounds of racism comes from the following brief interaction in which a young woman who has been wounded by racist insults comes home to her lover. At first she retains her pain, but he offers an awareness that leads to her soothing.

> Not knowing how to tell him, she tried to dismiss it with a shrug. His eyes narrowed shrewdly. 'What is it—somebody said something?' he asked sharply. 'One of those white people insulted you?' (Marshall, *Brown Girl, Brownstones*, p. 289)

And he was right. And the support coming from his awareness of the racial system and his understanding of her pain were helpful.

Gender, Age, Social Class, and Other Diversities

In the analyses in this book of how racism comes home to families, there are at places clear differences among family members by gender and age, and there are clearly differences across (and sometimes within) families in terms of social class as measured by economic well-being. (The novels do not seem to say anything explicit about sexual orientation, though one can see sexual orientation between the lines in James Baldwin's *Go Tell It on the Mountain*.)

In the novels, racism often impacts women and men differently, and those differences are part of what comes home to families. Most of the examples of police brutality and racism in the criminal justice system are about the targeting of African American men. In the novels, men are more likely than women to be jobless, are the only family members who become involved in extramarital sexual relationships, and are more likely to leave home in search of work. Women are the only people in the novels who are sexually assaulted by whites, more or less forced into concubinage with whites, or forced to flee from the sexual aggression of whites. Women are more likely than men to have work, but it is often work as domestics—maid word, caring for white children, doing laundry for whites. The income women receive from this kind of work is minimal, and the work often is described as physically and psychologically difficult as well as very time consuming. The work exposes some women to white male sexual advances. The work also gives women knowledge about white people, and in one novel that knowledge comes home in ways that make trouble in the family by creating unachievable aspirations. Also, with racism pushing many family members, especially men, out of the house, if someone has sole responsibility for children it is a woman—most often a mother.

In the novels, family elders may have wisdom and warnings to offer about racism. They also may have been so worn down by racism that they have little to offer younger family members. And some of their wisdom might be resisted by younger family members, particularly a religion-based acceptance of oppressive situations, with the hope of having a joyful eternity in a heaven free from racism.

In the novels, children are often the focus of family efforts to defend against racism. The children, when younger, may be kept innocent about racism, but as they get older, their struggles to understand racism and to find their way in a racist society can be central concerns to the children and sometimes to the adults around them.

In the novels, many families are not well-off, but in more recent novels, and even in some novels set in the relatively distant past, there are African American families who are comparatively well-off economically, with a home and financial resources. Being relatively well-off does not guarantee safety from racism, but it either helps to insulate a family from racism or is a symptom of being in a social and geographic location where African American families have some insulation from racism. So racism may come home less often, or in less obvious ways, to African American families who are better-off economically.

In the novels, people who are economically better-off are often depicted as having family members who are not well-off. The well-off family members may provide economic resources for the less well-off families, but it is not so simple. Less well-off family members may have resources of wisdom and love that the more well-off family members need, desire, and gain from, as in Gloria Naylor's *Mama Day*. And the more well-off family members may use their resources in ways that undermine the family life of the less well-off family members, as in Dorothy West's *The Living Is Easy*.

A comprehensive story of how racism comes home to families must be sensitive to diversity across and within African American families. In the novels there are substantial gender, age, and class differences in relationship to racism, and there are also regional (south versus north) and era (pre-civil rights era versus civil rights era versus more recent times) differences.

Family Systems Theory Helps to Illuminate the Effect of Racism

Family systems theory has been a useful tool in illuminating what happens in the novels to African American families. One example of that usefulness is the observation in Chapter 3 about the value of relatively open family boundaries when the racial system pulls a crucial player out of the family (the example given was of Sofia in Alice Walker's *The Color Purple*). Or to take an example from Chapter 4, linked to a discussion of Langston Hughes' novel *Not Without Laughter*, a person who is important to a family system does not have to be physically present to continue to be a strong force in what goes on in the family.

The analyses in this book show that from a systems theory perspective the oppressive larger system—what Bronfenbrenner (1979) would have called the exosystem—can have a profound effect on African American family systems by directly doing harm to families, by harming an individual family member in ways that affect the whole family, and by greatly limiting the options available to families. The racial system can even undermine family system rules. For example, as is described in Chapter 5, white-imposed poverty undermined the marital rule system in Ann Petry's *The Street* in ways that led to Lutie and her husband breaking up. Related to that, it was observed in Chapter 7 that it is difficult for families in an oppressive system to resist incorporating rules imposed by the oppressive system, which is presumably the key reason why colorism rules, values, and ideals operate in a number of African American families and communities in the novels. Or to take another example, the power of the racial system is such that it can override very strong African American community rules such as working together to deal with racism. The most obvious example of that is from Ernest J. Gaines novel, *In My Father's House*, when the white police chief used a father's concern about his son to undermine the father's leadership of resistance to oppressive practices by a white store owner.

From a systems theory perspective, another kind of harm created by the racial system is that it forces African American families in many of the novels to do much to adapt to the racial system. As Bateson (1979) pointed out, every adaptation can also be a mal-adaptation. For example, limiting the family's economic creativity and success in order not to threaten whites and invite their retaliation is a limitation on the family's ability to adapt economically to the demands of making a living. And then, among other examples that can be linked to Bateson's thinking, one can read Ann Petry's *The Street* (see particularly the discussion in Chapter 4) as a story of the downward spiral of Lutie and her family as each adaptation to their difficulties creates new problems that call for new adaptations that create new problems and so on to disaster.

Critical Race Theory

Looking at the novels through the lenses provided by critical race theory (Delgado and Stafancic, 2001; see Burton, Bonilla-Silva, Ray, Buckelew, and Hordge Freeman, 2010, for an overview of critical race theories as applied to families and family research) one can see the novels as collectively in accord with the critical race theory idea that race is a central, institutionalized organizing concept in society, pervading all aspects of life. This is so even as racism changes its forms and expressions, with the new racism (Bonilla-Silva, 2010) providing more covert, masked, and deniable (by those who perpetrate it and gain from it) processes for benefiting whites at the expense of African Americans. One can see that many of the interactions of African American characters in the novels with whites are at one level about white maintenance of and defense of the privilege, power, and entitlements that come to whites from the racial system. Thus, the heart of the racial system is about creating, maintaining, and insuring the relative advantage for whites and relative disadvantage for African Americans. One can then see, from the novels, that the racial system is built on an extensive history of white dominance but is not locked into the forms of the past. It is constantly being revised. From a critical race theory perspective, one can also see that among the ways that racism affects African Americans is that colorism, discrimination based on color and other racial features, is part of the racial system, and is so powerful that its standards may even operate within African American families.

The novels and the analyses of them in this book offer telling perspectives on critical race theory. Critical race theory is rooted in many lines of thought and the experiences of diverse people (Delgado and Stefancic, 2001; Zamudio, Russell, Rios, and Bridgeman, 2011, p. 7). But a case can be made that it was originally codified with leadership by progressive legal scholars, many of them African American, who were concerned about the slow and sometimes harmful processes by which the legal system moved toward providing justice and fairness to those who are marginalized in the racial system (Delgado and Stefancic, 2001; Mirza, 1999; Olmsted, 1998). Critical race theory was developed in part as a device for drawing legal scholars, jurists, and academics, most of whom were white, into greater awareness and understanding of the racial system, particularly as it pertains to law-making, the law, and the courts. Over time, the theory became incorporated into discussions of institutionalized racism in other areas, such as education. But in many novels analyzed in this book characters offer what are arguably critical race theory ideas, and that includes novels written long before critical race theory was codified. Hence, one can see critical race theory as representing what had long been widely understood and talked about in African American families and communities (Feagin, 2006, pp. 277–8; Zamudio, Russell, Rios, and Bridgeman, 2011, p. 147); the unfairness of the racial system, the apparent obliviousness of many whites to the unfairness, the ideology that at times is offered by whites to justify the unfairness of the racial system, and the specific ways in which the system's unfairness has played out in such areas as the criminal justice system and education. Being oppressed and often in danger made people astute observers of the racial system. And the astute analyses resembling critical race theory that could be found in African American communities and families can be found in the novels and can even be found in writings going back a century or more ago by the great African American thinker W.E.B. DuBois (Rashid, 2011).

Using Novels in Social Science Research

In Chapter 1 a case was made for using novels in social research, citing precedents from the sociology of literature and elsewhere in the social sciences. Arguments based on a substantial literature on the value of fiction as a source of ideas and data in the social sciences were marshaled as were ideas about the blurry boundary between fiction and social science. My hope is that the accounts in this book drawn from 27 African American-authored novels and the discussions based on those accounts will have strengthened the case that novels are a legitimate source of ideas and data. And my hope is also that this book has helped to codify what is in the novels about the impact of racism on African American families.

This book makes the case that if there is trouble in African American families, if there is poverty, if husbands leave wives and parents leave children, if family members are unemployed or are employed at menial, low-paying jobs, if there is trouble with the legal system, and so on, it is not as though these troubles arise spontaneously from the families. In contrast to writings that seem to blame African American families for their troubles, writings in which the Moynihan report received the most attention (Moynihan, 1965), the novels offer many instances in which an African American family's troubles stem from the operations of the racial system.

An important measure of a book like this is whether we can build on what is reported in it with further research. Can we add to the documentation and extend the analyses in this book in deeper and broader ways? Can we move research into domains where what is revealed is insightful and useful by the standards of social scientists and other readers? An obvious first step is new research to tap into the experiences and perspectives of multiple members of African American families about how racism might have come home to their family. Take, for example, how what is experienced as racist job denial impacts a family. With data from multiple family members across many families we might be able to pick up more of the family complexities, including the diversity and variability of support, economic anxiety, anger, and neediness among family members that arise from the job denial. Also, different family members may see, understand, and experience the job denial and much connected to it differently, and those differences could set off challenging family dynamics as family members deal with their differences. Further, across families there may be substantial differences, depending, for example, on their economic situation, variations in the availability of alternative good jobs, how much racism has previously injured the family member denied the job, and how much the family talks about difficult experiences.

Another kind of work to be done is conversation study. It could be quite useful and illuminating to know how the racial system is reflected, if it is, in African American family conversations. Included in that is the question of how much racism becomes a conversation burden in the family in the sense both of taking up conversation time that might otherwise be devoted to other matters and of leading to abrasive interactions. And if there is conversation about racism, what are the up-sides if any (for example, in terms of finding paths to a better life, feeling more connected, learning more about each other, and developing shared understandings of the ways that their difficulties are due to racism and not to family member failings)? How does conversation about racism contribute to developing family system scaffolding, such as clear roles, agreements, shared goals, and shared narratives? And African American family conversations about white people and racism would be prime locations for exploring how realities are talked into existence and clarity through conversation.

It also could be valuable to understand how the family impacts of racism develop over time and over repeated experiences with racism. To take one example, the novels offer very significant ideas about how the recurrent blows of racism prior to and following an arrest on trumped-up charges, help to weigh down a couple or family. The public discourse about police profiling and racial disparities in arrests and sentences for, say, drug possession, is about individual rights and perhaps implicitly about the association of race with crime. But family research, building on ideas in this book about how much harm the profiling and racial disparities in arrests and sentences cause to family, may extend the public discourse in useful ways.

This book also suggests that there is more to be learned about the impact on families of recurrent experiences of racism. How might recurrent experiences lead to a shared vocabulary and set of narratives, to a progressively greater avoidance of talking about what is so toxic, to an easy and quick understanding of one another, to a pattern of mutually reinforced anger, depression, or sorrow, or to myriad other possibilities? Intensive interviewing, perhaps with a longitudinal element, could be wonderfully helpful, but there are other sources of data available that could be helpful. For example, there are autobiographies and biographies with considerable information about experiences of racism over time. One biography that is particularly rich not only about multiple experiences of racism over time but also on the experiences of multiple family members (and friends) is Rampersad's (1997) biography of Jackie Robinson, the first African American to break the modern color line in organized baseball. And for reasons that say much about the pervasiveness of racism, many African American autobiographies and memoirs contain rich material on multiple experiences of racism and often on parent socialization to deal with childhood experiences of racism (for example,

Bray, 1998; Cobbs, 2005; Hayre, 1997). There is much more that may be learned about the impact of racism on African American families. The topic is of vital importance. And the knowledge resources yet to be tapped are diverse.

Appendix

The Novels

Baldwin, James (1963). *Go Tell It on the Mountain*. New York: Dell. (First copyright by James Baldwin, 1952. First hardcover edition by Doubleday, 1963. The edition I used was from Bantam Dell, New York, first printed in 1980.)

Baldwin, James (1974). *If Beale Street Could Talk*. New York: Dial Press. (The edition I used was from Vintage Books, Random House, New York, 2006.)

Brooks, Gwendolyn (1953). *Maud Martha*. New York: Harper & Row. (The edition I used was from Third World Press, Chicago, 1993.)

Campbell, Bebe Moore (1992). *Your Blues Ain't Like Mine*. New York: Putnam's. (The edition I used was from One World, a division of Random House, New York, 2007.)

Gaines, Ernest J. (1971). *The Autobiography of Miss Jane Pittman*. New York: Dial Press. (The edition I used was from Bantam, New York, 1972.)

Gaines, Ernest J. (1978). *In My Father's House*. New York: Knopf. (The edition I used was from Vintage Books, Random House, New York, 1992.)

Golden, Marita (1989). *Long Distance Life*. New York: Doubleday. (The edition I used was the first trade paperback edition, Doubleday, New York, 2006.)

Hughes, Langston (1930). *Not Without Laughter*. New York: Knopf. (The edition I used was the first Scribners paperback edition, Simon & Schuster, New York, 1995.)

Hunter, Kristin (1964). *God Bless the Child*. New York: Scribner. (The edition I used was from Howard University Press, Washington, DC, 1987.)

Hurston, Zora Neale (1937). *Their Eyes Were Watching God*. New York: Lippincott. (The edition I used was from HarperCollins, Harper Perennial Modern Classics, New York, 2006.)

Killens, John Oliver (1971). *The Cotillion or, One Good Bull Is Half the Herd*. New York: Trident. (The edition I used was from Coffee House Press, Minneapolis, MN, 2002.)

Marshall, Paule (1959). *Brown Girl, Brownstones*. New York: Random House. (The edition I used was the 2nd Feminist Press Edition, City University of New York, New York, 2006.)

McFadden, Bernice L. (2001). *The Warmest December*. New York: Dutton. (The edition I used was the first Plume printing, New York, 2002.)

McFadden, Bernice L. (2006). *Nowhere Is a Place*. New York: Dutton.

McMillan, Terry (2001). *A Day Late and a Dollar Short*. New York: New American Library.

Morrison, Toni (1970). *The Bluest Eye*. New York: Holt Rinehart and Winston. (The edition I used was from Washington Square Press, Pocket Books, New York, 1972.)

Morrison, Toni (1973). *Sula*. New York: Knopf. (The edition I used was from New American Library, a Plume Book, New York, 1982.)

Morrison, Toni (1977). *The Song of Solomon*. New York: Knopf. (The edition I used was from Signet, New York, 1978.)

Naylor, Gloria (1982). *The Women of Brewster Place*. New York: Viking Penguin. (The edition I used was from Penguin books, New York, 1983.)

Naylor, Gloria (1988). *Mama Day*. New York: Ticknor & Fields. (The edition I used was from Vintage Contemporaries Edition, New York, September, 1993.)

Petry, Ann (1946). *The Street*. New York: Houghton Mifflin.

Thurman, Wallace (1929). *The Blacker the Berry*. New York: Macaulay. (The edition I used was from Scribner Paperback Fiction, Simon & Schuster, New York, 1996.)

Walker, Alice (1976). *Meridian*. New York: Harcourt, Brace, Jovanovich. (The edition I used was the Harcourt, First Harvest edition, New York, 2003.)

Walker, Alice (1982). *The Color Purple*. New York: Harcourt. (The edition I used was the First Harcourt Harvest Edition, New York, 2003.)

West, Dorothy (1948). *The Living is Easy*. Boston: Houghton Mifflin. (The edition I used was from the Feminist Press at the City University of New York, Graduate Center, New York, 1982.)

Wideman, John Edgar (1983). *Sent for You Yesterday*. New York: Houghton Mifflin.

Wright, Sarah E. (1969). *This Child's Gonna Live*. New York: Delacorte. (The edition I used was from the Feminist Press at the City University of New York Graduate Center, New York, 2002.)

References

Alberts, J.K. (1986). The role of couples' conversations in relational development: A content analysis of courtship talk in Harlequin romance novels. *Communication Quarterly, 34,* 127–42.

Anderson, E. (1999). *The Code of the Street: Decency, Violence, and the Moral Life of the Inner City.* New York, NY: Norton.

Banks-Wallace, J., and Parks, L. (2001). "So that our souls don't get damaged": The impact of racism on maternal thinking and practice related to the protection of daughters. *Issues in Mental Health Nursing, 22,* 77–98.

Barr, S.C., and Neville, H.A. (2008). Examination of the link between parental racial socialization messages and racial ideology among Black college students. *Journal of Black Psychology, 34,* 131–55.

Bateson, G. (1967). Cybernetic explanation. *American Behavioral Scientist, 10*(8), 29–32

Bateson, G. (1979). *Mind and Nature: A Necessary Unity.* New York, NY: Bantam.

Baugh, J. (2001). Coming full circle: Some circumstances pertaining to low literacy achievement among African Americans. In J.L. Harris, A.G. Kamhi, and K.E. Pollock (eds), *Literacy in African American Communities* (pp. 277–88). Mahwah, NJ: LEA.

Berger, P., and Kellner, H. (1964). Marriage and the construction of reality. *Diogenes, 46,* 1–24.

Bernard, E. (2006). A familiar strangeness: The spectre of whiteness in the Harlem Renaissance and the Black Arts Movement. In L.G. Collins and M.N. Crawford (eds), *New Thoughts on the Black Arts Movement* (pp. 255–72). New Brunswick, NJ: Rutgers University Press.

Bertera, E.M., and Crewe, S.E. (2013). Parenthood in the twenty-first century: African American grandparents as surrogate parents. *Journal of Human Behavior in the Social Environment, 23,* 178–92.

Biernacki, R. (2012). *Reinventing Evidence in Social Inquiry: Decoding Facts and Variables.* New York, NY: Palgrave Macmillan.

Bonilla-Silva, E. (2001). *White Supremacy and Racism in the Post-Civil Rights Era.* Boulder, CO: Lynne Rienner.

Bonilla-Silva, E. (2010). *Racism without Racists: Color-Blind Racism and Racial Inequality in Contemporary America,* 3rd ed. Lanham, MD: Rowman and Littlefield.

Borenstein, A. (1978). *Redeeming the Sin: Social Science and Literature.* New York, NY: Columbia University Press.

Bouson, J.B. (2000). *Quiet As It's Kept: Shame, Trauma, and Race in the Novels of Toni Morrison.* Albany, NY: State University of New York Press.

Bowman, P.J., and Howard, C. (1985). Race-related socialization, motivation, and academic achievement: A study of Black youths in three-generation families. *Journal of the American Academy of Child Psychiatry, 24,* 134–41.

Boyd-Franklin, N. (2003). *Black Families in Therapy: Understanding the African American Experience,* 2nd ed. New York, NY: Guilford.

Boyd-Franklin, N., Franklin, A.J., with Toussaint, P.A. (2000). *Boys into Men: Raising our African American Teenage Sons.* New York, NY: Dutton.

Boyd-Franklin, N., and Karger, M. (2012). Intersections of race, class, and poverty: Challenges and resilience in African-American families. In F. Walsh (ed.), *Normal Family Processes: Growing Diversity and Complexity,* 4th ed. (pp. 273–96). New York, NY: Guilford.

Bray, R.L. (1998). *Unafraid of the Dark: A Memoir.* New York, NY: Random House.

Brinkmann, S. (2009). Literature as qualitative inquiry: The novelist as researcher. *Qualitative Inquiry, 15,* 1376–94.

Bröck, S. (1984). "Talk as a form of action": An interview with Paule Marshall, September 1982. In G.H. Lenz (ed.), *History and Tradition in Afro-American Culture* (pp. 194–206). Frankfurt, Germany: Campus Verlag.

Bronfenbrenner, U. (1979). *The Ecology of Human Development: Experiments by Nature and Design.* Cambridge, MA: Harvard University Press.

Brooks, G. (1984). Interview. *Triquarterly, 60,* 405–10.

Brown, T.N., and Lesane-Brown, C.L. (2006). Racial socialization messages across historical time. *Social Psychology Quarterly, 69,* 201–13.

Burrows, V. (2004). *Whiteness and Trauma: The Mother-Daughter Knot in the Fiction of Jean Rhys, Jamaica Kincaid and Toni Morrison.* New York, NY: Palgrave Macmillan.

Burton, L.M., Bonilla-Silva, E., Ray, V., Buckelew, R., and Hordge Freeman, E. (2010). Critical race theories, colorism, and the decade's research on families of color. *Journal of Marriage and Family, 72,* 440–59.

Burton, L.M., and Clark, S.L. (2005). Homeplace and housing in the lives of low-income urban African American families. In V.C. McLoyd, N.E. Hill, and K.A. Dodge (eds), *African American Family Life: Ecological and Cultural Diversity* (pp. 166–88). New York, NY: Guilford.

Burton, L.M., and DeVries, C. (1992). Challenges and rewards: African American grandparents as surrogate parents. *Generations: Journal of the American Society on Aging, 16*(3), 51–4.

Burton, L.M., Winn, D.-M., Stevenson, H., and Clark, S.L. (2004). Working with African American clients: Considering the "homeplace" in marriage and family therapy practices. *Journal of Marital and Family Therapy, 30,* 397–410.

Byerman, K.E. (2005). *Remembering the Past in Contemporary African American Fiction.* Chapel Hill, NC: University of North Carolina Press.

Bynum, J.E., and Pranter, C. (1984). Goffman: Content and method for seminal thought. *Free Inquiry in Creative Sociology, 12,* 95–9.

Carlin, A.P. (2010). The corpus status of literature in teaching sociology: Novels as "sociological reconstruction." *American Sociologist, 41*, 211–31.

Carolan, M.T., and Allen, K.R. (1999). Commitments and constraints to intimacy for African American couples at midlife. *Journal of Social Issues, 20*, 3–24.

Chiteji, N.S., and Hamilton, D. (2002). Family connections and the black-white wealth gap among middle-class families. *Review of Black Political Economy, 30*, 9–28.

Coard, S.I., and Sellers, R.M. (2005). African American families as a context for racial socialization. In V.C. McLoyd, N.E. Hill, and K.A. Dodge (eds), *African American Family Life: Ecological and Cultural Diversity* (pp. 264–84). New York, NY: Guilford.

Cobbs, P.M. (2005). *My American Life: From Rage to Entitlement.* New York, NY: Atria Books.

Collins Sims, C.M. (2013). *Towards a "New Way of Thinking" about African American Family Life in Urban Neighborhoods.* (Unpublished doctoral dissertation). University of Minnesota, St. Paul, Minnesota.

Cosbey, J. (1997). Using contemporary fiction to teach family issues. *Teaching Sociology, 25*, 227–33.

Crouter, A.C., Perry-Jenkins, M., Huston, T.L., and Crawford, D.W. (1989). The influence of work-induced psychological states on behavior at home. *Basic and Applied Social Psychology, 10*, 273–92.

Czarniawska, B. (2006). Doing gender unto the other: Fiction as a mode of studying gender discrimination in organizations. *Gender, Work and Organization, 13*, 234–53.

Daniel, J.L., and Effinger, M.J. (1996). Bosom biscuits: A study of African American intergenerational communication. *Journal of Black Studies, 27*, 183–200.

Davies, C.B. (1985). Mothering and healing in recent Black women's fiction. *SAGE: A Scholarly Journal on Black Women, 2*, 41–3.

Davis, T. (2002). Foreword to Sarah E. Wright's *This Child's Gonna Live* (pp. vii–ix). New York, NY: Feminist Press of the City University of New York.

Davis-Sowers, R. (2012). "It just kind of like falls in your hands": Factors that influence Black aunts' decisions to parent their nieces and nephews. *Journal of Black Studies, 43*, 231–50.

DeLamotte, E.C. (1998). *Places of Silence, Journeys of Freedom: The Fiction of Paule Marshall.* Philadelphia, PA: University of Pennsylvania Press.

Delgado, R., and Stefancic, J. (2001). *Critical Race Theory: An Introduction.* New York, NY: New York University Press.

Dilworth-Anderson, P., Burton, L.M., and Johnson, L.B. (1993). Reframing theories for understanding race, ethnicity, and families. In P. Boss, W.J. Doherty, R. LaRossa, W.R. Schumm, and S.K. Steinmetz (eds). *Sourcebook of Family Theories and Methods: A Contextual Approach* (pp. 627–46). New York, NY: Plenum

Dodson, J.E. (2007). Conceptualizations and research of African American family life in the United States: Some thoughts. In H.P. McAdoo (ed.), *Black Families*, 4th ed. (pp. 51–68). Thousand Oaks, CA: Sage.

DuBois, W.E.B. (1989). *The Souls of Black Folk*. New York, NY: Bantam. (First published in 1903 as *Reconsidering the Souls of Black Folk*. Philadelphia, PA: Running Press.)

Duck, W.O. (2012). An ethnographic portrait of a precarious life: Getting by on even less. *Annals of the American Academy of Political and Social Science, 642*(1), 124–38.

Duffey, K. (2002). "Writing" the wrong: The dilemma of the minority author. *Fresh Writing*, Fall. Retrieved June 28, 2007, at http://www.nd.edu/~frswrite/issues/2002-2003/duffey.shtml.

Dunham, S., and Ellis, C.M. (2010). Restoring intimacy with African American couples. In J. Carlson and L. Sperry (eds), *Recovering Intimacy in Love Relationships: A Clinician's Guide* (pp. 295–316). New York, NY: Routledge.

Durrant, S. (2004). *Postcolonial Narrative and the Work of Mourning: J.M. Coetzee, Wilson Harris, and Toni Morrison*. Albany, NY: State University of New York Press.

Ellena, L. (1998). Argumentation sociologique et referenes litteraires. *Cahiers Internationaux de Sociologie, 104*, 33–54.

Ellison, R. (1955). The art of fiction: An interview. *Paris Review, 18* (Spring), excerpts reprinted in H.A. Ervin (ed.) *African American Literary Criticism, 1773–2000* (pp. 105–10). New York, NY: Twayne.

Ensslen, K. (1984). History and fiction in Alice Walker's *The Third Life of Grange Copeland* and Ernest Gaines' *The Autobiography of Miss Jane Pittman*. In G.H. Lenz (ed.), *History and Tradition in Afro-American Culture* (pp. 147–63). Frankfurt, Germany: Campus Verlag.

Falk, W.W. (2004). *Rooted in Place: Family and Belonging in a Southern Black Community*. New Brunswick, NJ: Rutgers University Press.

Feagin, J.R. (2006). *Systemic Racism: A Theory of Oppression*. New York, NY: Routledge.

Feagin, J.R., and McKinney, K.D. (2003). *The Many Costs of Racism*. Lanham, MD: Rowman and Littlefield.

Feagin, J.R., and Sikes, M.P. (1994). *Living with Racism: The Black Middle-Class Experience*. Boston, MA: Beacon.

Ferguson, R.H. (2007). *Rewriting Black Identities: Transition and Exchange in the Novels of Toni Morrison*. Brussels, Belgium: P.I.E. Peter Lang.

Ford, K.R., Hurd, N.M., Jagers, R.J., and Sellers, R.M. (2013). Caregiver experiences of discrimination and African American adolescents' psychological health over time. *Child Development, 84*, 485–99.

Fox, M. (2009). Sarah E. Wright, novelist of Black experience in the Depression, dies at 80. *New York Times*. October 4, 2009, p. A28.

Frauley, J. (2010). *Criminology, Deviance, and the Silver Screen: The Fictional Reality and the Criminological Imagination.* New York, NY: Palgrave Macmillan.

Fry, W.F., Jr. (1962). The marital context of the anxiety syndrome. *Family Process, 1,* 245–52.

Garfinkel, H. (2002). *Ethnomethodology's Program: Working Out Durkheim's Aphorism.* A.W. Rawls (ed.). Lanham, MD: Rowman and Littlefield.

Gates, H.L., Jr. (2006). Afterword—Zora Neale Hurston: "A Negro way of saying." In *Z.N. Hurston, Their Eyes Were Watching God* (pp. 195–205). New York, NY: Harper Perennial Modern Classics.

Giggie, J.M. (2008). *After Redemption: Jim Crow and the Transformation of African American Religion in the Delta, 1875–1915.* New York, NY: Oxford University Press.

Glenn, E.N. (2009). Consuming lightness: Segregated markets and global capital in the skin-whitening trade. In E.N. Glenn (ed.), *Shades of Difference: Why Skin Color Matters* (pp. 166–87). Stanford, CA: Stanford University Press.

Goldin, M. (2008). Who said you could say that? Voice, authority and the writer. In B.M. Greene and F. Beauford (eds), *Meditations and Ascensions: Black Writers on Writing* (pp. 3–10). Chicago, IL: Third World Press.

Goldsmith, R.E., and Satterlee, M. (2004). Representations of trauma in clinical psychology and fiction. *Journal of Trauma and Dissociation, 5*(2), 35–59.

Green, T.T. (2009). *A Fatherless Child: Autobiographical Perspectives on African American Men.* Columbia, MO: University of Missouri Press.

Gresham, J.H. (1976). James Baldwin comes home, *Essence, 7* (June), 54–5, 80, 82, 85, reprinted in Standley, F.L., and Pratt, L.H. (eds) (1989). *Conversations with James Baldwin* (pp. 159–67). Jackson, MS: University Press of Mississippi.

Grewal, G. (1998). *Circles of Sorrow, Lines of Struggle: The Novels of Toni Morrison.* Baton Rouge, LA: Louisiana State University Press.

Griffin, F.J. (1995). *"Who Set You Flowin'?" The African American Migration Narrative.* New York, NY: Oxford University Press.

Grimes, W. (1996). A conference on black literature asks if the good times will stay. *New York Times* (late Edition, East Coast), March 21, C13.

Gubrium, J.F., and Holstein, J.A. (1990). *What is Family?* Mountain View, CA: Mayfield.

Guzzio, T.C. (2011). *All Stories Are True: History, Myth, and Trauma in the Work of John Edgar Wideman.* Jackson, MI: University Press of Mississippi.

Hannerz, U. (1969). *Soulside: Inquiries into Ghetto Culture and Community.* New York, NY: Columbia University Press.

Hare-Mustin, R. (1987). The problem of gender in family therapy theory. *Family Process, 26,* 15–27.

Harris, T. (1982). *From Mammies to Militants: Domestics in Black American Literature.* Philadelphia, PA: Temple University Press.

Hathaway, R.V. (2004). The unbearable weight of authenticity: Zora Neale Hurston's *Their Eyes Were Watching God* and a theory of "touristic reading." *Journal of American Folklore, 117,* 168–90.

Hayre, R.W. (and A. Moore). (1997). *Tell Them We Are Rising: A Memoir of Faith in Education.* New York, NY: Wiley.

Hegtvedt, K.A. (1991). Teaching sociology of literature through literature. *Teaching Sociology, 19,* 1–12.

Hill, S.A. (1999). *African American Children: Socialization and Development in Families.* Thousand Oaks, CA: Sage.

Hines, P.M., and Boyd-Franklin, N. (1996). African American families. In M. McGoldrick, J. Giordano, and J.K. Pearce (eds), *Ethnicity and Family Therapy,* 2nd ed. (pp. 66–84). New York, NY: Guilford.

Hochschild, J. (2006). When do people not protest unfairness? The case of skin color. *Social Research, 73,* 473–98.

Hochschild, J., and Weaver, V. (2007). The skin color paradox and the American racial order. *Social Forces, 86,* 643–70.

Hook, D., and Howarth, C. (2005). Future directions for a critical social psychology of racism/antiracism. *Journal of Community and Applied Social Psychology, 15,* 506–12.

hooks, b. (1989a). Feminist scholarship: Ethical issues. In b. hooks, *Talking Back: Thinking Feminist, Thinking Black* (pp. 42–8). Boston, MA: South End Press.

hooks, b, (1989b). To Gloria, who is she: On using a pseudonym. In b. hooks, *Talking Back: Thinking Feminist, Thinking Black* (pp. 160–66). Boston, MA: South End Press.

hooks, b. (1992). Representations of whiteness in the black imagination. In b. hooks, *Black Looks: Race and Representation* (pp. 165–78). Boston, MA: South End Press.

Hopkins, D.N. (2000). *Down, Up, and Over: Slave Religion and Black Theology.* Minneapolis, MN: Fortress Press.

Hornbostel, J. (1988). "This country's hard on women and oxen": A study of the images of farm women in American fiction. In W.G. Haney and J.B. Knowles (eds), *Woman and Farming: Changing Roles, Changing Structures* (pp. 109–19). Boulder, CO: Westview.

Howard, L.P. (1993). Introduction: Alice and Zora—"The call and the response." In L.P. Howard (ed.), *Alice Walker and Zora Neale Hurston: The Common Bond* (pp. 1–12). Westport, CT: Greenwood.

Hughes, D., and Chen, L. (1997). When and what parents tell children about race: An examination of race-related socialization among African American families. *Applied Developmental Science, 1,* 200–214.

Hunter, M.L. (2002). "If you're light you're alright": Light skin color as social capital for women of color. *Gender and Society, 16,* 175–93.

Hunter, M. (2004). Light, bright, and almost white: The advantages and disadvantages of light skin. In C. Herring, V.M. Keith, and H.D. Horton (eds),

Skin Deep: How Race and Complexion Matter in the "Color-Blind" Era (pp. 22–44). Urbana, IL: University of Illinois Press.

Hurston, Z.N. (1950). What white publishers won't print. *Negro Digest, 8* (April), 85–9.

Imber-Black, E. (2008). Incarceration and family relationships: A call for systemic responses. *Family Process, 47,* 277–9.

Jackson, D.D. (1959). Family interaction, family homeostasis and some implications for conjoint family psychotherapy. In J.H. Masserman (ed.), *Individual and Familial Dynamics* (pp. 122–41). New York, NY: Grune and Stratton.

Jackson, D.D. (1965). The study of the family. *Family Process, 4,* 1–20.

Jenkins, C.M. (2007). *Private Lives, Proper Relations: Regulating Black Intimacy.* Minneapolis, MN: University of Minnesota Press.

Jones, J. (2010). *Labor of Love, Labor of Sorrow: Black Women, Work, and the Family from Slavery to the Present,* revised ed. New York, NY: Basic Books.

Jones, S.L. (2002). *Rereading the Harlem Renaissance: Race, Class, and Gender in the Fiction of Jessie Fauset, Zora Neale Hurston, and Dorothy West.* Westport, CT: Greenwood.

Journal of Blacks in Higher Education (1995, June 30). News and views: Are American libraries closing the books on African-American authors? No. 8, 42–3.

Keith, V.M. (2009). A colorstruck world: Skin tone, achievement, and self-esteem among African American women. In E.N. Glenn (ed.), *Shades of Difference: Why Skin Color Matters* (pp. 25–39). Stanford, CA: Stanford University Press.

King, L. (2006). Introduction: Baldwin and Morrison in dialogue. In L. King and L.O. Scott (eds), *James Baldwin and Toni Morrison: Comparative Critical and Theoretical Essays* (pp. 1–9). New York, NY: Palgrave Macmillan.

Kvale, S., and Brinkmann, S. (2009). *InterViews: Learning the Craft of Qualitative Research Interviewing,* 2nd. ed. Thousand Oaks, CA: Sage.

LaGrone, K. (2009). *Alice Walker's "The Color Purple."* Amsterdam, The Netherlands: Rodopi.

Laurie, A., and Neimeyer, R.A. (2010). On broken bonds and bondage: An analysis of loss in the slave narrative collection. *Death Studies, 34,* 221–56.

Lesane-Brown, C.L. (2006). A review of race socialization within Black families. *Developmental Review, 26,* 400–426.

Levine, L.W. (2007). *Black Culture and Black Consciousness: Afro-American Folk Thought from Slavery to Freedom* (30th anniversary ed.) New York, NY: Oxford University Press.

Lewis, D., Rodgers, D., and Woolcock, M. (2008). The fiction of development: Literary representation as a source of authoritative knowledge. *Journal of Development Studies, 44,* 198–216.

Li, S. (2009). Becoming her mother's mother: Recreating home and the self in Audre Lorde's *Zami: A New Spelling of My Name.* In V. Theile and M. Drews (eds), *Reclaiming Home, Remembering Motherhood, Rewriting History:*

African American and Afro-Caribbean Women's Literature in the Twentieth Century (pp. 139–63). Newcastle upon Tyne: Cambridge Scholars.

Lipsitz, G. (2011). *How Racism Takes Place*. Philadelphia, PA: Temple University Press.

Long, L.A. (ed.) (2005). *White Scholars/African American Texts*. New Brunswick, NJ: Rutgers University Press.

Ludwig, S. (2007). Toni Morrison's social criticism. In J. Tally (ed.), *The Cambridge Companion to Toni Morrison* (pp. 125–38). New York, NY: Cambridge University Press.

Martin, P.P., and McAdoo, H.P. (2007). Sources of racial socialization: Theological orientation of African American churches and parents. In H.P. McAdoo (ed.), *Black Families*, 4th ed. (pp. 125–42). Thousand Oaks, CA: Sage.

May, V.M. (1996). Ambivalent narratives, fragmented selves: Performative identities and the mutability of roles in James Baldwin's *Go Tell It on the Mountain*. In T. Harris (ed.), *New Essays on Go Tell It on the Mountain* (pp. 97–126). New York, NY: Cambridge University Press.

Mayberry, S.N. (2007). *Can't I Love What I Criticize? The Masculine and Morrison*. Athens, GA: University of Georgia Press.

M'Baye, B. (2006). Resistance against racial, sexual, and social oppression in *Go Tell It on the Mountain* and *Beloved*. In L. King and L.O. Scott (eds), *James Baldwin and Toni Morrison: Comparative Critical and Theoretical Essays* (pp. 167–86). New York, NY: Palgrave Macmillan.

McDowell, D.E. (1997). Conversations with Dorothy West. In V.A. Kramer and R.A. Russ (eds), *Harlem Renaissance Re-Examined: A Revised and Expanded Edition* (pp. 285–303). Troy, NY: Whitston.

McHoul, A.W. (1987). An initial investigation of the usability of fictional conversation for doing conversation analysis. *Semiotica*, *67*(1–2), 83–103.

Meisenhelder, S.E. (1999*). Hitting a Straight Lick with a Crooked Stick: Race and Gender in the Work of Zora Neale Hurston*. Tuscaloosa, AL: University of Alabama Press.

Meyer, R.W. (1965). *The Middle Western Farm Novel in the Twentieth Century*. Lincoln, NE: University of Nebraska Press.

Mirza, Q. (1999). Patricia Williams: Inflecting critical race theory. *Feminist Legal Studies*, *7*, 111–32.

Mistry, R. S, Vandewater, E.A., Huston, A.C., and McLoyd, V.C. (2002). Economic well-being and children's social adjustment: The role of family process in an ethnically diverse low-income sample. *Child Development*, *73*, 935–51.

Mitchell, A. (2002). *The Freedom to Remember: Narrative, Slavery, and Gender in Contemporary Black Women's Fiction*. New Brunswick, NJ: Rutgers University Press.

Mitchell, V.D., and Davis, C. (2012). *Literary Sisters: Dorothy West and her Circle, a Biography of the Harlem Renaissance*. New Brunswick, NJ: Rutgers University Press.

Monteith, S. (2006). The never-ending cycle of poverty: Sarah E. Wright's *This Child's Gonna Live*. In S.W. Jones and M. Newman (eds), *Poverty and Progress in the U.S. South Since 1920* (pp. 83–97). Amsterdam, The Netherlands: VU University Press.

Morrison, T. (1987). The site of memory. In W. Zinsser (ed.), *Inventing the Truth: The Art and Craft of Memoir* (pp. 103–24). Boston, MA: Houghton Mifflin.

Morrison, T., and McKay, N. (1983). An interview with Toni Morrison. *Contemporary Literature, 24*, 413–29.

Mosley-Howard, G.S., and Evans, C.B. (2000). Relationships and contemporary experiences of the African American family: An ethnographic case study. *Journal of Black Studies, 30*, 428–52.

Moynihan, D.P. (1965). *The Negro Family: The Case for National Action*. Washington, DC: Office of Policy Planning and Research, U.S. Department of Labor.

Naylor, G., and Morrison, T. (1985). A conversation. *Southern Review, 21*, 567–93.

Newkirk, P. (2009). *Letters from Black America*. New York, NY: Farrar, Straus and Giroux.

Nobles, W.W. (2007). African American family life: An instrument of culture. In H.P. McAdoo (ed.), *Black Families*, 4th ed. (pp. 69–78). Thousand Oaks, CA: Sage.

Olmsted, A.P. (1998). Words are acts: Critical race theory as a rhetorical construct. *The Howard Journal of Communication, 9*, 323–33.

O'Reilly, A. (2004). *Toni Morrison and Motherhood*. Albany, NY: State University of New York Press.

Palmer, II., B.E.F. (2011). Man-to-boy becoming man-to-man: A son's reflection. In M.E. Connor and J.L. White (eds), *Black Fathers: An Invisible Presence in America*, 2nd. ed. (pp. 131–43). New York, NY: Routledge.

Parmer, T., Arnold, M.S., Natt, T., and Janson, C. (2004). Physical attractiveness as a process of internalized oppression and multigenerational transmission in African American families. *The Family Journal, 12*, 230–42.

Patton, T.O. (2010). Hey girl, am I more than my hair? African American women and their struggles with beauty, body image, and hair. In L.J. Moore and M. Kosut (eds), *The Body Reader: Essential Social and Cultural Readings* (pp. 349–66). New York, NY: New York University Press.

Peters, M.F. (1997). Historical note: Parenting of young children in Black families. In H.P. McAdoo (ed.), *Black Families*, 3rd ed. (pp. 167–82). Thousand Oaks, CA: Sage.

Petry, A. (1950). The novel as social criticism. In H. Hull (ed.) *The Writer's Book* (pp. 32–9). New York, NY: Harper.

Phillips, N. (1995). Telling of organizational tales: On the role of narrative fiction in the study of organizations, *Organization Studies, 16*, 625–49.

Pinderhughes, E.E. (1982). Afro-American families and the victim system. In M. McGoldrick, J.K. Pearce, and J. Giordano (eds), *Ethnicity and Family Therapy* (pp. 108–22). New York, NY: Guilford.

Pinderhughes, E.E., and Jones Harden, B. (2005). Beyond the birth family: African American children reared by alternative caregivers. In V.C. McLoyd, N.E. Hill, and K.A. Dodge (eds), *African American Family Life: Ecological and Cultural Diversity* (pp. 285–310). New York, NY: Guilford.

Porter, H. (1996). The South in *Go Tell It on the Mountain*: Baldwin's personal confrontation. In T. Harris (ed.), *New Essays on Go Tell It on the Mountain* (pp. 59–75). New York, NY: Cambridge University Press.

Prince, V.S. (2005). *Burnin' Down the House: Home in African American Literature.* New York, NY: Columbia University Press.

Putnam, A. (2011). Toni Morrison's *The Bluest Eye, Sula, Beloved,* and *A Mercy. Black Women, Gender, and Families, 5*(2), 25–43.

Ragan, S.L., and Hopper, R. (1984). Ways to leave your lover: A conversational analysis of literature. *Communication Quarterly, 32,* 310–17.

Rampersad, A. (1997). *Jackie Robinson: A Biography.* New York, NY: Knopf.

Rashid, K. (2011). 'To break asunder along the lesions of race.' The critical race theory of W.E.B. DuBois. *Race Ethnicity and Education, 14,* 585–602.

Ready, M.T. (2000). The tripled plot and center of *Sula.* In S.O. Iyasere and M.W. Iyasere (eds), *Understanding Toni Morrison's Beloved and Sula: Selected Essays and Criticisms of the Works By the Nobel Prize-Winning Author* (pp. 1–18). Troy, NY: Whitston.

Reynolds, C.V. (2003). Banned somewhere in the U.S.A. *Black Issues Book Review, 5*(5), 23.

Riina, E.M., and McHale, S.M. (2010). Parents' experiences of discrimination and family relationship qualities. *Family Relations, 59,* 283–96.

Riley, M. (1968). *Brought to Bed.* London: Dent.

Ritterhouse, J.L. (2006). *Growing Up Jim Crow: How Black and White Southern Children Learned Race.* Chapel Hill, NC: University of North Carolina Press.

Rober, P., and Rosenblatt, P.C. (2013). Selective disclosure in a first conversation about a family death in James Agee's novel *A Death in the Family. Death Studies, 37,* 172–94.

Rogers, M.F. (1991). *Novels, Novelists, and Readers: Toward a Phenomenological Sociology of Literature.* Albany, NY: State University of New York Press.

Rosenblatt, P.C. (1983). *Bitter, Bitter Tears: Nineteenth Century Diarists and Twentieth Century Grief Theories.* Minneapolis, MN: University of Minnesota Press.

Rosenblatt, P.C. (1990). *Farming is in our Blood: Farm Families in Economic Crisis.* Ames, IA: Iowa State University Press.

Rosenblatt, P.C. (1994). *Metaphors of Family Systems Theory: Toward New Constructions.* New York, NY: Guilford.

Rosenblatt, P.C. (2000). *Parent Grief: Narratives of Loss and Relationship.* Philadelphia, PA: Brunner/Mazel.

Rosenblatt, P.C. (2002). Interviewing at the border of fact and fiction. In J.F. Gubrium and J.A. Holstein (eds), *The Handbook of Interview Research* (pp. 893–909). Thousand Oaks, CA: Sage.

Rosenblatt, P.C. (2009). *Shared Obliviousness in Family Systems*. Albany, NY: State University of New York Press.

Rosenblatt, P.C. (2012). The concept of complicated grief: Lessons from other cultures. In H. Schut, P. Boelen, J. van den Bout, and M. Stroebe (eds), *Complicated Grief: Scientific Foundations for Health Professionals* (pp. 27–39). New York, NY: Routledge

Rosenblatt, P.C., and Barner, J.R. (2006). The dance of closeness-distance in couple relationships after the death of a parent. *Omega, 53*, 277–93.

Rosenblatt, P.C., Karis, T.A., and Powell, R.D. (1995). *Multiracial Couples: Black and White Voices*. Thousand Oaks, CA: Sage.

Rosenblatt, P.C., and Wallace, B.R. (2005a). *African American Grief*. New York, NY: Routledge.

Rosenblatt, P.C., and Wallace, B.R. (2005b). Narratives of grieving African-Americans about racism in the lives of deceased family members. *Death Studies, 29*, 217–35.

Rosenblatt, P.C., and Wieling, E. (2013). *Knowing and Not Knowing in Intimate Relationships*. Cambridge: Cambridge University Press.

Rosenblatt, P.C., and Yang, S. (2004). Love, debt, and filial piety: Hee Gyung Noh's view of Korean intergenerational relations when a mother is terminally ill. *Journal of Loss and Trauma, 9*, 167–80.

Royster, D.A. (2007). What happens to potential discouraged? Masculinity norms and the contrasting institutional and labor market experiences of less affluent black and white men. *Annals of the American Academy of Political and Social Science, 609*, 153–80.

Ruggiero, V. (2003). *Crime in Literature: Sociology of Deviance and Fiction*. New York, NY: Verso.

Rushdy, A.H.A. (2001). *Remembering Generations: Race and Family in Contemporary African American Fiction*. Chapel Hill, NC: University of North Carolina Press.

Russell, K., Wilson, M., and Hall, R. (1992). *The Color Complex: The Politics of Skin Color among African Americans*. New York, NY: Harcourt Brace Jovanovich.

Russell, S. (1990). *Render Me My Song: African-American Women Writers from Slavery to the Present*. New York, NY: St. Martin's Press.

Ryang, S. (2012). *Reading North Korea: An Ethnological Inquiry*. Cambridge, MA: Harvard University Asia Center.

Satter, B. (2009). *Family Properties: Race, Real Estate, and the Exploitation of Black Urban America*. New York, NY: Metropolitan Books.

Schryer, S. (2011). *Fantasies of the New Class: Ideologies of Professionalism in Post-World War II American Fiction*. New York, NY: Columbia University Press.

Schultz, E. (2007). Natural and unnatural circumstances in *Not without Laughter*. In J.E. Tidwell and C.R. Ragar (eds), *Montage of a Dream: The Art and Life of Langston Hughes* (pp. 39–51). Columbia, MO: University of Missouri Press.

Schulz, M.S., Cowan, P.A., Pape Cowan, C., and Brennan, R.T. (2004). Coming home upset: Gender, marital satisfaction, and the daily spillover of workday experience into couple interactions. *Journal of Family Psychology, 18*, 250–63.

Shapiro, H. (1988). *White Violence and Black Response: From Reconstruction to Montgomery*. Amherst, MA: University of Massachusetts Press.

Sherrard-Johnson, C. (2012). *Dorothy West's Paradise: A Biography of Class and Color*. New Brunswick, NJ: Rutgers University Press.

Shields, J.P. (1994). "Never cross the divide": Reconstructing Langston Hughes's *Not Without Laughter*. *African American Review, 28*, 601–13.

Simmel, G. (1955). *Conflict and the Web of Group Affiliations*. (K.H. Wolff, translator). Glencoe, IL: Free Press.

Smiles, R.V. (2010). Popular black women's fiction and the novels of Terry McMillan. In G.A. Jarrett (ed.), *A Companion to African American Literature* (pp. 347–59). Malden, MA: Wiley-Blackwell.

Spencer, S. (2006). Racial politics and the literary reception of Zora Neale Hurston's *Their Eyes Were Watching God*. In M.J. Bona and I. Maini (eds), *Multiethnic Literature and Canon Debates* (pp. 111–26). Albany, NY: State University of New York Press.

Squires, G.D. (2007). Demobilization of the individualistic bias: Housing market discrimination as a contributor to labor market and economic inequality. *Annals of the American Academy of Political and Social Science, 609*, 200–214.

Srubar, I. (1998). The construction of social reality and the structure of literary work. In L. Embree (ed.), *Alfred Schutz's "Sociological Aspect of Literature": Construction and Complementary Essays* (pp. 75–88). Dordrecht, The Netherlands: Kluwer Academic Publishers.

St. Jean, Y., and Feagin, J.R. (1998). The family costs of white racism: The case of African American families. *Journal of Comparative Family Studies, 29*, 297–312.

Stack, C.B. (1974). *All Our Kin: Strategies for Survival in a Black Community*. New York, NY: Harper and Row.

Stanfield, J.J. (2011). *Black Reflective Sociology, Epistemology, Theory, and Methodology*. Walnut Creek, CA: Left Coast Press.

Stewart, P. (2007). Who is kin? Family definition and African American families. *Journal of Human Behavior in the Social Environment, 15*(2–3), 163–81.

Story, R.D. (1989). Gender and ambition: Zora Neale Hurston in the Harlem Renaissance. *The Black Scholar, 20*(2), 25–31.

Suizzo, M., Robinson, C., and Pahlke, E. (2008). African American mothers' socialization beliefs and goals with young children. *Journal of Family Issues, 29*, 287–316.

Tate, S.A. (2009). *Black Beauty: Aesthetics, Stylization, Politics*. Burlington, VT: Ashgate.

Tatum, B.D. (1999). *Assimilation Blues: Black Families in White Communities: Who Succeeds and Why?* New York, NY: Basic Books.

Terkel, S. (1961). An interview with James Baldwin. Transcript of a broadcast on radio station WFMT, Chicago, 19 December, 1961, printed in Standley, F.L., and Pratt, L.H. (eds) (1989). *Conversations with James Baldwin* (pp. 3–23) Jackson, MS: University Press of Mississippi.

Thomas, K., and Dettlaff, A.J. (2011). African American families and the role of physical discipline: Witnessing the past in the present. *Journal of Human Behavior in the Social Environment, 21*, 963–77.

Troupe, Q. (1988). Last testament: An interview with James Baldwin. *The Village Voice, 12* (January), 36.

Ulrich, W. (1986). The use of fiction as a source of information about interpersonal communication: A critical view. *Communication Quarterly, 34*, 143–53.

Valk, A., and Brown, L. (2010). *Living with Jim Crow: African American Women and Memories of the Segregated South.* New York, NY: Palgrave Macmillan.

Valkeakari, T. (2007). *Religious Idiom and the African American Novel, 1952–1998.* Gainesville, FL: University Press of Florida.

VanWormer, K.S. (2012). *The Maid Narratives: Black Domestics and White Families in the Jim Crow South.* Baton Rouge, LA: Louisiana State University Press.

Vines, A.I., and Baird, D.D. (2009). Stress of caring for children: The role of perceived racism. *Journal of the National Medical Association, 101*, 156–60.

Wall, C.A. (2005). *Worrying the Line: Black Women Writers, Lineage, and Literary Tradition.* Chapel Hill, NC: University of North Carolina Press.

Washington, M.H. (1991). Introduction. In M.H. Washington (ed.), *Memory of Kin: Stories about Family by Black Writers* (pp. 1–8). New York, NY: Doubleday.

Washington, R.E. (2001). *The Ideologies of African American Literature: From the Harlem Renaissance to the Black Nationalist Revolt: A Sociology of Literature Perspective.* Lanham, MD: Rowman and Littlefield.

Watson, C. (2011). Staking a small claim for fictional narratives in social and educational research. *Qualitative Research, 11*, 395–408.

Watson, C.W. (1995). The novelist's consciousness. In A.P. Cohen and N. Rapport (eds), *Questions of Consciousness* (pp. 77–98). London: Routledge.

Watzlawick, P., Beavin, J.H., and Jackson, D.D. (1967). *Pragmatics of Human Communication.* New York, NY: Norton

Webb, E.J., Campbell, D.T., Schwartz, R.D., Sechrest, L., and Grove, J.B. (1981). *Nonreactive Measures in the Social Sciences*, 2nd ed. Boston, MA: Houghton Mifflin.

Welcome, H.A. (2004). "White is right": The utilization of an improper ontological perspective in analyses of black experiences. *Journal of African American Studies, 8*, 59–73.

Whitson, C. (2002). The sexual boundaries of race and class in working-class novels: Marrying up and living it down/Marrying down and living it up. *Race, Gender and Class, 9*(3), 101–20.

Wilder, J. (2010). Revisiting "Color names and color notions": A contemporary examination of the language and attitude of skin color among young Black women. *Journal of Black Studies, 41*, 184–206.

Wilder, J, and Cain, C. (2011). Teaching and learning color consciousness in Black families: Exploring family processes and women's experiences with colorism. *Journal of Family Issues, 32*, 577–604.

Willie, C., and Lane, J. (2010). Paternal mentoring models. In C.V. Willie and R.J. Reddick (eds), *A New Look at Black Families*, 6th ed. (pp. 125–40). Lanham, MD: Rowman and Littlefield.

Wilson, R.N. (1979). *The Writer as Social Seer*. Chapel Hill, NC: University of North Carolina Press.

Wright, L.A. (1995). *Identity, Family, and Folklore in African American Literature*. New York, NY: Garland.

Yancy, G. (2004). A Foucaldian (genealogical) reading of whiteness: The production of the Black body/self and the racial deformation of Pecola Breedlove in Toni Morrison's *The Bluest Eye*. In G. Yancy (ed.), *What White Looks Like* (pp. 107–42). New York, NY: Routledge.

Young, J.K. (2006). *Black Writers, White Publishers: Marketplace Politics in Twentieth-Century African American Literature*. Jackson, MS: University Press of Mississippi.

Young, R.S. (2009). Theoretical influences and experimental resemblances: Ernest J. Gaines and recent critical approaches to the study of African American fiction. In D.A. Williams (ed.), *Contemporary African American Fiction: New Critical Essays* (pp. 11–36). Columbus, OH: The Ohio State University Press.

Zamudio, M.M., Russell, C., Rios, F.A., and Bridgeman, J.L. (2011). *Critical Race Theory Matters: Education and Ideology*. New York, NY: Routledge.

Zuberi, T., and Bonilla-Silva, E. (2008). *White Logic, White Methods: Racism and Methodology*. Lanham, MD: Rowman and Littlefield.

Index